Steel on Stone

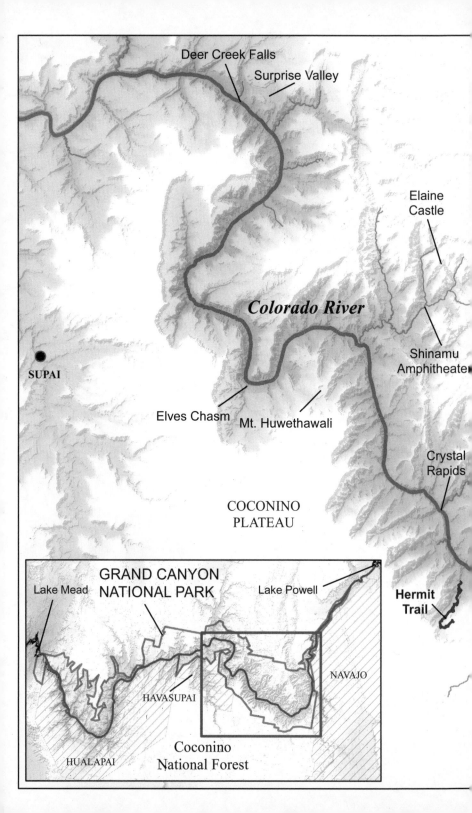

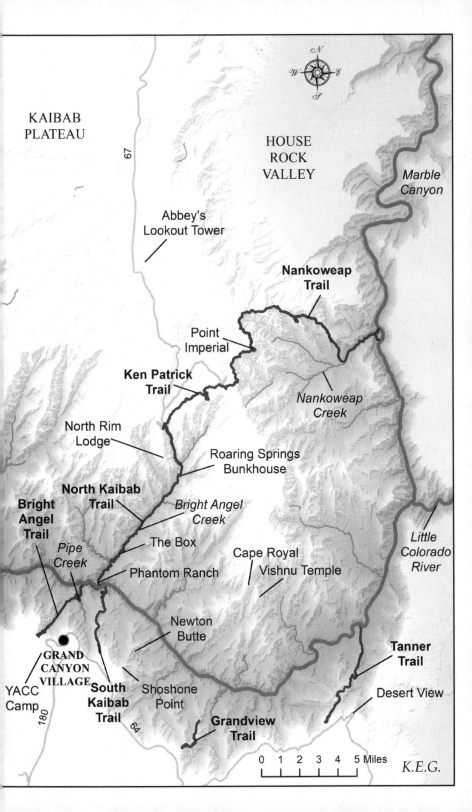

Steel on Stone

LIVING AND WORKING IN THE GRAND CANYON

NATHANIEL FARRELL BRODIE

TRINITY UNIVERSITY PRESS
San Antonio, Texas

Published by Trinity University Press
San Antonio, Texas 78212

Copyright © 2019 by Nathaniel Farrell Brodie

Book design by BookMatters
Cover design by Rebecca Lown

Cover image: River Trail construction by EWC
Company 818 enrollees. Man using a jackhammer on a
steep slope, circa 1934 NPS. Grand Canyon National
Park Museum Collection, no. 03968A.
Frontis: Map created by Kelly Gleason

ISBN 978-1-59534-860-9 paperback
ISBN 978-1-59534-861-6 ebook

Trinity University Press strives to produce its books
using methods and materials in an environmentally
sensitive manner. We favor working with manufac-
turers that practice sustainable management of all
natural resources, produce paper using recycled stock,
and manage forests with the best possible practices
for people, biodiversity, and sustainability. The press
is a member of the Green Press Initiative, a nonprofit
program dedicated to supporting publishers in their
efforts to reduce their impacts on endangered forests,
climate change, and forest-dependent communities.

The paper used in this publication meets the
minimum requirements of the American National
Standard for Information Sciences—Permanence of
Paper for Printed Library Materials, ANSI 39.48-1992.

CIP data on file at the Library of Congress

23 22 21 20 19 | 5 4 3 2 1

Printed in Canada

CONTENTS

To Mom and Dad,
for everything

So, the world happens twice—
once what we see it as;
second it legends itself
deep, the way it is.

—WILLIAM STAFFORD

"Oh, the Grand Canyon, that must be nice." The woman sips her cocktail, tilts her head to listen to the airport intercom, then turns to me again. "I have to ask, though: do you ever get sick of looking at it?"

I too take a drink. I want to tell her how, standing in line at a bank, I'll overhear people mention the Grand Canyon and I'll strain to catch their conversation; how I'll find myself studying a crack in the concrete and thinking of the sudden ease with which Havasu Canyon carves through the Coconino Platform. I want to tell her that I've split-second recognized the Canyon plastered on the side of a bus going the opposite way through five lanes of LA traffic; or that, skimming through a magazine, I'll stop, flip back a few pages, and study an advertisement containing a small picture of the Canyon in an attempt to identify where the photographer stood, at what season, at what time of day.

I want to tell her that I think the thermals coursing out of the Canyon's depths spread over the entire earth before collapsing, so that wherever I am in the world, threads of scent and longing from that piñon-juniper, scorched-rock air find me, move me. About

that drunken night at a bar in Chicago with Michael and his girlfriend, whom he had left the Canyon to live with, and how, when
she left the table to go to the bathroom, I said, "I think about going
back all the time," and Michael nodded and said quietly, "So do I."

I want to tell her about the feeling that I have, driving north
toward the Canyon on Route 64, a familiar pull that I've known
only one other time: when, driving to my childhood home in LA, I
finally pass through Barstow and swing southwest toward the city,
and nostalgia and homecoming swell to a crest, and right then, in
the searing aridity of the Mohave Desert, I'll swear I can smell the
ocean.

I want to tell her that the landscape painter Thomas Moran's
painting *Chasm of the Colorado* scarcely resembles the actual
Grand Canyon and yet, in the way it scrambles scale, time, and
place; fuses emotion and image; and exemplifies how one's memory
collages fragments of experience into a cohesive whole, it captures
the essence of how I came to know the Canyon: as a physical place,
yes, but also as mutable, shifting with time and angle, different to
every personality, mood, expectation, and experience, a timeless
mosaic of moments, stories, ecologies, histories, images, impressions, contradictions, and memories.

But I'm hesitant to reveal these things, and I figure, perhaps
ungenerously, that her question itself indicates she wouldn't understand, so I tell her, "No. I never do," and finish my whiskey in
silence.

SPRING

The heat seethed off the rock. I willed one foot in front of the other, my head throbbing in time to the trudge of boot on dirt. Step, step, step. The air shimmered like hot oil.

"So angry," I mumbled to myself. "Why so angry, sun?"

It was my first day of work on the Grand Canyon National Park Service Trail Crew. A few weeks earlier I'd been standing in the steady rain in Olympia, Washington, using a payphone to call Will, head of Trails at Grand Canyon National Park. He offered me a job. I'd recently exhausted my wanderlust and bank account after six months of travel through Asia and India, and having nothing else lined up, I accepted. I'd long since sold my car, so my girlfriend, Erika, drove me down from Washington. We slept in the woods outside the park, woke early, passed through the entrance gates, parked along the side of the road near Mather Point, ducked through the last strip of piñon-juniper between the road and the rim, and stared out at the Grand Canyon.

Technically, I had already once seen the Grand Canyon, as a three-year-old child. My mother tells me that I threw a tantrum because she didn't allow me to accompany my dad and older brother a few hundred yards down the Bright Angel Trail, and though I am pleased by this story, the entire trip has slipped from my mind.

I don't remember what I thought of the Canyon before I truly saw it, as though the flood of later experiences scoured away any earlier suppositions. But I suspect that the jaded arrogance of youth got the better of me and I thought the Grand Canyon would be overrated—a whole park made of viewpoints, every one of them named Inspiration Point; a park for fat Vegas tourists, overcrowded and anticlimactic. I tended to avoid icons, to be suspicious of their status and, for some lamentable reason, wary of the emotions they are expected to elicit. This was probably true concerning the hoopla over the Grand Canyon—all that Natural Wonder of the World, bucket-list hype had pushed it toward cultural cliché.

But this second time I saw the Grand Canyon—the first time I truly saw it—will not slip from my mind. If I had considered the Grand Canyon a cliché, my response to it ran the gamut of clichés: my breath failed and my mouth hung agape. It was one of those rare instances when one's surroundings still to the point of suspension, when each and every inanimate object seems imbued with an intrinsic presence, even a contentedness: the juniper berries clustered underfoot, the turkey vultures kettling on a thermal, the individual boulders spilling off the cliffs, all perfect, all perfectly in place. I leaned over the guardrail, slowly shaking my head, murmuring nothings, my hand occasionally, almost helplessly, motioning toward the river running more than a mile beneath us, the ten miles of naked rock that lay between us and the forested plateau of the North Rim.

In the years to come I'd witness people break into sudden tears at the sight. I'd see them laugh in disbelief, or blanch in fear, or stand in stunned silence. I'd see them shrug, or hold their cell phones up, take the obligatory selfie, then turn back to the car. That day I overheard the mother of the family next to us say, "Well, this sure is bigger than the meteor crater," and I looked at her and nodded, blankly, having no idea to what meteor crater she was referring but understanding and appreciating the sentiment, the way the riven earth before us reduced the rest of the world.

The family wandered off, and still Erika and I stood, riveted. I ran my eyes down the distant scar of the South Kaibab Trail, thinking of the position I was to take in and against the eroded expanse before me. For the first time in my life I understood how fear fits into the meaning of the word "sublime."

Almost twenty-four hours later I was lying on my back in the broken shade of a scrub oak in the bowels of the Canyon, barely bothering to brush aside the gathering flies, and watching a vulture spin loops in the heat-blanched sky above me. The fear within the meaning of "sublime" was no longer an abstraction; it was dripping down my face as sweat, burning through my calves as exhaustion.

That morning, my first day of work, had started out innocuous enough. Along with Sara, who was returning to the Canyon after a season working Trails in Denali National Park, and Johnny, a fellow newcomer, I had spent a bureaucratic hour being inducted into the National Park Service. Will met us afterward. Shaved head, goatee, tattoos of agave moths and canyon wrens sleeving his arms, and an understated demeanor, he barely looked us over.

"The rest of the crew's already started hiking. Roaring Springs bunkhouse. Devin will drop you at the trailhead. Have a good hike."

On the drive to the trailhead Sara explained that we'd be

working a nine-day tour "opening" the North Kaibab Trail, which sustains heavy damage every winter and spring. But since the road to the North Rim hadn't yet been plowed, we were to hike down the South Kaibab Trail, across the Colorado River, and up the North Kaibab to the residence at Roaring Springs. Sixteen miles. I nodded: I could do that. I was twenty-five and in good shape. I was excited and confident. I was doomed. I wore brand new steel-toe boots—a bit tight, too—because I erroneously believed that we were required to wear them at all times, not just when rolling rocks or swinging a sledge or running a rock drill. As nobody had warned me that I was to hike sixteen miles into and across the Canyon that day, I hadn't packed a lunch. A few snacks and two liters of water—enough to last a day in the Pacific Northwest, where I had lived the previous five years, but a paltry amount for a hot end-of-April day in the Grand Canyon.

The South Kaibab Trail plunges 5,413 feet in seven miles, passing through the eleven most common sedimentary layers of stacked rock strata that make up the walls of the Grand Canyon. It's a relentlessly steep descent—for good reason, the Canyon has been referred to as an "inverted mountain." On average, for every thousand feet of elevation that one descends, the temperature rises by 3.5 degrees Fahrenheit. Entranced by the raw, wild, impossible surroundings in which I was to live and work, I was slow in comprehending the increasing heat, in realizing that I wasn't drinking enough water or that the stiff leather of my new boots was hugging my heels like a vise. But seven miles later, when we crossed the Colorado River at Phantom Ranch, a series of rustic tourist cabins designed by the architect Mary Colter in the 1920s, my legs were weak with fatigue, my boots pressed like branding irons, and the heat, easily in the upper nineties, had caused my

brain to press against my skull. From Phantom the North Kaibab
Trail winds up the narrow confines of the side canyon that Bright
Angel Creek has cut through the glossy black, heat-lacquered
Precambrian schist. The thin river of sky above the towering walls
of Bright Angel Canyon had bleached white with heat, but the
2-billion-year-old schist only scorched a deeper black. The ribbons
of intruded granite resembled veins of fire. My head clenched, my
brain attempting to curl into a fetal position. I grew woozy. With
Sara and Johnny out of sight, I surreptitiously retched a thin drib-
ble of Clif Bar. Vomiting made me feel a bit better, but a half-mile
later, where the pressing cliffs opened into a valley flooded with
sunlight, I was damn near delirious. Johnny had fallen behind, and
Sara had forged ahead. Before she'd abandoned me, she'd told me
that the residence was on the other side of the next bridge.

I walked and waited for that bridge. No bridge. Only the unre-
mitting sun. A fuzzy brown caterpillar lay dead in the middle of
the trail, as though it had gambled from shade to shade only to die
of heatstroke halfway across. A raven hung still in the burning sky.
The hard plastic of my water bottles had softened in the heat, and
the last sloshes of warm water tasted faintly of petroleum. Every
time I stopped walking then started up again my heels seared in
pain. At Cottonwood campground I refilled my water bottles,
crouched under the running faucet, then lay stricken in the shade
of a scrub oak.

In the years that followed I'd work in staggering, stuporous,
stultifying heat: days when it was 114 degrees in the shade and
there was no shade. When steel tools burned bare skin and liters of
water, frozen solid at dawn, turned tepid by midday. Prickly pears
would have desiccated to flaccid and skeletal white pads; antelope
ground squirrels would have slipped into hypnotic trances of inac-

tivity called aestivation; condors would be defecating on their legs to reduce their body temperature; lizards would crawl atop rocks, do a few halfhearted pushups, and retreat from whence they came; and we'd be breaking rock in the full sun.

In the years that followed I'd see hikers wilt, falter, beg for help. I'd watch the heat and miles and aridity wring the life out of men and women, young and old withering and reeling alike. I'd offer encouragement, or water, or salty snacks, or carry them out on litters, or radio in helicopters to fly them out. I'd search for those whom the heat had killed; I'd find their dead bodies on boulders in the sun. Always, even subconsciously, their plight would remind me of this first day, of the lesson that sun and rock and gradient could break one like a brittle stick.

What I couldn't realize that first day was that I would come to love it all—not just the sadomasochistic craziness of the conditions, but the way my animal mind and body would scheme and adapt in order to survive this oppressive, crushing, glorious place. I couldn't realize what the Canyon would become in my life, that it would hone my ever-gathering sense of self, that I'd feel more at home in that fiery desert than I did in the Southern California city where I was raised. I couldn't have known that this love would change even my memory of that day, crafting it into a narrative of initiation.

After an incapacitated hour, with still no sign of Johnny, I figured he must have died. "Seemed like a nice guy," I thought, then shouldered my pack and resumed my somnambulistic shuffle uptrail. Eventually I turned a corner and saw a bridge. Within minutes I had collapsed on the residence porch and eased off my boots, wincing at the sight of my shredded heels, their half-dollar-sized wounds already weeping a thin, clear liquid.

The size of my blisters elicited some raised eyebrows and kindly murmurs from the crew, though most examined them more clinically than sympathetically. They regarded them as though they were blister connoisseurs. Which they were. These were kids whose tattered maps of the Canyon had webs of ink detailing their peregrinations through the layered rock. Who, after working eight days building trail down at Phantom Ranch, would hike the seven miles and five thousand vertical feet to the rim, remove all the work clothes from their backpacks, repack them with climbing gear, then hike back down to Phantom, all in a day, to spend their five-day break climbing the Canyon's buttes and temples. These were kids who, after a day clearing the North Kaibab of the winter-induced debris flows and rockfalls, would don wetsuits, lifejackets, helmets, and boogie boards, and, with others lining the cliffs above them, ready to toss rescue-line throw bags, would hurl themselves into the snowmelt torrent of Bright Angel Creek, cascade over a small series of waterfalls, and go coursing through a whitewater gorge.

So I suffered in silence. Every day for the next eight days I'd wake, break the bond that had formed between my pussing heels and my sleeping bag, pop five ibuprofen, stuff my maimed feet into my too-tight boots, hike an agonizing few miles to the work site, dig ditch all day, then hobble back. I never told a soul about how draining the hike had been. I suspected that it was important to prove myself tough and capable that first tour of work, which, in a small and ultimately meaningless way, it may have been, though this sophomoric aspiration took a hit when one of the crew, an anarchist with mohawked dreadlocks who the night before had graphically and articulately described the final cockfight scene in the book *Roots*, politely inquired what I was reading, which to my sudden horror was Larry McMurtry's *Leaving Cheyenne*, the thinnest volume I'd found to carry, and, as I sheepishly explained, a cowboy love triangle.

But many years later, with a full moon rising over Marble Canyon, John Hiller toasted my marriage by mentioning the enormity of my blisters, and the way I'd "soldiered" on, eventually hiking the sixteen miles back out of the Canyon in tattered moccasins. Even then, after I had stayed on for an additional seven seasons of those cross-Canyon hikes, after I'd had my ass handed to me year after year and hike after hike, the unending humbling being no small part of what kept me coming back; after, more importantly, realizing the danger posed by the machismo façade (though understanding the impetus behind it enough to later refrain from quoting the Koran to dozens of tyro trail workers struggling through their own ordeals: "Do you think that you shall enter the Garden of Bliss without such trials as came to those who passed before you?"), even then I was glad to know that I'd earned my place with the tribe and, maybe, in that singular space known as the Grand Canyon.

∻ ∻

At the end of my second tour that first season I was sitting in the shade of an overhanging boulder, eating my sandwich with hands white with rock dust, idly watching a fat black carpenter bee hovering by a nearly blooming agave spike. The bee dipped up and down, slowly orbiting the ten-foot stalk. Irritated by the bee's buzzing, I threw a small rock at it. Missed, but the bee darted in pursuit of the rock. Within seconds it returned to hovering. I lobbed another rock, with the same results. Other insects came zooming up, and in tiny fury the black bee chased them away. Whatever volatiles the agave's unopened flowers were emitting into the spring afternoon were remarkably effective—the bee was enthralled.

I marveled, as I ate, at the interplay between taxonomic kingdoms, the wonders of mutual evolution, until John Hiller's explosive laugh brought me back to the boys. Dee was shaking his head and grinning, and Blake's eyes were crinkled in mirth. I had missed what they were laughing at—something Blake had said—but couldn't help but smile at their smiles. And I knew then that I'd become captivated by the work, by my affection for my crewmates, by my growing passion for the Canyon.

I felt as though I had lacked without knowing what I was lacking or that I was lacking anything at all until that emptiness was filled. Filled with nothing more that particular day than the vibrancy of spring: the seasonal surge of snowmelt and landslide, flowerbud and insect hatch. On the Canyon rim above me the warming weather and waxing daylight roused the ponderosa pines from their winter dormancy, sap began to rise through their cambium, and the forest thickened with the scent of dry butterscotch. Kaibab squirrels, swollen with their own sort of sap, spiraled after one another so quickly their white tails seemed to wrap the pine trunks like maypole ribbons. Farther downcanyon the aspen began to form bright green buds, and farther still the redbud's fuchsia blossoms and fresh green leaves stood from the ochre slopes like scenes in a Japanese watercolor. Roaring Springs raged ten thousand gallons per minute out of its solid limestone cliff; seeps at the base of the surrounding cliffs bloomed riots of primrose, paintbrush, monkeyflower, and penstemon. Biting flies, gnats, and mosquitoes hatched and bothered; ouzels birthed chicks in grottos in waterfalls; ants busied themselves with their holes; crickets and beetles chirped ecstatically and took off in noisy and awkward flight; and the tree frogs' mournful cries mingled in deafening chorus in every drainage. And here, in front of me, the near-blooming stalk of a Kaibab century plant, a giant desert lily pollinated not only by overly attendant bees but also, later this evening, by bats. Bats!

Socrates advised one to pay attention to the "best possible state of your soul." The juxtaposition between seemingly eternal stone and brilliantly ephemeral spring moved me to that state. I'd already adopted the crew's custom of talking about "emerging" from the Canyon as though we had been submerged, in Lao Tzu's words, in "something nebulous / silent / isolated / unchanging and alone / eternal." For this the thousands of tourists descended the hiking trails; on this our jobs were based; for this I was to return, season after season, spellbound, enthralled.

᭽: ᭽

A turkey garbled, loudly, seemingly right beneath my head. I sat upright. Dawn. I could hear the turkey scratching the pine duff beneath my trailer. I lay back down. My breath fumed upward to hang in the frigid air of the spring morning. Erika slept beside me, one arm flung over her face, her honey-blond hair mussed over the pillow. I rolled silently out of bed, pulled on a pair of fleece pants, and took a few steps toward the bathroom before I realized that the unusual sensation I was experiencing owed to my hair standing straight up and sweeping the trailer's low ceiling.

After a few seasons of sharing a trailer or a room in the bunkhouse with other Trail dogs, I'd been excited about having my own trailer on the North Rim for a season, especially one a hundred yards from the Canyon's rim. But the trailer was a small and shitty old FEMA fifth-wheel, rumored to have been passed down from post-Katrina New Orleans. It only took me seven short steps to move from the bed through the kitchen to the bathroom. The bathroom was laughably small: I could lean against the wall as I pissed; the toilet bowl was so small that sometimes I'd fill it to the brim and have to stop, bend over, and flush before I could finish peeing.

I stood groggy by the sink, filling the kettle. The olive oil had fully coagulated overnight: temperatures had dropped into the teens. A dead deer mouse lay in the trap by the trashcan, and I recalled waking in the night to the snap and death thrash, and the small satisfaction this had given me before I had fallen back asleep. I cracked the door—the cold slanted in—and placed the mouse and trap on the top step. When I left in the morning I would lay the mouse under one of the big, lightning-scarred ponderosa snags as an offering to the ravens, just as I'd already done with a half-dozen of its relatives. That night I would rebait the same trap.

The specters of dead mice have never bothered me half as much as moving into a place that has been lived in by countless others. It would take a while for the place to be "mine," or "ours"—for Erika's and my energies to supersede the weird residues of those who lived here before, their smells and dust lingering in cupboards and corners, their dreams still saturating the soft mattress. Bleach helped, as did opening the windows wide for a week, despite the freezing temperatures.

I sat in the booth and drank my yerba maté and wrote in my journal. Crunching sounds outside made me look up to see fifteen mule deer, their heads down in the first spring growth. I tapped on the window with my finger and they all looked up at once, their white-tipped ears concaving toward me.

"You maté-ing without me?" Erika said from bed, without sitting up.

"Yeah, sorry; I thought you'd want to sleep."

"Mmmmm. I am sleeping. But I'll take a *há*."

I rose and handed her the steaming *guampa*. She sat up in bed and sipped from it, watching me as I moved about the trailer: putting on my uniform, fixing my lunch, filling my water bottles, stopping by the bed when it was my turn to drink.

Erika had dedicated her summer to applying to graduate schools. The previous fall she'd applied to study under a well-known canopy biologist. For years she'd worked as a canopy researcher, ascending old-growth trees in search of red tree voles and marbled murrelets, often with the professor's former students and friends, a few times with the professor himself, and she was confident that she'd be accepted. She wasn't: the funding fell through. She was crushed. But she's stubborn, and the following year—that summer in the trailer—she was applying to five schools. She'd also shifted her proposed research area, from nitrogen-capturing canopy lichens to ethnobotanical cultures.

The shift wasn't such a stretch, either. Since I'd known her she'd professionally and academically oscillated between botany, mycology, dendrology, ethnobotany, anthropology, and cartography. She often used the phrase "my new favorite." Her new favorite breakfast that summer in the trailer was a pile of barely wilted bitter greens with a single coddled egg on top. She'd delicately puncture the egg and watch the yolk run over the greens. Before that her favorite breakfast was a car-camping-style huevos rancheros quesadilla. Then savory crepes with avocado and cheese. The wilted greens breakfast was in turn supplanted by an egg sandwich creation involving sautéed tomatoes, prosciutto, and goat cheese.

This was succeeded by shredded zucchini fry, about which she'd close her eyes and moan, "It tastes like crab."

"Where're you working today?" she asked.

"Below the tunnel," I said, stuffing my backpack. "Few more days of digging ditch. What application are you working on?"

"Hawaii."

"Hawaii would be nice."

"Hawaii would be really nice," she said.

The plan, at that point still inchoate, was that Erika would go back to school for her master's degree and PhD, and I'd follow. I wasn't entirely sure how I felt about the idea. When we first came to the Canyon, Erika and I had been apart as much as we'd been together: she in Costa Rica for five months, then me in Southern Africa for four months; then me working in Glacier National Park for a summer while she climbed trees on Mount Rainier, then the same the following summer. After we graduated from college, we traveled together in Southeast Asia and India. That trip had been an assessment, a testing, and we underwent as many harrowing experiences as we did romantic ones, and all in all it was good for us: we had fallen further in love. But when we returned to the States, we again separated, Erika to climb trees, me to wander, then to work building trails for a season at Point Reyes National Seashore.

The together-then-apart pattern strengthened and defined our relationship. Our love was strong because it could survive, even thrive, thanks to the time spent apart. We were young, in our early twenties, with no real idea what the future held for us either individually or as a couple. Nor were we in any hurry to find out. We knew that we valued our independence; perhaps, in those early years, we valued it more than our compatibility. But also, almost intrinsically, we both needed novelty. We expected life to be fresh, or new, or exciting: we associated happiness with that sort of change. This extended into my love for the Canyon as well, for though I had committed to it as far as coming back—by that point for my third season—commitment did not require a constant physical presence. Indeed, during my first few seasons, my restlessness was stronger than the pull of the Canyon, and I spent most of my five-day breaks outside the Canyon: over to Colorado to climb "fourteeners," up to Montana to see my brother, back to LA to swim in the ocean, out to Florida to learn to scuba dive, up to British Columbia to climb, over to Utah or New Mexico or Oregon to hike. This pattern would be replicated on the bigger scale of my winter "off-seasons": a winter in LA, a winter in Santa Fe, two winters in South America, two winters in Tucson.

I wonder, now, what I thought then of true commitment. I probably thought of it in absolute terms. Descending slot canyons often required rappelling over successive dry waterfalls. Depending on the slot, you could leave your ropes up in case you later chanced upon a nasty keeper pool or a drop longer than your ropes; you could then retrace your steps and ascend the fixed rope to exit the canyon. But I never explored virgin canyons—I always followed a guidebook, or went with someone who knew the route, someone who knew whether there was an escape route downcanyon, or knew the size of the rappels ahead, and inevitably someone who'd be loath to jug back up a fixed line. So after rappelling we pulled our ropes. And yet every time I watched the rope come slithering through our anchor to fall down the cliff and lie slack at our feet, I felt a surge of excitement: there was no going back. I associated a relationship's commitment with this same sort of finality. I was in, trapped, with no guide, no idea of what surprises lay around the next bend, the only exit downlife, hidden from view.

Our time in the Canyon, though, was the beginning of true commitment—to a place, to one another. I remember the night at Erika's mom's house in Chico, California, when I'd accepted the job in the Canyon and was scheduled to board a bus to Flagstaff the following morning. Erika had no solid plans for the summer, though she was likely to be offered work climbing trees again. She loved that job, it paid fairly well, and around it she'd begun to build the myths that structure our lives. I can't remember the long discussions that night that led to her deciding to come with me, to move to Arizona and find a house and job in Flagstaff for the summer, to do what we'd not yet done in our relationship— make that leap of trust and faith and confidence. But the next day, instead of dropping me off at the Greyhound station, Erika drove us toward Arizona.

Following Erika to Hawaii, or wherever, was more than a way of returning the favor: I wanted to spend my life with her. But I loved working Trails. By that summer I'd earned a well-paid, mid-level position in the crew. I'd earned the respect of my peers and my bosses. And, like Erika climbing trees, I'd begun constructing myself around the work and place. I knew that, if I were willing, I could continue to move up the hierarchy. I could work year-round, earn benefits, find a nice rent-subsidized house on the South Rim, and maybe spend my summers in one of the cute little cabins on the North Rim. The National Park Service was a fine organization. I could live my life—a good life—in places indefinitely preserved for their natural beauty. I was tempted.

The deepening of my relationship with Erika is woven into my time in the Canyon as powerfully as is the work and rock. But that

morning, with Erika still in bed and me in uniform and a dead
mouse on the step and the day starting to warm and miles of ditch
to dig, I could sense there'd come a reckoning, a choice between
the two.

∾: ∾

Four windthrown trees—three ponderosa pines and a white fir—
lay atop one another like pickup sticks. A few of the ponderosa's
branches had broken off when the trunk hit the ground; they remained embedded in the earth as six-foot spikes. I hung my backpack on one of them, perched my chainsaw on one of the downed
trees, and topped it off with gas and bar oil.

Every spring we'd hike the North Rim's forest trails to cut
through the trees that the winter had downed across them. Long
sections of the Point Imperial Trail and the Ken Patrick Trail
wound through the aftermath of the Outlet Fire and were particularly impeded by windfalls—one spring, along less than five miles
of the Ken Patrick, I counted 105 downed trees. On this particular
day there had been windfalls every few hundred feet, and surely
more hidden within the bigger snowdrifts.

Movement in my side vision made me look up. Stretches of the
burnt, still winter-bare forest floor were covered in soiled snow
drifts, the sky was bruised with sleet clouds, the stands of dead
aspen were like photographic negatives: charred bark over bone-
white trunks, and against all that strolled Blake in vibrant orange
chaps, his saw slung over his shoulder, his eyes shining bright.

"Man!" he exclaimed, all fake chipper. "Those fire douches sure
are American heroes."

Blake, like many of the crew, wasn't overly fond of wildland
firefighters. There were countless reasons for this, from personal

histories to machismo competitiveness to traditional tribal conflicts to a more general consensus that firefighters got paid absurd
amounts of hazard and overtime pay only to fight fires that their
own myopic suppression policies had worsened. Or, at least, that
they shouldn't necessarily be hailed as heroes for the effort. There
was also the blasphemous fact that many of these fire guys had
worked in Grand Canyon National Park as long as some of us had,
and yet they'd never, not once, left the rim lands and descended
into the genuine Canyon. Anyway, in this case Blake was referring
to the Outlook Fire having been intentionally lit as a "prescribed
fire" designed to burn understory shrubs and smaller trees as a
"natural" fire would have done some few hundred years ago, before
we imposed our own ideas of how forest ecosystems should function. Instead the fire had grown out of control, forced the evacuation of the North Rim lodge, and incinerated fourteen thousand
acres before it hit the Canyon rim and ran out of forest to burn.
The fire was in 2000; six years later the dominant vegetation that
had recolonized the scorched earth was New Mexican locust, an
evil, wiry bush boasting two-inch thorns.

"I kinda like it," I said. "It's so…apocalyptic. I feel like the Road
Warrior."

"Brodie, this was a green forest filled with soft-eyed woodland
creatures! Haven't you seen *Bambi*? The fire scene?" He lowered
his voice. "Get up, Brodie. Get up! You must get up!"

"Yeah," I shrugged, grinning. "It'll grow back. And look: pocket
gophers." I pointed at the fresh gopher eskers rumpling the spongy
earth.

"Gophers," he deadpanned. "Great."

With that he turned and circled around the blowdown. He'd
hike until he got to the next windfall, and if he was still cutting

through it when I caught up I'd leapfrog past him, and in this way the four of us cutting trees that day would clear the trail.

I put in my earplugs and stood for a few moments, planning the cuts. The fir had fallen as though folding upon the earth, its root wad still snarled with rock and soil. I checked to ensure that the tree wasn't still rooted, that the trunk wouldn't spring upright once its limbs weren't entangled or its top cut off—I've seen downed but still-rooted trees rise back toward vertical like Dracula sitting up in his coffin. Beneath the fir were the ponderosas, the biggest easily three feet in diameter. It had shattered into huge segments, most bearing the tendriled inscriptions of termites and the stigmata impressions of sapsucker beaks. I looked to see if any of them were resting on stumps or rocks; I reckoned which ways the cookies would fall once I'd cut them loose; I kicked myself some footing in the underbrush. The burnt earth was perforated with holes where the fire had followed tree roots as though they were fuses. The blowdown was a tangled mess, but not overly complicated, and bucking it up was mainly a matter of anticipating the binds: how the tensions and compressions within the wood might pinch the chainsaw's bar as it passed through them.

I fired the saw, dug its dogs into the fir's bark-shorn, seared red trunk, gave it full gas, and let it rip through the trunk on its own accord. The chain was sharp. Fat woodchips spat back onto my chaps. Some of the cuts I'd start from the bottom, cut a third of the way up, then meet that cut from the top. Others I'd start from the top and watch to make sure the kerf opened incrementally wider; if it started to close, I'd either meet the cut from the bottom or slap a small wedge in the kerf to keep it from closing. I'd stop every once in a while and drag the cut limbs away; once I had cut a trailwide cookie out of one of the logs, I'd crouch behind it and roll it off-trail. Sometimes the round would go lumbering down a hill for a few hundred feet before slamming up against a log or tree. One of my favorite lines from one of my favorite books—*A River Runs through It*—goes: "One great thing about fly fishing is that after a while nothing exists of the world but thoughts about fly fishing." Bucking logs is similar, and I lost myself in the work of not pinching my bar or throwing my chain or dirting the tip or limbing my own limbs along with the trees'. But it wasn't completely engrossing: through the cracks in my concentration welled an easy joy, the thought of how good it was to be back on the North Rim.

The North Rim had become my Canyon home. I may hold certain places within the Canyon's walls—wildflower-draped springs, sinuous slot canyons, remote rock promontories—in a more sacred light, or cite them when asked why I kept coming back to the Canyon. But after visiting those places I'd return to the North Rim, to whatever room in the bunkhouse or trailer or cabin housed me over the five summers I was based there. From there I watched the sunset while I ate dinner; from there I looked up at the stars before I slept; from there I woke with the sun and pulled on my dirty denim pants and walked to work.

The North Rim is the southern end of the 8,800-foot terrestrial bulge known as the Kaibab Plateau. (Kaibab is a Paiute word meaning "mountain lying down.") As the plateau is the highest point in the whole 277-mile length of the Canyon, the Colorado River cuts its deepest course through it, providing what's arguably the most dramatic part of the Grand Canyon. From the Engelmann spruce and white fir forests on the plateau's summit one can descend through an impressive array of elevation-determined vegetation communities: down through the ponderosa and gambel oak forests, farther down through the piñon-juniper woodland, through the blackbrush and century plants of the Great Basin Desertscrub, though the acacia and barrel cactus of the Mojave and Sonoran Desertscrubs, until you stand amid the willows and sedges of the riparian areas where the Colorado River eases into Lake Mead, more than 7,600 feet below the Kaibab Plateau.

There were sprawling meadows broken by outcroppings of deteriorating white limestone and ringed by colonies of quaking aspen. Across these meadows roamed the occasional herd of invasive and exotic bison, as well as some of the biggest mule deer bucks in the country. There were open, old-growth ponderosa forests—some of the last in the Southwest—through which one could wander for miles before coming to a point overlooking a spectacular Canyon amphitheater and find, right on the uttermost edge, half a dozen five-point black-tailed deer antlers. There were squirrels with large brown bodies and tufted black ears and brilliant white tails that lived nowhere else in the world but on the Kaibab Plateau. In spring the woods filled with the deep, tribal thrum of dusky grouse. Preying on grouse and squirrel alike, northern goshawks—the forest's apex predators—swooped and folded through the spaces between the pines. Separated from the mainland plateau were sky-island pillars of rock on which the Old Ones had built dwellings that the intervening centuries had reduced to piles of rubble under the open sky.

The North Rim was far less crowded than the South Rim, attracting only about 10 percent of the park's nearly 6 million annual visitors. There was one lodge, one saloon where we paid too much money for whiskey, and one pub attached to the Employee Dining Room where we drank dollar PBRs and played pool and flirted with the foreign girls who worked at the lodge. Blake, for one, hated the North Rim because it was so isolated—a four-hour drive from Flagstaff or the South Rim, a four-hour roundtrip haul just to get groceries—and considered the lack of crowds and the limited services a bore. I considered it ideal.

I didn't generally work the winter season, and when I returned in spring it was for the "opener": when every person on Trails would come to the North Rim before it opened for the season to clear the forest trails of trees and the North Kaibab Trail of land-slides. So pretty much every year the North Rim was my welcome back to the Canyon, and a privileged one, as with the North Rim still closed to the public we could bike down the long causeway right out to Bright Angel Point, a place normally teeming with tourists, and sit on the rocks and watch the sunset with a six-pack and nothing but violet-green swallows for company.

At noon I caught up with Blake and we walked off-trail, toward the rim overlooking Marble Canyon. Snow and ice still encased most of the rimrock, but we found a burnt-over outcrop of partly bare rocks, and I took off my chaps and spread them out and sat on them. Sawdust clung to my hair, to the creases in my clothes. I poured water over my hands and rubbed them together and wiped them on my pants. Even so, my sandwich tasted of pine sap and saw gas.

Black clouds roiled about in the Canyon below us, obscuring the phenomenal view of Marble Canyon and ten-thousand-foot Navajo Mountain. My Park Service radio broadcast the park's daily soap opera of news and divisional melodrama, what a paramedic friend called "As the Canyon Crumbles." Most of it was South Rim's law enforcement chatter: a "significant language barrier" in helping a tourist's squirrel-bit finger, an "elk jam" (when tourists stop their cars in the middle of the highway to take pictures of elk), a "group in front of the First Amendment sign singing without a permit," a smoldering dumpster in Trailer Village, and so on, all of it blessedly distant. I reached over and turned the radio off. The wind keened against the rock.

My attention was caught by the rivulets of thaw water twist-slipping quickly, hypnotically, through the ice sheet that covered much of the rock I sat on. The drops followed grooves formed by other drops, and the faint sound of their movement through the grooves was like rain dripping off an overhanging rock. The drops would eventually dissolve enough of the connective tissue between the ice plate and the rock face and a section of the ice would pop up, and the water under the ice would run freely in sheets. Then it would hit thicker ice still melded to rock, and the water again formed into drops and rivulets, again sought paths to sever the bonds. The following tour, digging ditch in the Supai layer, some 1,400 feet below the rim, I'd watch as the same process caused huge lobes of ice to calve off the top of the Coconino cliffs and fall 300 feet to shatter, out of sight, on the shale slopes above me. But this was Kaibab limestone—the Canyon's caprock—and this ice had a long way to go before it sloughed off its rock.

From farther downtrail sounded the sharp whine of a chainsaw, spoiling my reverie. I glanced at my radio for the time. Twelve thirty on the dot. I looked over at Blake.

"Fucking Devin," he said, referring to our meticulous crew leader.

We reluctantly packed our bags, shouldered them, and wound back through the thorns to the trail. The wind had picked up. Eight hundred thousand acres of pine and fir and aspen shuddered about me. The burnt forest creaked and whistled in the wind, the trees swaying only as upright dead wood does—as a rigid, ready-to-snap whole. On one slight incline the wind had scythed the upper half

off every snag. The recurring weight of heavy snows had deformed
the trees' limbs downward, and having brittled in death they
moved in the wind like arthritic arms, scratching at their charred,
bark-scabbed trunks. They'd fall eventually, and we'd come back
eventually, and through them we'd cut the trail.

❧ ∾

The tracks were pressed so perfectly in mud as to seem intentional,
as though the cougar had chosen two strides to reveal itself. As
though it were winking at me.

It was the first of May and I was counting the trees that winter
had felled across the North Rim's Ken Patrick Trail. Later that
week we'd come back with saws and cut the trail through the
windfalls, but right then I had a whole day to walk an easy ten
miles. The North Rim was still closed to tourists; little chance I'd
encounter another human. I was happy to be alone. The bright,
high-altitude sun slanted through the spires of pines, and the first
burst of wildflowers—wild candytuft, golden peavine, mariposa
lily—caught the light, burning through the darkest patches of
forest. Thin drifts of snow remained in the north-facing drainages and deeper tree wells; the trail, still wet with snowmelt, was
stamped with animal tracks: squirrel, coyote, turkey, their tracks
glyphs of hunger, whim, instinct, territory. I'd stop from time to
time and study the spoor, and so walking and stopping I came
across a muddy divot displaying the lion's left forefoot and right
hindfoot, the tracks about three inches long by three and a half
wide.

I held my hand over them. As though they gave heat.

There is something special in coming across predator tracks—
the lion residue not only preserved in mud but hanging in air,

cuing some suddenly sensitive psycho-olfactory sense, exciting some long-dormant primal impulses. It is particularly pleasing coming across predator tracks on the Kaibab Plateau, the scene of one of the most storied predator-eradication campaigns in modern history.

In 1906 Teddy Roosevelt established the Grand Canyon Game Preserve, which encompassed much of the Kaibab Plateau. The logic behind a game preserve was simple—set aside a safe haven for game animals so that, free from human hunting, they could reproduce and repopulate other areas, thus ensuring a continual source of wildlife for hunting or tourist viewing. By that time, deforestation and unregulated hunting had severely reduced the populations of every major game species in the United States. Elk, once the most widespread of all North American ungulates, had been extirpated from the eastern United States. Bison, reputedly once the single most numerous species of any large mammal on earth, teetered on the brink of extinction. The endling passenger pigeon, the last of a species that had flown overhead in billion-bird flocks once estimated to be a mile wide by three hundred miles long, would die in captivity within eight years.

And yet, as the logic of the times dictated, protecting game animals in a game preserve necessitated not only the elimination of human hunters but also the elimination of natural predators. So between 1906 and 1923 federal government hunters on the Kaibab Plateau trapped, poisoned, and shot 781 mountain lions, 4,849 coyotes, 554 bobcats, the entire population of 30 wolves, and an unknown number of great horned owls, golden eagles, California condors, badgers, and foxes.

A century later no one knows how many cougars roam the Kaibab Plateau. The Forest Service, based on "harvest" information and observed lion sign, now estimates there to be roughly sixty to eighty cougars on the Kaibab Plateau, a population deemed "healthy and robust" enough to allow hunters to hound, tree, and casually shoot for sport a dozen cougars a year. Mountain lions have probably realized that the National Park's arbitrary boundary forms a safe haven—especially considering how heavily logged and extensively roaded the adjacent Forest Service lands are—and thus may not be accounted for in the Forest Service's "harvest" tallies. But according to the Park Service, "Research has not yet determined the exact number of lions [on the South Rim], nor has it concentrated on other areas of the park."

Thus it was a treat to come across cougar sign in a place where they had been systematically slaughtered, to follow the tracks and find a pile of scat. I probed the shit with a stick: it was at least 90 percent fur. I continued walking, pleased to tread the same trail as a cougar had, to slide under the same deadfalls, to be yelled at by the same Steller's jay. The trail switchbacked down a steep slope, crossed a sunlit meadow, and wound up a thickly wooded draw. In the middle of the trail lay an object that my eyes, struggling to readjust to the darkness of the timber, could not quite recognize. A long moment passed before I recognized it as a deer leg.

Enough fur had been gnawed off to expose the still-articulated femur, tibia, and fibula. A tuft of fur remained where bone met hoof. Moving slowly uptrail, I found another leg, similarly ravaged, then the rest of the kill: the spinal column, the scattered ribs, the halved lower jaw. In a hollow off the side of the trail lay the antlers, a fine dichotomous pair still attached to a large portion of skull.

I picked them up. Maggots burst like a broken pustule from the brain cavity.

I gagged, dropped the antlers, and looked around nervously. The drainage was choked with downed trees and hemmed by steep slopes rimmed by outcroppings of Kaibab limestone. Earlier in the day I had taken my knife out of my pocket and replaced it with my binoculars; now I took the knife back out of my pack. The rational part of my brain suspected that the cougar wasn't still around—the scat was days old, the kill well worked over. But it didn't require much imagination to envision the lion watching me from a dark hollow. The quick stab of fear I'd felt at the maggots was a primordial feeling, one of the root human feelings, a feeling now as rare as a cougar sighting. It was a fear that may have helped me if I'd actually come face-to-face with a cougar, an occasion I have fiercely longed for.

I have no doubt that I have been in the presence of mountain lions, that they have seen me and that I'd have seen them if I had only looked in the right place at the right instant; if, rather than being "lost" in thought, I had been present in the way that fear makes me present, heightens my senses; in the way it made me hike the rest of the trail with my head up, looking not at the ground or the façade of surrounding trees, but through the trees, into the shadows of the woods. There: a gnarled, anthropomorphic aspen snag. There: the flit and parabolic swoop of a jay. Here: the dry butterscotch scent of a yellow pine and the giving crunch of its litter underfoot.

The fear was more than a reminder to be attentive to the world around me, of course. But it was also a warning that our particular species of hominid is neither the center of this world nor ever apart from it; that, to a number of nonhuman animals, our brilliant, dominant species remains nothing more than meat.

The inherent indifference and austere conditions of the Grand Canyon kept me humble, true, but not in as visceral a manner as the thought of a 130-pound cat bursting from a bush and crushing my windpipe. And not just cougar: in autumn, the South Rim's thousand-pound bull elk swell with testosterone to the point that they'll stand in the middle of the road and stare down passing cars with bloodshot eyes and open mouths, almost hallucinating with anger. Once, at my trailer on the South Rim, I watched a rutting bull antler the absolute hell out of what looked to me like a rather unoffending metal trashcan. I was amused at the time, but biking back to my trailer that night I could hear the clack of antlers and moan of bulls battling in the roadside meadows and feared that in the dark an elk would mistake me for a charging rival.

My fear, in this specific instance, was rooted in an indelible moment that occurred when I was sixteen, working on a ranch bordering Idaho's Sawtooth Mountains. Wandering through the sagebrush hills, I spied an elk herd grazing in a meadow. I slipped from pine to pine to the meadow's edge, then inch by inch moved into its grass, barely breathing, hoping—what? To slap an elk ass? To stand amid them as Elk-Man? I don't know what I was thinking. It didn't matter. I was ten paces into the meadow when a six-point bull elk emerged from the aspen grove on the far side, snorting and tossing his head, his eyes stripping my soul. Fear ran down through me. I whispered prayers to gods I don't believe in and inched slowly backward, ever calculating the distance between the bull elk, me, and the closest tree capable of bearing my weight.

As I reached the first pine the bull swung its massive neck to the west and bugled, and as one the twenty or so cows streamed past him. Once the last of his harem had passed, the bull, without deigning a last look, followed, his chin up, his antlers pointed back at me like raised middle fingers.

Contrary to what one might expect from living so long in one of the biggest national parks in one of the more remote sections of the world, I never enjoyed a similar, direct, slowed moment of interspecies communication in the Grand Canyon.

Oh, there were times, even times of fear, but most of my animal encounters in the Canyon lacked that wild edge, the animals both boring and bored by acculturation. There was the old ram calmly chewing its cud in the middle of Bright Angel Trail, impatient crowds backed up on either side. There were the wild turkeys, gorged on Cheetos and territorial hormones, who attacked tourists and mule trains down at Phantom Ranch. The coyote gagging on road-killed carrion, the rattlesnake with its head crushed by a rock, the condors tagged like retail products. The time Michael felled a dead aspen whose rot-hollowed core hosted a squirrel's nest made of fiberglass insulation. The bushy-tailed woodrat who'd made a nest out of our mason twine. The feral "beefalo"— bison brought down from Yellowstone to be bred with cattle in the House Rock Valley—now grazing in the delicate meadows of the North Rim.

But cougars, cougars cannot be made boring, or fat, or tainted by previous contact. They cannot be controlled except by being killed. Which is, of course, why they are killed, and why I loved them and so wanted to see one, on its own terms. I may have seen one, once, in the Klamath Mountains of Oregon. I clattered around a dirt road bend in my jalopy and saw a tawny back end slink quickly into the downslope brush. So quickly it could, in fact, have not been a cougar at all, and despite what I swear were the distinctive scratching-at-the-road motions of a panicked feline, maybe only my desperate want made a cat out of an ungulate ass. Regardless, if it was a cougar, it was a split-second sight of a creature consumed by fear, not exactly what I have in mind when I long to fill, as D. H. Lawrence put it, the "gap in the world, the missing white frost-face of that slim yellow mountain lion!"

And yet the potential cougar's fear was fitting, too. At one point both cougar and Canyon embodied the sublime; both emanated power, silence, beauty; both had the ability to induce awe, astonishment, and reverence as easily as they did the shock and ecstasy of terror, horror, passion. Though both Canyon and cougar still retain these traits, their power, in a remarkably short time, has become debased, diminished. They have become capable of being overwhelmed; they have become overwhelmed.

The Grand Canyon is an integral component of American mythology—a vast, titanic, and wholly unique landscape; a tabula rasa that embodies the dramatic natural and human histories of the West. I bought into that myth for a while, bought the narrative the park sells so well: the Canyon's opened earth as unspoiled as the day the first human looked across it. Many of us did. When Ray, barely eighteen, came to work on Trails in the Canyon after a conservation corps summer in the Yosemite backcountry, he was thrown in with Michael—a wry Chicago realist—and Wayne—a libertarian Christian. Looking out across the great expanse of bared rock, Ray casually mentioned something about places like Yosemite or the Canyon being the real world, and everything outside of them as elaborately constructed fallacies.

"Bullshit," said Michael, without looking up from his work.

Ray stared at him, stunned.

"The world on the rim is the real world," said Michael.

"Yeah, the Canyon is the fucking bubble," I said.

"But, but—" Ray stammered.

"No. They're right," said Wayne, cutting him off, and so another debate began, this one noteworthy largely in that it may have been the only time that Michael, Wayne, and I had ever uniformly agreed.

The Canyon, we figured, is inextricably bound to the surface world; it is permeated with humanity's historic and current presence. This permeation, this presence, has had, and still has, its effects, and not just the effect of animals grown accustomed to humans. There's the dam, releasing the silt-strained waters of the Colorado in accordance with Phoenix's use of air conditioners. There's the air pollution: whereas at one time one could stand on the North Rim and look across seventy miles at individual trees on the San Francisco Peaks, during the years I worked in the Canyon the nearby Navajo Generating Station dispersed so much particulate matter over the region that, along with natural dust and smog blown in from Los Angeles, Phoenix, and China, on most days the peaks were only a hazy pyramid. There's light pollution: while the Grand Canyon region is still one of the most and last starbright places on the continent, its night sky is increasingly washed out by the city lights of Phoenix, 220 miles away. So much other evidence of our inescapable presence: the roads and trails; the fire-suppressed forests; the petroglyphs and potsherds, dendroglyphs and miner's trash; the mines contaminating the river; the helicopter-spewed fire retardant leaching off the rim to stain the fulvous Kaibab red; the fact that even much of the water emanating from the Canyon's springs is irradiated, hot with tritium from decades of nearby nuclear weapons testing.

This is our world: where even in a national park the skein of our presence is laid as thick as the desert vegetation. A world in which nature no longer has a monopoly on the sublime. Where the Canyon is less relevant to our daily lives, less impressive in a way, than what Leo Marx dubbed the "technological sublime": the dam plugging the Colorado, the knowledge that the weight of the impounded water behind such dams has shifted the way the world spins on its axis. The dominant catalyst for indescribable awe tinged by terror is neither Canyon nor cougar but the sheer quantity of pavement laid across the desert basin of Los Angeles.

This is far more terrifying to me than the fear of a cat in the woods. A cat I could flee from or fight. At least try. If I had encountered that lion that day in the woods, I like to think that my fear would have been instinctive, open, even enlightening. It would have been far less pernicious than my fears of the violence that humans so readily inflict on other humans, and far more honest, even reassuring, than my intellectual fears of ocean acidification, or antibiotic-resistant superbugs, or any of the other forms of slow violence that we have wreaked on the world.

In *The Thunder Tree: Lessons from an Urban Wildland*, Robert Michael Pyle writes: "If we are to forge new links to the land, we must resist the extinction of experience." This comes in the context of his greater discussion about "the state of personal alienation from nature in which many people live," in which he argues that "we must save not only the wilderness but the vacant lots, the ditches as well as the canyonlands, and the woodlots along with the old growth."

The extinction of experience may be why I attempted to infiltrate that elk herd at the idiotic and wonderful age of sixteen: being raised in Los Angeles, I had never before been blessed with such an opportunity. The extinction of experience is why I left Los Angeles, seeking to live in the last places that offered such experiences. And yet even in these last places we encounter this lack, this negative feedback loop: I can't help but think that if we had more face-to-face experiences with cougars and wolves and grizzlies we might be less afraid of their presence—or future presence—in our midst.

Or maybe not. The renewal of experience could easily have the opposite effect, providing the old forms for our now-general fears to reinhabit. Numerous studies have shown that people—even the Inuit—are evolutionarily hardwired to fear snakes and spiders. This could certainly be true of lion and wolf as well. If the wolf's tooth "whittled so fine / the fleet limbs of the antelope," as Robinson Jeffers put it, it also shaped my mind to start at shadows and my hands to grasp for knives. Certainly more experiences with mountain lions would likely lead to more attacks on humans, and thus rekindle and renew the urge to exterminate and eradicate. If I may consider the occasional cougar attack a small price to pay for a more genuine and balanced coexistence, I'd obviously be rather upset if Erika were carried off and consumed by a large carnivore. From a distance, often an urban distance, it's easy to speak blithely of restitching our frayed relationships to the nonhuman world, to speak positively of abstractions like keystone predators and trophic cascades and ecological communities. Yet picking through the rent and rotting flesh of a deer carcass, it's far more difficult to ignore the potential for the sudden and striking peril that shadows these creatures.

But that's the point. Even if the fear persists, even *as* the fear persists, we can learn from it. Accepting fear is not about ignoring it, and certainly not about eradicating the external trigger, but about coming face to face with it, addressing the internal source: in this case our primal insecurities, the relict terrors of beasts beyond the reach of the cave's firelight. It is remarkable to consider how many of our current ecological calamities arose—and are sustained—not simply through ignorance or anthropocentric worldviews, but also through our attempts to overcome our ancestral fears. Likewise, it is interesting to consider the possibility that, as Gary Snyder posited, "ignorance and hostility toward wild nature set us up for objectifying and exploiting fellow humans." If this is true, we can gain some solace in the Jeffers line "Old violence is not too old to beget new values"—it may be that by replacing these anachronistic fears and hostilities with new, ecologically based values and ethics, as well as humility, empathy, attentiveness, acceptance, courage, and discipline, future generations may still live with cougar and wolf and bear and elk. It may be that they will be kinder to one another.

I realize that most people would not embrace even the ecological violence of the cougar kill with the same edged joy I experienced that day. But I know that I'm not entirely alone. After all, and somewhat ironically, the Grand Canyon Game Preserve, and the subsequent eradication of predators to protect game species, was created in large part because, as Daniel Justin Herman points out in *Hunting and the American Imagination*, upper- and middle-class New Englanders who considered themselves "sportsmen" were looking back "on the exploits of real men like Daniel Boone, and fictional hunter-heroes like Natty Bumppo, with a nostalgic longing to recapture for themselves the spirit of independent, self-reliant manhood they sadly lacked in their own urban, industrial lives." A century after these sportsmen decided to protect game animals by killing predators, I was following in their atavistic footsteps, longing for the old days when one could wander across the Kaibab Plateau and come face to face with wolves, bear, and cougar. I suspect that this longing impels the millions of people a year who visit national parks and wildlands; I know that Ray, Michael, and Wayne felt the same way, no matter what we felt constituted the "real world."

Those days may come again; I may yet have the chance to walk through a rewilded Kaibab Plateau. In October 2014—years after my encounter with the cougar kill—a female gray wolf was spotted on the Plateau, having traveled at least 450 miles from her home in the northern Rocky Mountains. She was the first wolf on the plateau since the 1940s, when the government destroyed the local population. Still, her visit may be a onetime occurrence: if the US Fish and Wildlife Service—the modern-day iteration of the same agency that helped systematically exterminate wolves from the lower forty-eight states—removes Endangered Species Act protection for all wolves, there is little chance that wolves will be able to recolonize the areas they once roamed, even prime habitat like the Kaibab Plateau.

In his essay about the extinction of experience Pyle says, "We must become believers in the world." The world as it is: for human, wolf, and cougar. As much as I agree with this, it's difficult. Sad. I once heard a mule wrangler leading her tourist wards down the North Kaibab Trail say, "Teddy Roosevelt had to come and kill all the wolves and cougar on the North Rim because they were killing our deer." Our deer. Three months after the itinerant wolf graced the Kaibab Plateau, she was shot dead in Utah by a man intending to collect the fifty dollars that Utah pays per coyote pelt. This is the world we must believe in. That day I found the cougar kill, I finished my hike at a parking lot crowded with Park Service law enforcement. They were mostly young white men, all uniformed, all with an undercurrent of aggression, a hint of provocation, emanating from the way they gathered around their vehicles. They had just finished firearm training, and the parking lot was littered with empty shell casings. I skirted through the woods to avoid them, feeling more vulnerable than I had all day.

～ :～

Thinking of National Park Service law enforcement brings to mind the story of Cameron ramming a small ponderosa pine with his pickup truck. Over and over he'd rev the engine, hit the gas for six feet or so: *bam*, right into the tree. It was a scraggly little pondy, no more than twenty inches around, and it'd shudder violently with every hit, and its bark was chipped and wounded, but according to onlookers there was clearly no way it'd break or uproot. This did not deter the onlookers' encouragement. Cameron finally stopped his automotively assaulting the ponderosa when his truck's bumper began to cave. Eventually the tree was cut down or uprooted as collateral damage when YACC camp—the cluster of trailers we lived in on the South Rim—was demolished to make way for "high-efficiency" housing, but for years we knew it as "Cameron's Tree," and sometimes in mock solemnity one of us would point at the tree and slowly shake our head and say, "That tree kicked Cameron's truck's ass."

To this day I'm not sure why he was ramming the poor tree. Even among all the wild boys and adrenaline junkies and neopagan lunatics that made up the crew, the man's bestial eccentricities set him apart. He once tried and tried and finally succeeded in throwing an entire picnic table over the five-foot fence surrounding the Phantom Ranch bunkhouse patio. He once demanded that the crew stop the work truck; before it had come to a complete stop he'd bolted out of it and was running as fast as he could across the roadside meadow toward an astonished turkey. He inserted one of the tracking devices the National Park Service fish biologists used to identify individual fish into his own flesh; his infectious, irrepressible wildness was such that if he'd handed me one I'd have slid it into my own skin in solidarity. Cameron had grown up in the Grand Canyon. He'd climbed more of the Canyon's peaks than anyone I'd ever met; he'd descended the Colorado River through the Canyon hundreds of times; he'd worked Trails, worked at Phantom Ranch, worked as a river guide—it was hard to imagine him ever leaving the Canyon region. He viewed it with a certain proprietary edge, which may explain his actions that night. The poet Mary Szybist writes of how troubadours "knew how to burn themselves through, / how to make themselves shrines to their own longing," and that captures something in Cameron, something about many of us on Trails.

But really it was simpler than that: what was burning through him was bourbon.

We'd drink rye or Scotch or Irish whiskey or, for that matter, vodka, wine, gin, tequila, grappa, ouzo, or whatever liquor was at hand to complement the ubiquitous beer, but most parties or end-of-the-tour evenings that later turned into parties or continued as contained, concentrated drinking sessions usually involved bourbon. We drank bourbon because it was delicious. But also because we could pass around the bottle and, before tossing back our heads for a healthy chug, blow quickly across its open lip and send intemperate toots into the night. Because we smacked our lips and grinned or grimaced at the bite and burn in the throat, a burn that warmed on a cold night and tore one's shirt if not pants off on a warm night. A burn and a pain that corresponded to the gripe of thighs after a long hike, the sear of sunburned necks in spring, the dull throb of a rock-torn fingernail.

Years before I came to work in the Canyon, I made a necklace out of incisors I ripped from cape fur seal skulls on Namibia's Skeleton Coast. Between the teeth are scarabs, bloodstone, shells, turquoise, cow bone beads, and rattlesnake vertebrae. The seal teeth lie flat against my chest and don't bite, but the rattlesnake vertebrae are needle sharp and stab into the soft flesh of my neck.

I like the feeling.

For in the worst of times the Canyon—life itself—seemed as flat as a façade, and I'd have trouble believing in the reality of its presence or my own, and the pain helped gather me back. The desert offers the conflicting senses that there is a fundamental beauty in the struggle to survive and cast seeds into the world and, simultaneously, that life is so fragile as to be futile amid the enormity of the nonliving expanses. Pain, like the desert, reaffirmed us even as it reminded us of the inevitable.

Death wasn't the only inevitable: the bourbon delivered a belated pain decidedly more unwelcome than the burn in the throat. But in the heat of the night, with the alcohol coursing through us, with Cameron ramming a tree, or Blake tossing the kitchen trailer's moldering couch into the fire pit and it going up in a mushroom cloud, or John Hiller trying to jump over the bonfire and stumbling right at the lip and crashing down into the flames, or somebody tossing a Mason jar of old chainsaw gas on the fire, or the coyotes opening up their throats in thanks for the kill and us responding in kind, or whatever, really: the morning was far away, the hangover either impossible or worthwhile, the life to be lived being lived, right then.

And right about then the cops would come. For the most part, National Park Service law enforcement rangers weren't nice bearded naturalist fellows quick with charming anecdotes about desert bighorn sheep. They weren't Ranger Rick types who happened to be carrying firearms. These were cops right out of the Federal Law Enforcement Training Center, where whatever sympathies they may have had for good-timing trail crew types had been brainwashed out of them by counterterrorist goons. They'd come to the Canyon crewcut and stiff-necked, twitchy and starchy, trained to be suspicious, eager to advance their careers by racking up arrests. They'd run Google searches on permit holders to the North Rim's winter yurt. They'd create fake Facebook personas or fake avatars on Grand Canyon hikers' web forums to try and coax hikers into revealing unpermitted hikes. They'd lurk in the bushes with binoculars, waiting for someone to spark a joint. They'd circle the campfire in the darkness and then all at once step into the firelight and demand to see our IDs (once they pulled Lake aside and questioned him at length; as it turned out, another Eric Lake in the world happened to be a pedophile). Blake referred to them as though they were clones, every one of them named Ranger BuzzKillington. "Put down the fun and step away from the good times," he'd mutter, his voice warbling like a megaphone.

To be fair, there was a small group of cool rangers: the "Canyon rangers," whose duties were to hike the backcountry trails and off-trail areas, checking on hiking permits, monitoring and protecting "cultural resources," and the like. Because the Canyon rangers passed through our work sites and saw that we were actually well-meaning and hardworking young men and women shaping and shaped by the Canyon stone, they were a kinder and more forgiving bunch than the South Rim robots.

Most of us had no problem with the hierarchical structure of Trails—differing wage-grade levels, permanent versus term versus seasonal positions, the informal acknowledgments of years worked and technical skills—and most of us respected that structure and our places within it. And, obviously, in the egregious and aberrant treatment of park resources exemplified in the case of *Cameron v. Ponderosa*, we had earned the increased attention, if not arrest, by law enforcement. We may have been sensitive, proud, antiauthoritarian ragamuffins inclined to wrestle, drink bourbon, occasionally ram small trees with automobiles, and generally follow our own rude and open code of life, but we could handle scrutiny and pressure. As when they had one of us in handcuffs and threatened to haul him to jail unless the bonfire party stopped and everybody in unison shouted "Haul him off!" We could handle being regarded as delinquents or miscreants because many of us had been viewed as such our whole lives.

But in the end we couldn't forgive these South Rim law enforcement rangers for viewing us, the Canyon, the world, through suspicion, aggression, and fear. Their fear wasn't of the humbling kind, as I felt in coming across the fresh cougar kill; on the contrary, their fear fueled the same arrogance and need for control that had fueled the annihilation of predators on the North Rim. To us, this fear tainted their view of the world: as though they heard, no, *felt*, different than we did when the coyotes sang to the night.

We saw Trails and Law Enforcement as inhabiting different ecologies of presence: they belonged to, or were at least paying obeisance to, a world that had been grafted onto the rimrock to lure tourist dollars. It may have been the real world, but it wasn't a world we wanted to inhabit or for that matter truly believed in, in no small part because of the strictures and rigid codes of conduct that it was these cops' duty to enforce and uphold. We believed that our roles in the Canyon tied us into greater cycles: stacking stones in a retaining wall was a ritual of fitting them into a puzzle that described or mimicked patterns of the natural world.

Take the fuel we used for our bonfires: we burned old check steps, those critical trail structures shoring up the tread on every trail in the Canyon. We had once cut them from living junipers in the same forest where we'd later burn them. We had carried the checks into the Canyon, plugged them into the trail, and decades later, after they had bowed in the middle or cracked with rot, we pried them out of the ground and loaded them onto mules to be hauled out of the Canyon, dumped by the barn, then loaded into our personal trucks and carried here to be burned hot, brilliant, and brief, just as we all burned against the ancient, indifferent rock of the Canyon walls, or beneath the ancient, indifferent light of the starbright night.

Framed in the sober red and blue strobe lights of the South Rim's Ranger Empire, that was only so much pretentious and self-righteous Buddhist nonsense. And to be fair, the rangers' general fear and suspicion wasn't *entirely* unwarranted: the South Rim village, with a large overnight population and an even greater daily transient population, bore many of the minor transgressions associated with a small city, as well as a few storied instances of violence and armed lunacy. In 1992 Danny Ray Horning, serving four consecutive life sentences for bank robbery, kidnapping, and aggravated assault, escaped from the Arizona state prison. On the lam, he kidnapped a couple from Flagstaff and made them drive him to the Grand Canyon. He stayed at the El Tovar and enjoyed room service. The next morning, after trying and failing to kidnap another family, he disappeared into the South Rim woods. Despite the efforts of some four hundred officers from a dozen different agencies, he remained at large in the park for four more days. He then kidnapped another couple, passed through a few checkpoints, got involved in a high-speed chase and shootout, disappeared yet again into the woods, and was finally captured fifty-four days after his prison break.

Then, in 2008, two men intentionally drove their car off the rim of the Canyon. Their car got hung up in a tree. According to horrified onlookers, the two men exited the vehicle, pulled out full backpacks, casually smoked a few cigarettes, and then disappeared into the forest. Turns out they were the Twiggs brothers, one of whom—Tebeaux—was a highly decorated Marine combat veteran who, after one tour of duty in Afghanistan and four tours in Iraq, was suffering PTSD-induced hallucinations. Apparently Tebeaux was a martial arts instructor, weapons expert, and skilled combat tracker, and both brothers were rumored to be heavily armed and planning a "suicide by cop." Needless to say, the rangers were on high alert—terrified, it seemed to us—and the South Rim swarmed with paramilitary law enforcement personnel. Eventually, like Horning, the brothers carjacked a tourist near Desert View, exited the park, and got in a high-speed chase down in southern Arizona. Using their only weapon—a .38 pistol—Tebeaux first killed his brother and then turned the gun on himself.

Compared to that, some Canyon kid on the trail crew ramming a small tree in a sea of trees should have been—had they caught him in the act—a laughable arrest, another roll-the-eyes-and-shrug-the-shoulders-with-the-other-cops-back-at-the-base.

After all, what was the point of cloistering us in our own cluster of decrepit trailers at the edge of a virtually endless piñon-juniper forest if we were not free to celebrate at the end of each tour our knowledge that life is a lit fuse progressing toward death?

:~ :~

Getting back to our quick dismissal of poor Ray that day. It's not that I didn't understand where he was coming from, I understood exactly where he was coming from: we had both grown up in Southern California. I have no doubt that at one point, perhaps high in a California live oak in the hills above my house, looking down on the cybernetic grid of LA, I'd derided the city as Ray had derided the surface world: as an elaborately constructed fallacy, a bullshit Babylon.

In 1951 my grandparents paid seven thousand dollars for a one-third-acre lot on a narrow ridge in the Santa Monica Mountains. They built a house on the lot, and raised my father and his siblings in that house. When my grandparents died, my father and my mother raised my brother and me in that house. When my grandparents built our house, there were few other houses along the road, but by the time I left home the last remaining parcels of undeveloped land were developed: the neighbor's avocado grove was uprooted and replaced by a mansion that sold for $3 million, and the old ranch with the emus, peacocks, horses, and sprawling prickly pear was replaced by one of the most aggressively large houses I've ever encountered.

But the house my grandparents built remains, and my parents still live there, never to leave. I've now lived longer away from the house as I did growing up in it, and, like most homes that one leaves to never truly return, it's home and it's not home: its influences are deep and inescapable, but further influences and experiences have shaped my life since I lived there. I make annual pilgrimages back, and the first few days of my return are submerged in memories, every object shining with a rich patina of experience, every sense a repository of and gateway to remembrance and emotion: the su-surrus of eucalyptus leaves, the alarm call of a California quail, the oily glint of poison sumac leaves, the desiccating Santa Ana winds, all as evocative as Proust's madeleine.

The deepest influence of all was up the road a steep half-mile past our house, where the pavement ended and a dirt fire road continued into the rumpled hills of Topanga State Park, my primal landscape of California coastal sage and chaparral. We referred to the fire road and the mountains as "The Hill," just as we'd later refer to the Grand Canyon as "The Canyon": as if there were no other. There was no other. Trails branched off the fire road and led down to dry creekbeds crunchy with sycamore leaves. Farther upstream the creekbeds offered actual surface flow, and the water fell over bare cliffs. There was a shallow mouth in a sandstone cliff into which I'd crawl and make the slightest humming in the depths of my chest and the whole cave would resonate and thrum. There was an overlook from which I could see every mountain range ringing the LA Basin, then turn and look far across the ocean to the Channel Islands. There was a grove of hoary California live oaks that seemed as mystical and powerful as any old English pedunculate oak under which druids used to sacrifice children. There were animal trails that tunneled through the usually impenetrable wall of ten-foot-high ceanothus, and I'd slide through these game tunnels, some-times down entire hill slopes, the dust and dry leaves catching in hair and nose and mouth. There were hawks and owls and coyotes and bobcats and foxes and rattlesnakes and deer and cougars.

And later, older, in high school, my friends—those brilliant fools, artists, reprobates, pranksters, dreamers, addicts, lunatics, lovers, and drunks who preceded, foreshadowed, the characters I'd befriend on the trail crew—and I would go up The Hill, or to similar spots in the surrounding hills where we could drink and smoke and boast and wrestle. At the end of many of those nights a friend and I would butt-board down the miles of steep roads, down the S curves of Tuna Canyon or Carbon Canyon or Mandeville Canyon, the moonlight flooding the road in front of us, the night drowned out by the song of skate wheels on concrete.

And in the day during high school, suffocating under flickering fluorescent lights, bored into a stupor, I could gaze out many of the classroom windows and see shining through the maritime fog a single blooming yucca like a torch calling me back to the dark hills. All too often in those last few years of high school I'd ditch school to heed the call. Those hills were my home as much as the house amid them was. They were a refuge. As an adult, I love LA; love discovering and sampling its diverse offerings of food, music, culture. Yet when I lived there my relationship with the city was exactly what I would come to criticize in others' relationship with the Canyon: I rarely delved too deeply into the messy, vibrant, difficult, and interesting immediacy of the place, and thus never absorbed those details of immersion that come closest to what could be called the truth of the place. Some of this was simply a matter of circumstances: there was little reason for me to ever leave my neighborhood. I spent most of my life in school, and when I was not in school I was either up in the hills or at the beach. I was too young to go to the bars or music venues that would have drawn me deeper into the machinery of the city. I never bothered to obtain a driver's license when I lived in LA, which severely curtailed my ability to explore.

But the point is that I did not want to explore the city. I was not interested in exploring the city. The Hill was a refuge because it was not the city. I had constructed the city largely from the generalizations that the detached, synoptic view from those hills allowed, the same truthful but shallow stereotypes that so many strangers and casual acquaintances would later offer about LA: a crowded hive of smog, snobbery, heat, violence, traffic, plastic surgery, caged rivers, and endless concrete. But at the time, generalizations served me well: I needed a convenient vessel into which I could pour my adolescent derision, a symbol I could distance myself from, feel superior toward.

In hindsight, what I really hated was not the city but the culture as a whole. It's been said that the purpose of culture is to provide an image of what it is to be a man or woman of substance and merit, yet the images I received were spawned of materialism, commodification, competition, overconsumption, superficiality; an obsession with power, celebrity, and affluence; a slavish devotion to technology, private interest, profit. As much as our love for the Canyon, this is what connected me to Ray, or John Hiller, or Michael, or any of those other feral Trails kids: a shared loathing for how our myopic, solipsistic, and anthropocentric worldview has led to the rape and heedless plunder of the natural world; how so much of the surface world was invested in so little of true value; how there was something incredibly, abhorrently insubstantial about the whole system.

When juxtaposed against the Canyon's bare rock—the youngest sedimentary layer of which was deposited roughly 25 million years before the dinosaurs existed—the world on the rim seemed an increasingly fragile and assuredly temporary artifice. The temporal immensities represented by that rock had substance, merit.

Not television and pop culture. Not politics or financial markets. Stepping off the rim into the Canyon gave one the feeling, as Wendell Berry noted in his essay "An Entrance to the Woods," that "I am alive in the world, this moment, without the help or the interference of any machine. I can move without reference to anything except the lay of the land and the capabilities of my own body....I am reduced to my irreducible self."

More important than Berry's words, at least in the way they'd brought so many of us to the Canyon, in the way they illuminated the Canyon as something, finally, to which we could give ourselves to, were the words of Ed Abbey. As a teenager in Los Angeles, raging against the confines of adolescence and urbanity, ol' Cactus Ed—shooter of television sets, explorer of slot canyons, defender of wolves and wild rivers—modeled the life I wanted to live: a life where one's trails, as he put it, were "crooked, winding, lonesome, dangerous, leading to the most amazing view." When I came to work in the Canyon, I found myself part of a tribe of Abbey devotees, a brotherhood of those who had also followed his crooked trail away from what he had deemed the "clamor and filth and confusion of the cultural apparatus." Like us, Abbey had drifted between seasonal positions at national parks and monuments across the country: Canyonlands, Everglades, Lassen, Death Valley, Lees Ferry, Atascosa, Organ Pipe Cactus. Like us, he had proclaimed himself a Grand Canyoneer; he claimed to have made at least one descent into the Canyon almost every year of his adult life. We received his exhortations to "explore the forests, climb the mountains, bag the peaks, run the rivers" as scripture from a desert prophet. We read his books as though reading our lives. When he wrote: "Beyond the wall of the unreal city there is another world waiting for you. It is the old true world of the deserts, the mountains, the forests," we nodded our heads in agreement.

But later in my life, no longer that burning teenager, and having lived "beyond the wall" for many years, I saw it in a different, apostatic light: as an argument that veers awfully close to sanctimonious bullshit. (It's also disingenuous, at least coming from Abbey, who would have been horrified if people en masse were able to surmount the various economic, social, and logistical barriers that impeded them from invading his "old true world.") The city, the surface world, is real. Further, a great deal of similarity exists in the regard for nature in terms of "old true worlds" and in the regard for wolves and cougars as craven and bloodthirsty killers. Neither of these polarities is complete, adequate. And finally, the deserts, mountains, and forests of the world have been so altered by the forces of the surface world that, in many cases, they can no longer be considered apart or "beyond."

This is, of course, a common debate. It's also, as Colin Fletcher, the first white man to walk from Lees Ferry to Havasu Canyon in one attempt, rightly put it, a spurious one. "Dedicated urbanites 'know' beyond shadow of doubt—because doubt never raises its disturbing head—that civilization is the real world: you only 'escape' to wilderness. When you're out and away and immersed, you 'know' the obverse: the wilderness world is real, the human world a superimposed façade.... The controversy is, of course, spurious. Neither view can stand alone. Both worlds are real."

Abbey's argument, or Ray's intimations of it, lacks this mutualism. It too readily gives up on the surface world. In *The Thunder Tree*, Robert Michael Pyle wrote, "I believe that one of the greatest causes of the ecological crisis is the state of personal alienation from nature in which many people live." In this light, what matters is not only the nature of some "old true world," but the nature where people live, the nature with which they make daily contact: the abandoned lot, the fire road, the city park, or, in Pyle's case, a drainage ditch.

And yet these places were not enough for us. Even Fletcher, after carefully stating that both worlds were real, couldn't help but end with: "But the wilderness world is certainly older and will almost certainly last longer. Besides, [it] seems far healthier for a human to embrace." So we did. We could accept, intellectually, Pyle's argument for shifting our cultural ideals of nature as only represented by hairy wilderness and national parks to that of ditches and fire roads, but we agreed, viscerally, with Abbey's embrace and virulent defense of those wild, uninhabited, and subjectively real areas.

Why, then, did the three of us give Ray such a hard time that day?

For one, we weren't about to tolerate a kid who didn't yet have his Canyon legs under him coming in and telling us with such rectitude about the real world. No. Maybe after he had been annealed by the Canyon as the rest of us had, we would have allowed him to preach its righteousness. But even then, considering that Wayne and Michael were two of the most pugnacious sons of bitches on Trails, he'd have been engaged in heated debate.

But I like to think that the Canyon itself—where solid earth melts and the green river flashes brown; where within an hour one can go from heart-stricken to hypothermic—had taught us the fallacy of declaring with any certainty: this is the world. People say such things when their position—on the rim, or up in the oak tree, or on the trail crew—affords them the opportunity to think of themselves as detached. We are never detached. The world is in-

terrelated—the park was a bubble, or, as it was so impacted by the
surface world, an illusion of a bubble. Occasionally the National
Park Service will spend thousands of dollars to eradicate tamarisk,
the Canyon's most insidious invasive plant. And every year the up-
wind groves massed along the Little Colorado River send trillions
of seeds floating into the park. You cannot separate yourself from
the world. We may have taken pride in our lives apart from the
surface world, but we brought it with us wherever we went.

The only way that I was even partly as detached from the city
as I liked to fancy myself in high school was that my house was
located in one of the richest and whitest neighborhoods in the
greater LA area. This sort of economic and racial distance was not
exactly what I had in mind when I liked to think of myself as apart.
But there it was. My parents were not rich; I figured they were,
as George Orwell described his parents, within the "lower upper
middle class." Nonetheless, I was a child of privilege: both of my
parents had PhDs; I never knew economic pain or familial strife; it
was assumed that I would graduate high school with high marks,
go to a good college, get a good job.

After I graduated from high school I traveled down the west
coast of South America with my brother. My privilege was revealed
to the point that I was embarrassed by (and, still an adolescent,
even resented) the happenstance good fortune of my time and
place of birth. Once, waiting for a bus by the side of the road after a
trek through the Cordillera Blanca, a friend began feeding the last
stale heels of our bread to a pack of skeletal dogs. A campesino who
was also waiting for the bus approached my friend and asked for
the bread. He walked back to his spot, broke the bread in pieces,
and shared those pieces with his compañeros. The ground shifted
under my feet more powerfully than in any earthquake. Over and

over again in my travels, in the life I'd chosen to live in the decades
out of high school, I'd experience those tremors, those reminders
that my assumptions about myself, the world, myself in the world,
needed to be continually examined, challenged, reworked.

Years into my time in the Canyon, drunk at Phantom Ranch,
I scrawled on the Ranchers' bathroom chalkboard: "What is?"
Later that night I came back to find that one of those postmodern
hedonist philosophers moonlighting as a rancher had written:
"Context." Rolling rocks in the depths of the Canyon with a tribe
of likeminded savages, it was easy to dismiss the surface world as
a bunch of bullshit. So too, standing on the rim amid the motion
and noise of the tourist hordes, it was easy to recognize and appreciate the isolation the Canyon offered. As a hippie kid in LA,
I felt that I had no place in the System; as a white American male
in sub-Saharan Africa, it was obvious that no matter what I *felt*, I
was a product of that System. It took a long time and a lot of territory before I truly understood and appreciated how nuanced and
interconnected the world is. I knew that Wayne had been through
his own such journeys, as had Michael. All three of us had our
issues, our prejudices, our blind spots and failings. All three of us
writhed with the tensions of wilderness and domesticity, wildness
and control, wanderlust and rootedness, self and other, freedom
and responsibility. As Proust wrote: "We do not receive wisdom,
we must discover it for ourselves, after a journey through the wilderness, which no one else can make for us, which no one can spare
us, for our wisdom is the point of view from which we come at last
to regard the world." As much as it's a betrayal of my own self-as-
sured eighteen-year-old self, and as unfair as it surely was to him,
we figured that Ray, essentially right out of high school, where the
"received wisdom" had been pounded into him as into the rest of

us, simply hadn't yet journeyed enough through the wilderness—
of desert *or* city—and thus not yet earned our uncritical respect
for his regard of the world.

❦ ❧

Whaling away at a fat slab of Coconino sandstone with a single-jack sledge and chisel, I noticed one of the European volunteers watching me. When the rock cleaved in two and I set my
tools to the side he said with a thick accent, loud enough for me to
hear, "Badass," and then shyly put his head down and went back
to shaping his own rock. He'd choked his hand so far up the helve
of his hammer it snugged against the head. He hesitantly tinked
it at his chisel.

I smiled, remembering my first tour, how I'd watched Devin
beat at a sandstone boulder with a double-jack, and how when
winded he'd handed me the sledge, saying, "Your turn," and
nodded for me to follow the hammer dints he'd scored into the
wandering rock. I'd looked from him to the sledge to the rock,
thinking, "Yeah... fucking right."

Devin was my crew lead for my first three seasons in the Canyon.
He taught me almost everything I knew about building trails in
that precipitous, highly dissected, highly erodible landscape: how
to run mason string to set up a work site; how to determine trail
grade with a clinometer; how to row a rock with a rock bar; how to
take the measure of a rock, split it, and fit it against another to line
the trail. He taught me riprap and cribbing and steps and water
bars. He taught me how to read the trail: he once pointed out a
retaining wall that held up a section of the South Kaibab Trail
and described how he and two others had built it, side by side,
and how different their building styles were, and right away I saw

the marks of the individual craftsman: one section with untrued faces and knobby with protruding deadmen, one section clean and tight, almost ashlar quality, the final section a solid hodgepodge of the two styles, and as those things go in life, once I knew how to look I never saw walls the same.

My first experiences in the Canyon were settling like sediment atop a similar and fairly solid bedrock persona: before I came to work Trails in the Canyon I'd hiked hundreds of miles in the backcountry, summited dozens of peaks; built trails in California, farmed in Washington, worked construction in Alaska; and sought adventure in Africa, Asia, and South America. I liked physical labor, I liked beer, I liked whiskey and wrestling, I could boast and banter and bullshit with the best of them, I knew what I was getting into on Trails, and I was getting into it because I loved it and I was good at it. In short, Devin didn't need to teach me how to swing a sledge; he needed to show me that it could be done against a rock and that rock would split.

I hefted the double-jack, my right hand near the head, my left hand down the length of the handle. I centered Devin's beat-line between my spread feet, then in one unbroken motion flexed my knees, swung the sledge behind my back, and arced it over my head, my right hand sliding down the shaft to join the left hand just as the sledge head smacked atop the rock. The eight-pound hammer head bounced back into the air, the wooden handle shivered with the strain, and the impact rang my wrist bones like a bell. It felt good. I swung again. And again, and again, the air thickening with the smell of brimstone and the dull sound of steel on stone, the boulder dumbly absorbing the blows, though every strike made cracks in the stone and every further strike rooted those cracks farther through the stone, until, with a last blow, the network of cracks coalesced into the dark smile of the cloven rock.

I let the sledge fall to my side and, breathing hard, looked up at Devin. He nodded and smiled.

Working on a trail crew was like that: an interweaving of instinct and education, of explicit and implicit knowledge. After all, humanoids have been using tools for 4 million years; Darwin surmised that our hominid brains enlarged as a result of hands being used for purposes other than to support the body. My simian fingers quite comfortably wrapped around the three-foot-long handle. Watching other kids on Trails swing sledges over the years, it was obvious that they too felt, as the famous French alpinist Gaston Rebuffat put it, "that mind and muscles were fulfilling their intended function." Everybody had their own form, evolved through the work, through their own mechanics of body and experience, through the way they went through life. Take Michael. Michael had gray-green eyes and a sweet half-smile, and tears shone in his eyes listening to Dylan sing "Desolation Row," but he was also built like a tugboat, was blunt in his opinions, frequently modeled his personality after John Goodman's character in *The Big Lebowski*, and paid little attention to even the crew's infrequent social graces. He insistently hated agaves because he once happened to fall on one. What Michael lacked in height he made up with intensity, and when busting a rock he'd hoist his whole center of gravity into his swing. I'd crouch by a rock with a slab splitter and he'd rain his sledge atop it with a rhythm few others could attain or maintain.

This Dutch kid, on the other hand, was clearly terrified of raining his sledge on his thumb. But it wasn't just that he lacked skill and confidence and familiarity with his tools—he didn't know the rock. The Colorado carved the Canyon out of a remarkable diversity of rock: sandstone, limestone, mudstone, shale, schist, gneiss; lumpy chert nodules on the rim and slick schist flutings along the river; basalt slabs scabbing over the western Canyon's cliffs and Cárdenas lava vomited forth in the earth's infancy. Knowing the nature of each rock type was a vital aspect of much of Canyon life. John Wesley Powell, the first man to run the river through the length of the Canyon, noted in his journal on August 5, 1886: "We have learned to closely observe the texture of rock. In softer strata, we have a quiet river; in hard, we find rapids and falls." What held true for boating also held true for climbing: you had to know, generally, what rock you could trust; as there was little rock in the Canyon you could truly trust, you had to closely observe the specific rock on which you intended to place your full weight.

Knowing the materials from which you were going to attempt to build a wall or line a trail was also critical, especially when shaping them. Muav limestone was iron-hard and wholly uncooperative; a chunk of Muav could absorb a hundred sledge blows before a crack shanked straight to the closest edge, the obdurate rock popping off in awkward, unusable pieces. If anything, Redwall limestone was even harder, damn near impossible to shape. I had learned caution when crushing Redwall into trail tread, as any overhead swing of the double-jack that didn't hit the rock perfectly square could blast the uncrushed rock back into my shin. The Kaibab limestone, a friable mix of sandy limestone and calcareous sandstone, often fractured unevenly around its exceptionally hard chert nodules. The Coconino sandstone—which this Dutchman was working on—was so soft that I could abrade its frosted sand grains with the force of a calloused finger, and thus, in the long run, wasn't the most durable material for building trail. But one could carve it like butter.

The eastern Canyon's four-hundred-foot-tall cliffs of Coconino sandstone are the lithified remnants of an ancient, Sahara-sized desert. The dunes in this desert were made of pure quartz sand. For 10 million years wind had whisked the rounded sand grains off the top of dunes and deposited them either on the same dune's slip face or on a downwind dune's windward flanks. As the dunes migrated, these minute shifts in sand were preserved as distinct lamina, some millimeters apart, some feet apart, some stacked parallel, others in beveled cross-beds. Two hundred seventy million years later, these layers are still so distinct that geologists can determine the direction of the ancient winds, just as this kid could have placed his chisel edge along one of the seams and with a few blows split his stone as neatly as opening a book.

But how was he to know? Nobody had shown him. I'd learned to read many of the signs and signatures that make up the endless tome of knowledge that is the Grand Canyon, but only after years of working and climbing and rafting, and only with the Canyon having taught me *how* to read them. Geology, for example. Before I came to the Canyon my knowledge of geology was virtually nil. Which is embarrassing, because unlike this Dutch kid, hailing from a land sorely lacking in the great quantities of exposed rock that often spur one's interest in the study of the solid earth, I had no excuse: the Santa Monica Mountains in which I was raised were a geologic wonderland.

A *complicated* geologic wonderland: a witch's brew of sea floor sediments and volcanics that have been severely crushed, crumpled, twisted, and folded by the shifting, settling, and subduction of the North American and Pacific plates. At the Grand Canyon, one can view more than five thousand vertical feet of exposed rock as easily as scrolling one's eye down a chart; one's interest in geology is piqued exactly because, for the most part, the Canyon's strict, layer-cake sedimentary strata serves as a geology textbook: first this, then this, then this, settling atop one another oh so neatly. The overhead geological map of the Santa Monica Mountains, on the other hand, shows a tumult of different-colored splotches signifying different rock: shale, mudstone, pebble-cobble conglomerate, slag-like diabase intrusions, dramatically folded volcanics, resistant beds of coarse-grained sandstone overlaid on less resistant beds of fine-grained sandstone, on and on.

Easy now to cite the complicated geology as justification for my ignorance; closer to the truth is that I simply didn't care. I was too young and too busy running, climbing, smoking ganja, and drinking beer atop that geologic tumult to pay attention to the rock's origin story. Certainly at that time in my life I'd have shunned the stilted scientific terminology as an inferior epistemological approach to that of my own sensory elations. All I knew was the feel of those narrow ridges and steep slopes under my bare feet and open hands. All I knew was what the mountains taught me to see; or, as at 4:31 a.m. on January 17, 1994, they forced me to see.

I woke to the sound of the window not half a foot from my head shivering violently in its frame. My belongings were shuddering off my shelves and crashing to the floor. I rolled out of bed and crouched on the convulsing floor. From down the hall I could hear the sustained shatter of glass. Outside, great flashes of light from exploding electrical transformers arced across the night. The earth trembled like an animal in fear.

When the shaking subsided my father, mother, and I picked our way through the broken glass and strewn clutter of our lives and made our way to the lawn. The lawn overlooks a large swath of the Pacific Ocean and the city of Los Angeles. Practically every day of my life for eighteen years I stood on that lawn and looked to where ocean met shore, where alluvial plain began and city sprawled across it in every direction. Night provided the most marked juxtaposition: the glittering, lighted city pressing against the somber, sable ocean; on the one hand a teeming, gridded metropolis and on the other a vast, crescent blank.

But that night of the Northridge earthquake the city was black as the sea. The only difference between the two was the flames of a few structure fires. It was as though there were no city, had never been a city, as though giant ground sloths and saber-toothed cats still roamed the plains. As though the ocean had moved up to bury the basin, as it had some 5 million years ago. It was my first true experience with deep time; the first time I saw that the grid could be so easily extinguished.

The Northridge earthquake featured some of the strongest ground accelerations ever recorded, resulting in one of the costliest seismic disasters in US history—and it wasn't even caused by the San Andreas Fault, that slip-strike tectonic trigger that will unleash "the Big One" earthquake that will devastate LA. The San Andreas haunted my childhood with an unsettling combination of wonder and terror that many feel while regarding the depths of the Grand Canyon.

Obsession creates suspect patterns through which to see the world, and perhaps the threads that stretched between Canyon and city, the threads that stitched me to both, are threads only of my own spinning. But I was pleased, and found it fitting, when I later discovered, among the many shifting stories by which geologists explain the creation of the Canyon as we know it, one that gives prominence to the San Andreas Fault. This theory posits that the ancestral Colorado River used to flow the opposite direction than it does now (so, to the east and north), while a smaller river— separated from the Colorado by a small mountain range—drained more or less the direction the Colorado now flows (west and south). But at some point in the last 10 million years, the San Andreas Fault shuddered, significantly lowering the Gulf of California (into which the smaller river flowed). This lower terminus granted the smaller river tremendous power to eat headward, through the small mountain range, until it eventually "captured" the ancestral Colorado, reversing its flow, a process known as stream piracy. The combined waters gouged the Canyon to its current depth.

I love that LA and the Canyon may have common roots in a single tectonic strain, just as my love for the Canyon is tangled in my strains against metropolitan LA. I love that my knowledge of both required a steeping, a continuous presence, as any true knowledge does. This Dutch kid never had such an opportunity. When he looked up again, I said, "It gets easier with time" and walked up-trail to point out the lamina lines on his own rock.

ॐ ॐ

When I first came to the Canyon, Trails seemed an exclusive fraternity, a tribe with its own hierarchy, rituals, and customs. And language. They communicated with words or terms I knew little or nothing about: single-jack, pionjar, mantee, Supai, and so forth. Even worse was their frequent use of acronyms—LE, EDR, BA, JHA, LCR—or otherwise abbreviated words that might as well have been acronyms: Nanko, Zoro, rez.

I burned to know this language.

In time I knew the acronyms; I used the word "crush" as a noun; I realized that a "mantee" is a canvas tarp; a "pionjar" is a gas-powered rock drill; a "single-jack" is a six-pound hammer. Most of the formerly arcane words now conjure whole worlds of emotion and memory: "opener" invoking those first weeks of spring repairing the North Kaibab Trail, "Lava" summoning the hollow-gut feeling of fear, "Phantom" conjuring naked women in turkey feather headdresses and languid summer evenings on the river beach drinking Tecate.

I burned, too, to know the place-names.

For the crew addressed the various trails' points, outcroppings, flats, ridges, walls, and switchbacks with individual names and titles. The North Kaibab Trail alone was known and described by places with names such as Smell Tree, Cinchup, Monday Morning Rock, the Dirtpit, Coconino Overlook, Ohmygod, Crow's Nest, Freeway, Pipeline Corner, Boulder Corner, Picnic Table Rock, Supai Tunnel, Zeus's Mullet, Dog Spring, Cave of the Pools, Mossy Cove, Three Steps to Heaven, Needle's Eye, Temple of Redemptor (also known as Castle Grayskull), Jasper Falls, the Residence, Crack Rock, Asinine Hill, Microwave, Beaver Pond (which later became the Bog Bridge), Fourth Bridge, Tony's Wall, Third Bridge, Second Bridge, Boulder Corner, First Bridge.

The place-names functioned as markers, as symbols of old stories and experiences present in our daily lives. Memories fused to the physical life of the trails. We called a certain rock "Monday Morning Rock" because one mule wrangler was so hungover every Monday that he wouldn't speak to his tourist wards until he reached the rock, dismounted, and puked. We called a certain switchback "Pearl's Drop," or "Peg's Landing," because Pearl, a trail crew pack mule, slipped and fell off a small cliff, dragging Peg, the mule she was tied to, along with her. Pearl died, but Peg survived the fall.

By linking geographic features to historical events, the names revealed the Canyon's deeper scope and scale: we weren't merely walking along a random section of trail but were following the footsteps of the earliest natives, explorers, miners, tourists, and trail crews who also walked down this section of trail, sat on this promontory, and claimed it with a name.

Names reveal much about those who did the naming. As Gregory Crampton explains in *Land of Living Rock*, Native Americans overlaid few names on the landscape; when they did, the name described a definite physical feature. This applies to the Grand Canyon region's native tribes; for example, the Paiute name Kanab means "place of the willows." Even tribal names relate to natural features: Havasupai means "people of the blue-green water," Hualapai means "people of the pine." Crampton attests that, to a native, using a name for a feature of the landscape that was not descriptive of its central character would have been artificial and unnatural. Not so to the later denizens of the Canyon, the explorers, miners, and developers. Whereas the natives named themselves for the surroundings, those of foreign descent graced the surrounding with their own names.

In November 1892 Buffalo Bill Cody guided a group of English hunters on the North Rim. To honor the member of their party who killed the first buck, the group named a point on the rim MacKinnon Point. Flushed with the hunt and the novelty of the vast, unnamed landscape before them, they proposed naming the tributary canyon directly below them "Buffalo Bill's Coliseum."

The Canyon is rife with names left behind by men with no more attachment to the Canyon than a shot buck. Many of these names proved as ephemeral as the presence of those who did the naming. Declared by one and not known by the next, names layered over each other: MacKinnon Point became Widforss Point; what was initially dubbed Buckskin Cascade became Bridal Falls, then Surprise Falls, and is now Deer Creek Falls.

Even when a name has withstood the shifts of culture and years, the story behind the name occasionally slips from collective memory. Few now know of the O'Neill behind O'Neill Butte or the fey story that named Haunted Canyon. The casual chain of people, rumors, and stories that sustain and give relevance to the dubbing falters, and the person and story are forgotten, leaving the name rootless even as the original ridge recedes like O'Neill Butte, now disconnected and alone.

When a name stood in isolation, severed from its original meaning by the passing of time and the decay of memory, we'd craft a new, more relevant name, or we'd attribute meanings of our own invention to the rootless name. Take "The Chimney," a dramatic set of switchbacks ascending the Kaibab layer of the South Kaibab Trail. Because of its narrow and switchbacked ascent, I always associated the name with the rock-climbing technique known as "chimneying," which involves bracing one's legs, arms, and back in opposing angles of pressure as a way of ascending a body-width crack. But Blake insisted that it's called The Chimney because the switchbacks' narrow confines draw wind like a chimney. His interpretation was probably closer to the original intention, but with that intention forgotten, the meaning was ours for the making.

Possibly in response to the conventional (and often petty) nomenclature exemplified in MacKinnon Point, the geologist Clarence Dutton came up with a system known as "heroic nomenclature" in the late 1800s. Dutton was trained in science, architecture, and poetry and drew his place-names from a wide range of classical, mythological, and religious sources. So the modern visitor looks out over Canyon formations known as, to name but a handful, Buddha Temple, Vulcan's Throne, Siegfried Pyre, and Tower of Ra.

Though the "heroic nomenclature" system describes the dramatic landscape more appropriately than the haphazard nomenclature it supplanted, it also clouds the link between names and the region's history. Before this tradition, and still to a large extent, to know the names was to know the diverse history of the land; a name was an accretion of the different languages and cultures that touched, however briefly and lightly, upon the Canyon.

For example, the designation "Coronado Butte" sounds simply of Spanish origin, like "Colorado" and "canyon" (from *cañon*), yet in fact owes much to the French trappers of the early Western frontier. There was no word in English for the ubiquitous, steep-sided, flat-topped forms rising from the western plains, so the French word *butte* was adopted into the English vernacular. So in present-day Arizona, a Spanish name attached to a noun of French origin may be spoken in English by a Japanese tourist.

Most of the Canyon's prominent features have now been named. Although the established nomenclature is subject to dispute and evolution, the National Park Service and the Board of Geographic Names have loaned their authority to certain names. But specific features—unique pinnacles, distinct rocks, bends in the trail— had yet to be officially named, and we named them.

In the reference style of the natives, many of our names were practical, verbal representations of physical landmarks: The Flat Spot, The Sandpit, Mossy Cove, Beaver Pond. In the spirit of the miners, we named a spot after one of our own: Quilter's Shade, where a Trails brother rested in a sliver of shade shortly before his death. In our own continuation of the "heroic nomenclature" tradition, we named features Castle Grayskull, the Skybridge, Zeus's Mullet.

Names arise out of familiarity. Though they may progress from personal monikers to commonly used names to officially recognized titles, for the most part they remain close to the individual and the event. At times, for reasons that are not entirely clear, individual names attach to the Canyon and long outlast our brief movements within it. Other times, successive generations of trail crew may not refer to the same object or section of trail with the same name.

This lost continuity is fitting. We knew that nothing has a true name, that our naming was merely dubbing. The philosopher Saul Kripke called the original act of naming an "initial baptism." But in a land occupied for more than ten thousand years by varying tribes and tongues, that which we named had been noted and named before. The initial baptism was irrelevant. What was important was the naming of the world for ourselves before that world faded, and we faded, and only the rock remained.

ᴄ: ᴄ:

I leaned backward over the cliff, my legs braced on the cliff lip, my ass over air, my hips and torso supported by harness and rope, my hands working a four-foot rock bar at a desk-sized boulder. Using the cliff lip as a fulcrum and the tapered tip of the rock bar, I rowed the boulder inch by inch until it trembled and teetered at the edge. I stopped, got my footing, took a breath, and then in one motion nudged the boulder off the cliff and pendulum-ed out of the way. The boulder dropped, hit a shelf, bounced off, and, front spinning wildly, began bounding over terrace after terrace, the seconds between impacts stretching longer and longer as the boulder bounced faster and faster, farther and farther. It launched off the last cliff as though shot from a cannon. A held-breath silence... and only then the impact, a *BOOM* thundering downcanyon and rolling around the hollowed-rock amphitheaters, lingering and lingering before slowly fading into the greater silence of the desert morning.

I looked up at the crew.

"Good one," Abel said. "Wow. Good one."

In the mythology of Trails, the North Kaibab Trail was eternally doomed to suffer the wrath and devastation of winter. Our role was to resurrect it come spring. For the most part, the NKT openers were relatively benign, requiring a tour or two of "cyclical maintenance": digging ditch and cleaning water bars, raking the trail of debris and smaller rockslides, repairing a blown-out retaining wall here or there. But passing through Flagstaff or visiting the South Rim during a winter I'd taken off, especially in the span of summers that I became Trails' "North Rim guy," the crew would tell me in mock horror about snowfall totals on the North Rim—"dude, like two hundred inches"—and thus how thrashed the trail would be. In actuality, the years I worked were years of drought, the majority of winter precipitation alarmingly below average. Only one winter—2005—saw significant snowfall; the rest had remarkably low totals. But fidelity to the meteorological record was not the point: the stories of heavy snow were invocations. Let the volunteers dig ditch; we wanted to trundle rocks and hang in harnesses while reconstructing retaining walls.

And so at one point early in the spring, some of us would walk the trail and survey the damage wrought by storms and thaw. It was my favorite day of trail work in the Canyon. I'd hiked the North Kaibab Trail so many hundreds of times that it held little mystery, but that one day the world sparkled with opportunities— we'd round a corner to find the trail entombed beneath a jumble of boulders the size of refrigerators, or a bedrock section of trail so sheathed in ice it'd be too dangerous to cross without crampons, or the trail simply gone, having sloughed into the void.

A certain section of trail passed under a generally dry waterfall in the Redwall cliffs known as Jasper Falls, where the crew before my time had constructed a causeway of log cribbing capped by stone riprap. One winter we rounded the corner to witness where boulders had cannonballed onto the causeway, denting the riprap and crushing the cribbing. All but one of the boulders had bounced farther downcanyon: ghost boulders, I thought of them, evidence of a past presence, like cougar tracks, or the trace fossils abundant in the more fossiliferous strata layers—the footprints of lizards and amphibians, the burrow marks of marine worms. Sometimes the only evidence of these boulders' passing were craters encircled by a spray of mud. Sometimes the rocks splatted so deep into the muddy trail they stuck and, months or weeks later, remained embedded six inches into the dried tread. (There is a boulder on the South Kaibab Trail that is an example of this same phenomenon occurring some 545 million years ago, when rocks fell into mud and the mud was covered by ocean silt, all of which eventually compressed into a new rock containing both mud and old rock.) Sometimes we'd round a corner to find a giant semicircle of empty space and recently exposed soil yawning beneath our feet, the wreckage of the blown-out retaining wall strewn downslope.

These were caused not by ghost rocks or rockfalls but by mud-slides, or debris flows, or slope collapses. Most of these occurred in the Supai layer.

If we'd constructed a mythology around the cycle of closing and opening of the North Rim—The Ceding to Winter, The Spring Resurrection—the Supai was an integral character in that mythology. You'd walk almost two miles and fourteen hundred feet down through the Kaibab, Toroweap, Coconino, and Hermit Shale strata without all that much damage to the trail, and then you entered the Supai and it was as though all the erosive forces had merely been gathering power in order to detonate on the six-teen switchbacks that descended the six-hundred-foot-tall Supai layer.

Structurally, the Supai resembles the greater Canyon in which it's embedded: a series of staggered cliffs and slopes, with loosely consolidated rock slopes overlying different, more cohesive rock cliffs. But the greater Canyon, averaging a mile deep and ten miles wide, at least appears to have achieved some sort of equilibrium regarding depth and width. Not so the Supai: its rubbly mess of unconformable sandstones, siltstones, mudstones, conglomerates, shales, and limestones, all poised at a steep angle of repose, gives credence to the geomorphologist's term "mass wastage."

The Supai's current dynamism owes much to its dynamic ori-gins: all of its rock was laid down during one of the world's great ice ages, when Africa, Australia, India, South America, and Antarctica were locked together in the supercontinent Gondwanaland. At the time, Gondwanaland sat squarely atop the South Pole, and the land that would eventually (like, 200 million years into the future) become the Canyon region of the southwestern United States was near the ancestral Pacific Ocean. As Gondwanaland's massive glaciers waxed and waned over 25 million years, the Pacific correspondingly receded from and then encroached on the Canyon region. The Canyon region was thus covered by marine sediments and then (geologically speaking) relatively rapidly covered by arid, aeolian sediments, then more marine sediments (augmented by continental river and stream sediments), on and on, all these deposits in time lithifying into the Supai's interbedded strata.

One spring, in the three-quarter-mile section of trail that switchbacks through the Supai layer, slope failures bowled through twelve retaining walls as though they'd been made of cardboard. A single flow took out four walls, one on each consecutive switchback, and by the time the slurried earth hit the last wall it must have been moving pretty fast and carrying a good load because it punched a twelve-foot-long by seventeen-foot-high hole in the final wall. To the left of this blowout, not ten feet downtrail, was a wall we'd rebuilt three years earlier. Nearly adjacent to it was a wall we rebuilt four years earlier. Between those two walls yawed yet another blowout. Across the drainage from this switchback of blown-out walls were the faint traces of the old North Kaibab Trail, running straight and then disappearing into the monstrous slurry of liquefied Hermit Shale that had poured down the Supai layers in the infamous winter storm of 1966.

Where Abel and I were trundling rocks that day was just a few hundred feet upcanyon of this slurry: yet another rockslide in the Supai had obliterated more than a hundred feet of the water pipeline that runs from Roaring Springs to the North Rim.

Devin had sat our crew in the shade of a blooming redbud tree to inform us that it was our responsibility to clear up the pipeline rockslide. From where we sat we had a great view of the slide:

though much of the debris had crashed a few hundred feet down to the Roaring Springs Canyon creekbed, a gigantic pile of slabs and boulders—including a trailer-sized boulder—remained perched on a narrow and steeply inclined terrace where the pipeline had once run. As the pipeline supplied the North Rim with all its water, and the water in the North Rim's storage tanks was running low, and the North Rim would be officially open to tourists in less than two weeks, there was building pressure to get the pipeline repaired and the water flowing.

"Why don't the pipeline guys do it?" I asked Devin.

"Because they're too old," said Blake.

"And they get paid too much," said John Hiller.

"They can't clear slides like that," Devin replied. "That's not their job. Once we clear it, they'll fly in and repair the pipe."

So it was our responsibility. Devin's responsibility. As I was the North Rim crew leader that season, my responsibility. My annoyance must have shown, for John Hiller wrapped a huge arm around my neck in a half-hug, half-headlock and said, "C'mon Brodie, think of all the trundling."

"True," I said.

"And the blasting."

I smiled.

Trails hadn't used explosives in Grand Canyon for at least twenty years—not since the crew reconstructed the section of the South Kaibab Trail known as The Chimney. So by "blasting," John Hiller meant boulder busting. A boulder buster, technically called a Mechanized, Nonexplosive, Hydro-Fracturing Rock Fragmentation Device, is, as the name implies, a tool for fracturing big rocks. You drill a hole deep into the rock and fill the hole with water—in this case captured from the same melt stream that had triggered the slide, now flowing innocently through the rubble. You then drop a shotgun-shell-like cartridge into the hole, screw a firing mechanism onto a metal box, place the metal box over the hole, put a blast mat over the boulder to muffle fly rock, lay out a lanyard, and take cover, then pull the lanyard. The box shoots a charge into the cartridge, and the small explosion forces the water out through the fractures it makes. The rock breaks in pieces.

The boulder buster was equally efficient at exploding the thin barriers between adulthood and childhood, and we burst with excitement as the rocks burst with water. Before pulling the lanyard we'd yell "Fire in the hole!" or "Blasting!" or Michael would sing out the refrain from Tchaikovsky's 1812 Overture and blast the rock as the last percussive note. We'd prattle happily about pouring pionjar gas into the hole instead of water, or how we could best use the boulder buster on a ranger car. Given how the slide perched on the terrace, I thought that if we could get one of the big underpinning boulders to collapse, it might take much of the slide out in one domino-like collapse. So I told Blake, a *Star Wars* fan, in my best Admiral Ackbar voice, to "concentrate all firepower on the superstructure rock." All day, between blasts, he hummed the Rebel Fleet theme or muttered quotes from the various intergalactic battle scenes.

The sun blazed and the boys traded dirty proverbs about the heat; then came wind, then came horsetail clouds, then rain, then a day of snow, the flurries boiling downcanyon, the snow lining the blooming redbud trees, then sun again—typical springtime weather on the Kaibab Plateau. And all the while we trundled.

Years later Abel and I would reminisce about that trundling, that glorious trundling. The slide provided the perfect conditions: a huge pile of dense, blocky stones perched on the lip of a terrace a few hundred feet above a dry and deserted creekbed. Because of the staggered landscape, any rock we released provided the perfect pattern of explosive impacts and leapfrogging freefalls. More so: since it wasn't on a trail, or in a place where one would wander off-trail, there was no chance of anybody being below, and thus no need for extensive safety precautions. We could trundle with utter abandon.

When trundling on a regular trail we'd always get a fair number of disapproving looks from passing hikers. They'd peer over the edge, look back at us in suspicion, and ask, "You sure there's nobody down there?" It's understandable—throwing or rolling rocks into the Canyon's depths can be reckless and destructive. It's illegal for those very reasons. But it was a critical and fairly common part of our job. And many hikers were downright envious. I remember one small woman witnessing a particularly satisfying trundle and asking, "You get paid to do this?" I suspect that a large number of people find trundling an irresistible or barely suppressible urge. Zane Grey, on one of his first visits to the Canyon, couldn't resist heaving a boulder off the rim and celebrating its "most awful bellow of a thunderous roar." Even Ed Abbey, the staunch defender of unspoiled wilderness, came to the Grand Canyon and claims to have promptly hurled an old tire off the rim, watching it "bounce over tall pine trees, tear hell out of a mule train and disappear with a final grand leap into the inner gorge."

After all, not many places in the world allow one the opportunity to launch a rock and wait nine seconds before the sound of impact rises out of the void. Trundling allowed us to plumb the depths of the chasm: watching the bounding rock and hanging onto every last reverberation made, for a brief moment, in an empathetically tactile and audible manner, the scope and scale of the Canyon accessible—we knew it was deep, but now we *really* knew it was deep. We rarely witnessed the Canyon's creational processes. We'd come to a slide and see all that wonderful kinetic energy constrained by the level surface of our trail, each individual rock suspended, latent with the pull of gravity. Trundling not only continued the erosional process momentarily pent by our trail, but also allowed us to witness and participate in the ongoing creation of our beloved Canyon.

But really, concerning our particular exuberance, trundling shared the same common denominator as blasting: we were probably the most weathered bunch of whiskey-drinking children you'd ever come across. I'd rest in my harness and watch Michael and Abel, on the other side of the house-sized rock, send rocks down a chute they had cleared. Occasionally the rocks piled up on the lip of the cliff until one powerful trundle tore through them like bowling pins, at once sending half a dozen rocks over the edge and crashing down the cliffs, Michael's and Abel's faces alight with puerile joy.

Four of us rolled giant rocks off of giant cliffs for four straight days, and on the fifth day Devin made his way out to the slide. We happened to be lying about in various positions of snacky contentment, enjoying our federally mandated fifteen-minute afternoon break. He looked at us and then he looked at the slide and then he looked at us again, and I could see the pressure twitching through the muscles in his face.

I loved Devin; I really did. He is a good person and was a great boss. But he drove me crazy. He drove all of us crazy. He was incredibly meticulous, and his meticulousness, in conjunction with his deep reservoir of knowledge about working Trails, often brimmed over into obsessive-compulsive, tight-assed, nit-picking micromanagement.

Since he knew so much about trail work, he needed things to be done the absolute correct way. He really, really needed them done the correct way: the man spoke of constructing water bars as though his dreams at night were illuminated by perfect erosion-control structures. As excruciating as it was to deal with this kind of perfectionism in the moment, he taught me one of the most valuable lessons I took from Trails: pay careful attention to what you do and make the most perfect object you know how. This is important from a utilitarian perspective—the wall will hold, the tree will not fall back on you—but it's also one of the only ways to take pride in what you do, to make your work worthwhile and fulfilling.

Still.

That season Little Tommy Boyle and Devin and I were sharing a mobile home on the North Rim. Devin's duties as a field supervisor required him to be in constant flux between the two rims, and he hadn't spent much time in the trailer. But LTB and I had fallen into a mutual morning routine: waking early, caffeinating and breakfasting in silence while listening to NPR. The first morning Devin arrived, he entered the kitchen at 5:50 a.m. We eyed him warily.

Devin was notorious for his early-morning eccentricities. There was genuine debate among the crew about whether his habits of "organizing" the bunkhouse pots and pans at six in the morning, or stomping throughout the sleeping bunkhouse in his steel-toe boots, were born of simple obliviousness or puerile spite.

He walked in that first morning and tried to fill his water bottle with ice from the refrigerator's dispenser. Nothing happened. He looked at me accusingly.

"The ice machine doesn't work."

"Nope."

"Did you try and fix it?"

"Nope."

Before I could tell him that there were ice trays, he'd opened the door and begun fiddling with the internal mechanism. When this failed he proceeded, with no small effort, to pull the entire refrigerator-freezer unit from the wall. He started tinkering with the wiring in the back.

LTB and I looked at each other.

Devin stepped away from the refrigerator. He was muttering to himself. He turned, walked over to the closet, opened it, grabbed a broom, and walked back to the refrigerator corner. He began sweeping the walls. As the walls had been obscured by the fridge/ freezer unit for lord only knows how long, thick clouds of dust billowed into the kitchen and living room, splintering the first shafts of dawn. With a glance at LTB, and another at the lunatic sweeping the kitchen walls, I went to my room and shut the door.

In general, it wasn't so much Devin's borderline-spectrum be- havior but his haughty criticism that had us cursing him as we tore up the stonework he'd deemed inadequate. He had to comment on everything, and usually his comments were, or at least came across as, critical or condescending. Or both. To be fair, I really can be the same way, my irrepressible habit of correcting other's gram- matical mistakes—"No, Abel, you're inferring what I'm implying, not vice versa"—also surely considered condescending, and simply the tip of the iceberg. Though I like to believe that my criticism is cutting in a helpful striving-for-a-better-world sort of way, Erika has always been quick to point out that my petty bitching is not exactly Gandhian. Still, whereas my critical quibbles come with a certain degree of friendly jest, Devin could be a straight-up finicky dick about them.

Nevertheless, social niceties aren't necessarily an essential leadership trait. And anybody who really worked for Devin for multiple seasons had few reasons to doubt his leadership skills. He'd earned our respect. For one, he worked and sweated in the field alongside us. He could hoist a jack with the best of us, wield a chainsaw better than most of us. His proven skills earned him legitimate authority. This was no small matter. Second, he cared: his nit-picking stemmed from an abiding mindfulness to the relationships between a section of trail and its geography, between Trails and the Canyon. But I also respected him because he would realize, after the fact, that he'd been overly critical, and over the years he honestly and to my mind successfully attempted to rein in that side of him.

He didn't bother reining it in that day at the slide.

"You guys haven't gotten very far."

I tried to remain calm.

A few hours before he'd arrived we'd been drilling, horizontally, into an enormous boulder with a four-and-a-half-foot-long drill bit. The difficulty in using such a long bit on the horizontal was that the sixty-pound pionjar bent the bit ever so slightly. All was well as the bowed bit bored into stone, but it was exceedingly difficult pulling the bit out in the same manner it had twisted in. So Abel, Doc, and Michael had had to hold up the running pionjar to prevent its weight from bending the bit. But the deeper the four-foot bit augured into the rock, the more the pionjar struggled to blow the dust out. It kept bogging down and stalling, so they were constantly having to pull the long bit out of the hole to clear the dust. The process was exhausting just to watch, and though the combined bicep circumference of those boys rivaled the diameter of pine trees, they were exhausted.

"We've been blasting for five fucking days, Devin. We've actually cleared a lot. There're only four of us. There's only so much we can do."

He looked at me.

"And we're being safe," I said.

Safety was the trump card. I knew it and Devin knew it, and he respected it, but he didn't like it. My job was to keep the crew safe and get the job done; his job was to see that I got the job done while keeping the crew safe. Different enough.

"Well, I'm going to have to call Zion," he said, obviously disappointed.

Zion National Park still employed a real blasting crew. Like, dynamite. Devin had already warned them that we might need their services.

"Sounds good," I said, in an offhand, I-don't-give-a-shit way, though I was disappointed in myself for disappointing him, and then loathed myself for feeling disappointed when I didn't think it was deserved. But that's how it was sometimes. In writing about the first Powell expedition down the Colorado through the Grand Canyon, Wallace Stegner notes that John Wesley Powell "represented military discipline and the officer class," while his men represented "frontier independence and a violent distaste for discipline of any kind." This was not too far removed from my—and much of the crew's—relationship with Devin: our professional respect for hierarchy was always muddled with emotions, petty rivalries, and other interpersonal strains.

The Zion crew drove over two days later. One of our mule packers, Abner, loaded their explosives onto a mule string and hauled it two miles downcanyon to the site. They stuffed the trailer-sized boulder—by then well perforated with holes—and the tunnels we'd dug into the rubble with over 150 pounds of explosives. We shut down the trail; half of the crew went downtrail, the other half climbed out on a promontory well above the blast site. The trail guards radioed "All clear" to the blasting crew. The "Blasting!" call went out over the radio.

Silence.

Occasionally, during a spell of writer's block or boredom, I'll find myself watching the shaky video that Doc filmed of the blast: the house-sized boulder is distant and looks small in the frame; there are tinny voices on the radio, then the pregnant pause. And then in an instant the slide crumples, a great plume of dust punches into the sky, a tremendous shockwave shakes the camera, and a roar consumes the audio for a good four seconds. A cascade of rock can be seen crashing down into the creek. Beneath the sustained rumble of falling rock is the crew's hollering and cheering. When the dust cloud has finally entirely whisked upslope, the shot of the slide reveals only small rock, shattered and whitened by the blast.

Fifteen minutes later, back at the site, we were still giddy. The blasters were giddy. Devin was giddy. Seeing him so bubbly re-minded me of the time he'd told me, wistfully, that his last sum-mer as a work leader—the summer that he, Blake, Lake, and I lived for three tours at the Roaring Springs residence, the summer before he moved up the ranks to become a field supervisor, with far more responsibility and office work—had been the best sum-mer he'd had in the Canyon, and how life and work had been so simple then. As he told me I could see the longing in his eyes, the acknowledgment that to move up professionally often means a loss of the good, honest, and simple work that is the heart of Trails.

And later, clearing the last of the rubble from the blast site, I thought of how one of the best things about trundling was the synthesis between mind, body, rock, rock bar, and release. Any fool with any degree of hernial straining can shift a rock with a rock bar, but only the best of us could walk up to a boulder, take in its measure, find the perfect leverage point, and, with a gentle ease within the active strain, cant the bar back and forth to move the rock. Counterintuitive to its simple design, to work a rock bar is to think, and by thinking determine the perfect position to place the bar and fulcrum, but also to test, probe, and problem solve. In shaping a stone to fit another stone, one develops a cyclic pattern of fitting then shaping, fitting then shaping, testing, retesting, until the rock finally falls perfectly into place. Working a rock bar involves the same praxis—knowledge informing practice, practice informing knowledge.

And when you work a rock bar well, nothing compares: the simple marvels of mechanical physics helping you row, one-handed, a two-hundred-pound boulder. It's what the classic Greeks meant when they spoke of *technē*, from whence came "technique." Technē is often translated as craftsmanship or art but, according to the scholar Ellen Dissanyake, more fully means having "a correct understanding of the principles involved." Thus Plato and Aristotle believed that technē "applied equally to angling, chariot driving, and other mundane activities." Experience honed the use of the rock bar into skill, but the root of the skill was a simple and elegant understanding of what was required and why, a way of being effective and efficient and consistent and coming, at last, through hand on bar and bar on rock, to a unique and ephemeral unity of focus and practice and, in the case of trundling, release and joy.

We all had ways of working toward those moments, and some ways were easier or more difficult than others, and some of us were more or less successful than others, and if Devin, like few others on the crew, seemed to struggle with himself—his at times snooty intelligence and need for strict control frequently grappling with the rock-climbing, beer-crafting, mischievous side of him—well, down there, after the blast, that unity shone through him, a job he'd seen through, seen done right.

~: ~

And after blasting and trundling all day we'd hike back down to the Roaring Springs residence. The residence was originally built for the "pump master" in charge of the pumps that forced spring water to the North Rim, but technology had rendered that position obsolete, so Trails stayed in half of the residence; the other half was reserved for rangers and the occasional pipeline crew. Deep in Bright Angel Canyon, seven miles off the rim, the residence was the nicest housing in the Grand Canyon: full kitchen, two baths, hot water, a green lawn edged by iris, a long porch, a basketball hoop, a horseshoe pit, and a helicopter pad perched over Bright Angel Creek to both receive our supplies and provide a sleeping platform.

And when the temperature spiked toward summer and the spring runoff stopped rolling rocks downstream, we'd hike a half-mile uptrail to the succession of emerald pools the creek had bowled out of the Tapeats sandstone. After plunging down the slickrock waterfall and sliding through the gauntlet of pools, we'd bask and drowse on the flood-smoothed and sun-warmed sandstone banks.

And back at the residence we'd drink cocktails or beer and compete in ferocious games of croquet or horseshoes or basketball. Tourists hiking past on the trail or filling water at the trailside spigot would stare openmouthed as we grappled, cursed, and

balled in the depths of the Grand Canyon, the rocky court occasionally zinging the basketball sideways across cottonwood roots,
down the slope, and into the creek, where it bobbed merrily along
until whoever had raced downstream managed to fish it out. And
after playing basketball I'd take my shoes off and put my feet up
and for vespers crack a beer and watch the failing sunlight slip up
the west-facing walls. We were usually there during the longest
days of the year, when the sunsets yawned long and slow, the back-
scattered light casting everything warm, aglow, the final sliver of
sun catching the Kaibab afire.

And about that time we'd eat dinner. Every tour each person
made one dinner for the entire crew—Mexican night, Italian
night, barbeque night, pizza night—and we'd all sit outside at the
table or on the porch and tear wolflike, ravenous, into our food.
All would be dark but for the lights on the porch and the first
few stars and the last blue light behind the silhouettes of pines
on the rim, and still we'd sit, lazing, sated by the food, the day,
talking quietly, perhaps reverentially, perhaps simply wearily, after
the day's work. A bat would flutter and fold down the length of the
lighted porch, loop out into the night, then come twitching back
down again, and people stepping out of the residence would duck
and flail at its near passing. After dinner one of us did dishes and
the others made lunch and filled our water bottles and stuck them
in the freezer for the following day.

And early—eight, nine, ten o'clock—we'd crawl into the bunk
beds inside, or set up our sleeping pads and sheets or sleeping
bags on the helipad, and read for a while by headlamp, then sleep,
then wake to the sudden flood of milky light as the moon cracked
past the rim, or, on moonless nights, to the million stars spattered
across our half-dreams.

In this manner the days passed.

~: :~

When do you belong to a place? When your personal geographies of experience, memory, and identity overlay the physical geography? When the day's landscape becomes the night's dreamscape? When you've spent a decade ingesting a place's earth, its water, its earth in water? A lifetime?

At times, and only half in jest, I ascribed my life's blessings and burdens to being raised in a house filled with books. The long hallway I walked a few dozen times a day every day of my young life was lined with hundreds of books. I remember when my high school friend Ali, whose parents fled Iran during the revolution, stopped in my hallway and said, astonished, "Look at all these books. How many have you read?"

I had read many.

The content of those books influenced my development as a person as deeply as did the patience and wisdom of my mother and father and the patience and wisdom of those chaparral hills. In those books I first learned resistance. From Ferdinand the Bull ("He liked to sit just quietly and smell the flowers") to W. Somerset Maugham's Larry Darrell ("You see, money to you means freedom; to me it means bondage") to Jack London's Martin Eden ("But I am I. And I won't subordinate my taste to the unanimous judgment of mankind") to Hunter S. Thompson ("Life should not be a journey to the grave with the intention of arriving safely in a pretty and well preserved body, but rather to skid in broadside in a cloud of smoke, thoroughly used up, totally worn out, and loudly proclaiming 'Wow! What a Ride!'"), these characters and authors first described, criticized, and offered alternatives to what I would come to categorize as the System.

But it wasn't just the exhortations and criticisms of those pessimists and misanthropes, idealists and dreamers, revolutionaries and adventurers that helped shape the boy I was, the man I became. It was also their rambling ways. As a child I was obsessed with Tintin, the boy reporter who was motion and adventure incarnate, traveling the world via ships, trains, planes, automobiles, submersibles, rockets, camels, elephants, horses. As an adult, my literary heroes now include those who put down roots and who know a place deeply: Thoreau in New England; Robinson Jeffers in Big Sur; Wendell Berry in Kentucky; Gary Snyder in the Sierras. But as a youth and young adult I cared only for those restless, ravening spirits, to read about Ed Abbey's stateside peregrinations, Jack Kerouac's "crazy ventures," D. H. Lawrence's "savage pilgrimage," Walt Whitman's "perpetual journey."

And so I found myself, seventeen years old, stepping onto the cracked tarmac in Guayaquil, Ecuador, with a tropical storm casting purple lightning into the night, wet palm trees lashing against wet banana trees, and the utterly unfamiliar, pelagic weight of humidity enveloping me in embrace. Just as unfamiliar was the surge of flight-or-fight emotion that coursed out of me in response, an invigorating and, as it turns out, wholly addictive sensation: over and over in my life I'd strive for that sense of stepping off a threshold, of throwing myself into what J. W. Powell described as "the Great Unknown."

And so I spent four years bouncing from LA to South America to Washington State to Alaska to Glacier National Park to Southern Africa to Southeast Asia to India to Burma to Point Reyes National Seashore and back to LA. I had happily become what Wallace Stegner, in his essay "A Sense of Place," described as a "displaced" person, "always in motion," "adventurous, restless, seeking," "nomadic, unrooted," a person born into a "culture of movement without place."

But to Stegner, this is not a good thing: "Neither the country nor the society we built out of it can be healthy until we stop raiding and running, and learn to be quiet part of the time, and acquire the sense not of ownership but of belonging.... Only in the act of submission is the sense of place realized and a sustainable relationship between people and earth established," he argued.

That's a common refrain these days.

As the writer John Daniel put it, "Our rootlessness—our refusal to accept the discipline of living as responsive and responsible members of neighborhoods, communities, landscapes, and ecosystems—is perhaps our most serious and widespread disease.... We don't stand much chance of restoring and sustaining the health of our land, or of perpetuating ourselves as a culture, unless we can outgrow our boomer adolescences and mature into stickers, or nesters—human beings willing to take on the obligations of living in communities rooted in place, conserving nature as we conserve ourselves." Or, as Gary Snyder more succinctly put it, "Find your place on the planet, dig in, and take responsibility from there."

The problem with these well-articulated arguments was that the rooted life of which they spoke so convincingly sounded so damn boring. Or at least seemed like a very good thing for other people. Old people, really—those who'd already burnt through their wanderlust. Wendell Berry could plant wheat in Kentucky; I wanted to ride camels in Rajasthan. Stability and responsibility weren't merely boring, they were downright dangerous: from newspaper headlines to good friends' bankruptcies, everywhere I saw signs of how an act of submission like what Stegner advises could become subjugation to something more pernicious, to the mechanisms of the cold, callous System. I also suspected that a strict sense of place and belonging could abet possessiveness, jealousy, and callousness and, on a larger scale, lead to ethnocentrism and xenophobia.

No, I preferred Snyder's description of the beliefs of the Beats: "Better to live simply, be poor, and have the time to wander and write and *dig* (meaning to penetrate and absorb and enjoy) what was going on in the world." This fit me fine. This is what the seasonal worker lifestyle offered. If one did actually spend enough time to "penetrate" (and this I self-servingly reckoned to be about a seven-month stint), then it was better to experience the world— all the world—with the eyes of the traveler, the newcomer, the vagabond. I agreed with Paul Shepard, that subversive ecologist-philosopher, who noted that "we are space-needing, wild-country Pleistocene beings, trapped in overdense numbers in devastated, simplified ecosystems." We can't expect ten thousand years of sedentariness and, far more recently, civilization to eclipse the wandering that millions of years of evolution has encoded in our genes.

But in time I began to have my doubts about the Beats' beliefs. One season I shared a trailer for a few weeks with a crewmate named Ben. He worked Trails in the Canyon for a winter season; by the time I returned that spring, he was already preparing to head to the Tetons for the summer. Ben happily referred to himself as a "perpetual motion machine": he's worked Trails in parks across the West, from Grand Tetons to Saguaro, Lassen to Olympic. In seventeen years he hasn't lived in a single house for more than five months. (Though truth be told this isn't entirely indicative of Ben's life. A perpetual motion machine, sure, but also one drawn back to Grand Tetons National Park, to which he's dedicated twelve seasons. We all have our places.) At one point in my life Ben's restlessness may have sounded romantic, even ideal, but even at twenty-five, with only five years of itinerant working and rambling under my belt, and an unknown number more looming ahead of me, this sort of ceaseless flux was beginning to seem exhausting.

The seeds of my doubts were sown long before I became friends with Ben, before I'd even truly started the seasonal life. For a few years in college, I pursued the idea that I'd be a farmer. Fed up with what I saw as the interesting but ultimately purely academic knowledge imparted during my first year of college, I figured that the best thing I could learn would be the tools of self-sufficiency that I'd never needed to know in Los Angeles but that were so critical and evident in the lives I had witnessed in my travels. I happened to be attending a college with a five-acre organic farm on which I could learn how to make food rise and blossom from the earth. So I worked on this farm, and studied everything from soil science to small engine repair to scales of efficiency. I took in the notions of rootedness, bioregionalism, localism, villages. For the first time I thought about what it meant to become, in Wes Jackson's phrase, native to a place. For the first time I wanted this. For the first time I realized that, for all my travels, I was always a traveler, tourist, stranger, a consumer of experiences; that always escaping, always flitting here and there, meant I was nowhere, really; that my knowledge of those locations was as shallow as the Dutch kid's knowledge of the Canyon's rock.

Paul Shepard, for all his trumpeting about the absurdity of Pleistocene nomads stuffed into business suits, also paraphrased the psychotherapist Erik Erikson: "Belonging is the pivot of life, the point at which selfhood becomes possible—not just belonging in general, but in particular. One belongs to a universe of order and purpose that must initially be recognized as a particular community of certain species in a terrain of unique geology." This hit me hard. For all the ways travel and motion helped me develop a sense of selfhood, this statement about purpose and specific terrain rang true, in the way the chaparral hills and salted air of my childhood were true.

But there was nowhere in particular that I belonged. As much as I liked to believe that one controls one's outlook on life, as much as I liked to think that every gift ostensibly granted by a place like the Canyon—the sense of peace or excitement, enoughness or extravagance—actually blossomed from within, so that the greatest wonder is not the Canyon but our ability to wonder, the truth of it was that my sense of belonging was far less consciously malleable. I'd loved, deeply, passionately, so many of the places I'd "penetrated": the hanging valleys of Glacier National Park, the solemn groves in the Olympic rain forests, the long sweep of coast of Drakes Bay, the high alpine expanses of the Sierras. But as much as a part of me still resides in all those places, as much as parts of me still belong to those places, none pulled me to them with an irresistible magnetism, an unshakeable spiritual affinity.

And perhaps that expectation of place and belonging was exactly the problem. Maybe I expected too much, a lightning-bolt eureka moment, like the way Daphne, pursued by Apollo, turned instantly into a laurel tree, and so too my restless feet would suddenly, thankfully, grip the earth as roots. After all, many of my literary heroes wrote passionately about specific places, and many of these writers knew these places as their places as soon as they arrived. The poet/trapper John Haines declared, "From the first day I set foot [on Richardson Hill] I knew I was home. Something in me identified with that landscape. I had come, let's say, to the dream place." Paul Bowles, before settling into Algeria, declared that he "had always been vaguely certain that sometime during my life I should come into a magic place which in disclosing its secrets would give me wisdom and ecstasy—perhaps even death."

What I *had* felt, in many of these places, was that I belonged not so much through a mystical magnetism, but through the people who had also made their way to the same places. I belonged because I was accepted into, and liked by, and participated in, a community, a tribe, a family. In this regard the camaraderie and cohesion and community of the Canyon trail crew fit me like a well-worn work glove. There were kids on the crew who loved Trails and stuck around the Canyon exactly for that social sense of belonging. But this was not the sort of belonging I figured would be good for me, wholesome, nor the belonging that contained the ecological and moral virtues of rootedness. After all, I could continue on as a perennial tourist, belonging to a tribe of fellow backpackers and expats, but I'd always be in some mode of escape, rarely truly understanding or participating in the cultures I moved through. Same in the Canyon: I could drink bourbon and shoot the shit with my tribe of seasonal workers for decades without understanding the ecological underpinnings that supported my corporeal obliviousness.

Regardless, the Canyon was my place to try to belong. The Canyon never completely reconciled my mutually exclusive longings to roam the world and to settle deeply into place; what Stegner dubbed the "excitement of newness and possibility [and] the dissatisfaction and hunger that result from placelessness." But in many ways my relationship with the Canyon was the best of both worlds. Here was a place I recognized in that epiphanic, lightning-bolt way I had sought. Here was a place I could return to, again and again; stand on that rim and feel that surge of awe course through me, again and again. The rim was always a threshold. I could hike a new route and feel both the pleasure of discovery and the warmth of familiarity. Here, certainly, was Shepard's "terrain of unique geography," Stegner's place to know deeply and truthfully, through work and adventure, through a commitment to learn the lessons that one learns only with time. It was a time in my life and a place in my life when Erika and I were simply, easily, and deeply happy. That first painful, bloody, dizzying hike had been a baptism, and perhaps the whole of the Canyon could serve as a crucible into which I could cast a new self. It did not matter that the Canyon did not work on me at once. If the Hopi believe that they ascended through three worlds to emerge through the sipapu into the Little Colorado River gorge, just like that, I reckon I was more like the Diné, the Navajo, the Athabaskans who after a thousand-mile journey from the boreal forests of northwestern Canada felt some inexplicable and innate affinity with the Colorado Plateau, and slowly, over generations, abandoned their nomadic, hunter-gatherer lifestyle for one closer to that of the sedentary, agrarian Hopi. So too my own process of belonging to the Canyon happened, as Stegner put it, "by slow accrual" of quiet moments and small epiphanies and great swelling feelings of contentment.

⌁ ∻

I was sitting on a bench outside the General Store on the South Rim watching tourists. Memorial Day was approaching, the zenith of tourist season, and Japanese, German, French, Dutch, and various English dialects babbled about me. People were talking on cell phones, piling into and out of their RVs, and blustering out of the store with Grand Canyon T-shirts featuring Kokopelli, the Puebloan flutist petroglyph now as cartoonishly commercialized as Mickey Mouse.

To my left, between the post office and the crowded parking lot, was a placard for an exhibition at Kolb Studios, the local historic photography studio. The placard portrayed an Edward Curtis photograph of a Native American face. Beneath the face were the words "I Am the Grand Canyon." The placard was the title and front cover of a book by Stephen Hirst, a man who had lived with the Havasupai tribe for over a decade. I had recently read the book, and I easily recalled the scene from which the book's title stemmed. In 1971 the National Park Service put forth a master plan designed to consolidate the patchwork of federal landholdings adjacent to the Grand Canyon—national monuments, national forests, Bureau of Land Management parcels—into a significantly larger national park. Astonishingly, the Havasupai Indian Reservation, which would be entirely embedded within this expanded park, was not mentioned in the master plan.

At a public hearing for the plan on May 18, 1971, Lee Marshall, a five-term Havasupai tribal chairman, stood, surveyed the room, and said, "I heard all you people talking about the Grand Canyon. Well, you are looking at it. I am the Grand Canyon."

In five words he revealed the gulf between how two cultures understand the same piece of land. In one culture's conception, the land was put aside as an "other," everybody's and nobody's. In the other, the land had been home for nearly a thousand years, and man and the land were inextricably connected.

I studied the photograph on the sign: the sad, sepia-tinged

face of a Havasupai named Waluthma. According to Hirst, Waluthma's "affable nature and command of English made him a favorite among non-Indians." He was even given an Anglo name: "Supai Charlie." In 1907, seven years after the picture was taken, "Supai Charlie" was lynched by a gang of ranchers who accused him of killing a calf. He was killed because of a cow. Before he was killed his face was painted with red zigzags. Chicken feathers were stuck in his hair. He was castrated. His body was stuck in an old carton and buried in a shallow grave outside Flagstaff.

For all the ways my years in the Canyon worked against both my own nomadic tendencies and our restless American culture as a whole, and thus, in my eyes, allowed me a tenuous claim on Canyon knowledge and belonging, for all that there is this: an injustice, the fact that the establishment of Grand Canyon National Park was predicated on the forced removal of a people whose claims of belonging stretch across centuries.

For eight hundred years the Havasupai lived in the Grand Canyon, farming in the numerous side canyons in the summer, gathering piñon nuts and hunting deer throughout the plateau lands in the autumn and winter. But after the Civil War and with the encouragement of the Homestead Act of 1862, white settlers flooded into the region. By 1880, hoping for protection from encroaching settlers, the Havasupai agreed to a treaty that granted them a 38,400-acre reservation, a fraction of their estimated 7-million-acre traditional homeland. Within two years, President Rutherford B. Hayes, swayed by ranchers and miners, cut the reservation to a mere 518.6 acres—less than a square mile—within Cataract Canyon. Little more than a decade after being consigned to this tiny reservation, the majority of the Havasupai's former homelands became the Grand Canyon Forest Reserve, a precursor to Grand Canyon National Park.

The incipient Park Service only intensified the removal of the Havasupai from the new park. To be fair, the Park Service perceived any privately owned land within national parks as a threat to the preservationist mandate of the Park Service, and the Park Service forced rural landowners and communities, white and native alike, from Shenandoah to Death Valley, from their homes in what had been abruptly designated an area to be left "unimpaired for the enjoyment of future generations." Within Grand Canyon National Park, administrators struggled to integrate the patchwork of private holdings—impoverished native plots as well as rich, white landholdings—into the park. As the government did not consider the Havasupai to be US citizens, they were much easier to remove than whites. Arizona state senator Ralph Cameron battled the Park Service for years for control of Indian Garden and the Bright Angel Trail. According to the former NPS trails historian Mike Anderson, William Randolph Hearst taunted the Park Service with "rumors of luxury hotels and other grand developments on his two hundred acres of prime real estate" on the rim for two decades before the Park Service forced him out.

This relative view of history—that everyone, regardless of race, was removed from national parks—is exactly how the Park Service presents the Grand Canyon to the public: belonging at once to everyone and no one. Even the system of "heroic nomenclature"— the Egyptian, Greek, Teutonic, Hindu, Persian, and Arthurian names draped over the landscape—constructs the Grand Canyon as a universal treasure, unbound by time or culture. But this view masks an inherent injustice. One cannot justly compare the loss of Hearst's land claim to the loss of the Havasupai's traditional homeland. The long view tends to whitewash history, to make it an abstraction, to justify specific tragedies by placing them in universal frames, as though to say, "Well, there have always been extinctions. The loss of the bonytail chub is natural," or "Cultures have always come into conflict; there has always been oppression and injustice."

I can blithely claim I belong to the Canyon because I'm a descendant of the conquering culture. Because I have the luxury of looking at history as a benign or neutral force, as opposed to history as viewed by a people, in the words of the historian Patricia Limerick, "undergoing conquest and never fully escaping its consequences." As a Park Service employee, a wilderness enthusiast, a rider of the Southern Pacific Railroad, a Californian of Estonian, Norwegian, and Scottish descent, I am the beneficiary of the historical injustices. It's not necessarily an exercise in self-loathing to characterize my presence in the Canyon as that of an invasive-exotic species. Like tamarisk and zebra mussels, European Americans like myself have not only outcompeted the native flora and fauna, but with our unique baggage of cattle, concrete, and cars have irrevocably altered the country's ecosystems.

But then again, it's not entirely fair to blame the European hordes, especially on a global and taxonomic level. Don't blame the color of the hand but the hand itself, capable of grasping bow and gun, hammer and chisel. It is entirely plausible that, had they had the technology, the Hopi and Havasupai would have exploited the environment to the same degree the Europeans did, long before they even arrived. Significant ecological changes took place in North America as soon as the first humans crossed the Bering land bridge, as evidenced by the poor Harrington's mountain goat, which had lived in the Canyon region for at least nineteen thousand years and survived various ice ages, volcanic eruptions, and saber-toothed tigers but was pretty quickly hunted to extinction once the first humans arrived.

My point—again—is that nothing is ever simple. I'm fiercely glad for the parks as islands of relatively undeveloped ecosystems, yet I don't think a small band of Native Americans in the West should have had to suffer the repercussions of white man's over-hunting in the East. If I find joy in the park, in the conservation of land, in a place where cougars cannot be hunted, where housing developments and casinos don't mar the rim, where I could be so possessed by a place without possessing *it*, I also feel that as a culture we may have lost a great deal with the Park Service's stipulations against belonging.

Take what Powell wrote of the Paiutes, to whom he turned again and again for guides: "There is not a trail but what they know; every rock and every gulch seems familiar. I have prided myself on being able to grasp and retain in my mind the topography of a country; but these Indians put me to shame. My knowledge is only general, embracing the more important features of a region that remains as a map engraved on my mind; but theirs is particular. They know every rock and every ledge; every gulch and canyon; and just where to wind among these to find a pass; and their knowledge is unerring." This deep knowledge of place is not unlike the way Polynesian and Hawaiian sailors once used their knowledge of the sea and stars to navigate thousands of miles of open ocean without instruments. They knew the rhythms and patterns by which over two hundred named stars rose and set and shifted from latitude to longitude from hour to hour. As we use landmarks, they used seamarks—pods of porpoises, driftwood, individual whales, or "a region where flying fish leaped in pairs, a zone of innumerable jellyfish, an area of numerous terns." They knew how clouds mass above islands, how white sand beaches or calm green lagoons reflect light onto the bellies of those clouds, how swells refract around or reflect across islands, so that when the night sky was dark and the direction of the swells couldn't be read by sight, the master sailor could lie in the bottom of the canoe and distinguish the intended direction between the motions of five different swells.

What they knew, we have lost. Or we never knew it and now never will. Sadly enough, they too—Polynesians and Paiutes alike—have largely lost their intimate knowledge and associated skills of place. Though these ways of knowing have been replaced, even by ways of knowing the Canyon that the ancients never had— the Colorado River guide's ability to read the river's features, or a geologist's understanding of the origins of rock—all too often these are specialized skills, almost too particular. In his essay about a sense of place, Wallace Stegner praised Wendell Berry for "talking about the kind of knowing that involves the senses, the memory, the history of a family or a tribe. He is talking about the knowledge of place that comes from working in it in all weathers, making a living from it, suffering from its catastrophes, loving its mornings or evenings or hot noons, valuing it for the profound investment of labor and feeling that you, your parents and grand-parents, your all-but-unknown ancestors have put into it."

Trails came so close to this knowing. Through our stories, our own names on the land, the unique opportunity of being able to call the Canyon home, the Canyon opened itself to us in ways the vast majority of visitors will never experience. Yet even that only went so far. After all, as NPS employees our income was drawn from the faraway coffers of the federal government. Our food,

our energy, our material possessions, our entertainments, our re-
ligions—almost all arose out of sources apart from the Canyon.
By making the Canyon a park, and by making the Park Service
so dependent on seasonal employees, we forfeited, or at best
transmitted in diluted form from one generation of trail crew to
another, the rich foundational knowledge of place and belonging
that indigenous peoples passed down in place from parents and
grandparents and ancestors.

But it went deeper than a lack of intergenerational continuity: our modern Western consciousness is structured in terms of
distinctions and isolations rather than connections and affinities.
Blame it on Descartes, or on a Judeo-Christian belief system,
which, in opposition to the pagan belief systems that viewed the
earth itself as sacred, tends to reserve sacredness within marked-
off sanctuaries. Blame capitalism, our market god of commodification, which confuses belonging with ownership. These cultural
foundations have provided grist for criticism of national parks and
wilderness areas; the eminent environmental historian William
Cronon, for example, argues that "we seem unlikely to make much
progress in solving [critical environmental] problems if we hold up
to ourselves as the mirror of nature a wilderness we ourselves cannot inhabit." Whatever the reason, suffice it to say that we've been
hobbled, perhaps even partially blinded, in a way that prevents us
from more fully seeing and knowing and belonging to a place like
the Grand Canyon.

Yet blaming the ideas underlying national parks and wilderness
areas as contributing to our dire litany of modern environmental
crises strikes me as a red herring. Though they may occupy an important space within the American psyche, national parks occupy
only 3.4 percent of the actual landmass (and a huge percentage of

that national park land is in Alaska). The true problem lies not in
the existence of a national park, in managing a place like the Canyon
as apart; the problem lies in what we hold it apart *from*. To pass
through the park gate is to enter a sanctum—suddenly there are
elk, bison, condors, silence, dark nights, slowed time, and the natural rhythms and intricacies of generally minimally impeded ecological systems. I wouldn't want to sacrifice any of this to experiments
in adjustments toward greater societal environmental stewardship.
Nor would I want to give much or any of this up as reparations for
historical injustices. As it is, I applaud the delicate efforts Grand
Canyon National Park has made in trying to alleviate some of these
past injustices while still maintaining the Park Service's mission.

Jan Balsom, who served as the deputy chief for science and resource management at Grand Canyon National Park for over three
decades, wrote of how "the relationship Grand Canyon has with
the Havasupai and Hualapai are among the most complicated and
vexing relationships the NPS has, largely due to conflicting legislation and diametrically opposed management concerns." While
"concerns over development, conflicting management strategies,
natural and cultural resources, economic development, and the
preservation of sovereignty are core issues," Grand Canyon NP
has made a "concerted effort to change the legacy we have inherited
regarding resource management and relationships with our tribal
neighbors." In the end, perhaps Lee Marshall's dramatic phrase "I
am the Grand Canyon" helped sway those who designed the eventual 1975 Grand Canyon Enlargement Act. For while the park was
expanded by 1.2 million acres, the Havasupai Indian Reservation
was also expanded by 185,000 acres, the tribe was afforded use of
an additional 95,300 acres *within the park* for traditional activities
such as hunting and gathering.

Cronon condemned the idea of wilderness because "as we gaze into the mirror it holds up for us, we too easily imagine that what we behold is Nature when in fact we see the reflection of our own unexamined longings and desires." But I don't see this as entirely problematic: knowing that national parks and wilderness areas are cultural creations laden with complicated and vexing cultural baggage only makes me love them all the more. I'm blessed that National Park Service allowed me the time and space—hell, even paid me—to examine and work through my longings and desires, my tensions and oppositions, in a place beset by its own complicated and conflicted terrains.

~: :~

The rain, insistent all morning, began to course from the low clouds. Four miles out on the North Rim's Walhalla Glades Trail, Erika and I took shelter in the lee of a large spruce tree. Thinking of that moment now, years later, I don't think of being damp and cold and what that meant for the remaining miles, as surely I thought at the time, but remember instead the way the rain sheeted down outside the tree's dripline, and how Erika's face shone with happiness at being out in the forest in the rain.

I am prone to nostalgia.

Nostalgia, from the Greek *nostos*, "returning home," and *algos*, "pain or ache," was coined in 1688 by a medical student studying severe homesickness among Swiss mercenaries living far from the Alps. Nostalgia was originally seen as a debilitating sickness, a pathological pining, synonymous with indolence and melancholy, though it is now more commonly understood as a benign longing for things past, often enough a longing for a past that only and ever existed in the capricious halls of memory. Nostalgia casts

the past in a revisionist light that minimizes the pains and frus-
trations while illuminating the minor joys with ostensible meaning. Our nostalgic constructions help shape us as individuals: I
pick and choose, quite unconsciously, what to remember, and by
these selected fragments, manipulated or not, I construct myself.
Nostalgia in this case isn't an exercise in dissatisfaction and regression; it is evidence of how the past continues to shape our present:
I like to think of Erika as oblivious to the cold and happy in the
rain because it pleases me to be in love with such a woman.

But I have another memory of that day. The rain had abated,
and we had followed the trail to its terminus at Francois Matthes
Point. The rainclouds had collapsed into the Canyon and become
boundless, amorphous, gaseous traces of form drifting slack
and easy amid the Ottoman Amphitheater's towers and ridges.
Different clouds were moving different directions at once: the
higher, still-distinct thunderheads armada-ing northward on a
common plane, a lower windplane sliding others to the northwest,
with various clouds within the Canyon drifting upslope and rising
straight out of the Canyon like raptured souls reluctant to leave
earth.

Looking into that vast, churning chiaroscuro of white, inky
black, and smoke-blue gray clouds, Erika asked me: "Well, what
do you want?"

I had no answer.

I knew—at least I thought I knew—what I did *not* want: I did not
want to move to Gainesville, Florida, and live there for two to five
years as Erika attended the University of Florida, working first
toward her master's degree, and then her PhD. I did not want to
move anywhere in Florida. For that matter, I did not want to move

anywhere east of the Rocky Mountains. And yet she was almost
assuredly Florida bound. She had already visited the university, she
was excited about working with a young professor doing interesting
ethnobotanical work, and they were likely to offer her a good teaching appointment. In a bald attempt to court my future presence, she
had taken me to visit Gainesville and the university before whisking
me toward the ecological charms of central Florida: to the freshwa-
ter springs, then to the Atlantic coast, and then down to Key Largo
to scuba dive. All of which I found exotic, often beautiful, and
frequently fascinating—as a vacation. The thought of living there,
immersed in that humidity, that political conservativism, that ach-
ing, irredeemable flatness, was the stuff of nightmares. Literally. In
what later became a recurring joke between us, I had a dream that
I had indeed moved to Gainesville, only to spend my days waiting
tables at Red Lobster. Night terrors. What I remember most about
that visit to Florida was how uncharacteristically physically disori-
ented I was, how difficult it was for me to gain a mental map of the
unbroken landscapes we passed through. The cardinal directions
spun round, unmoored by topographical references: there were no
elevated landmarks to which I could consciously, then eventually
unconsciously, orient myself. There were no mountains or hills or
ridges that I could climb in order to piece the lowlands together:
all was lowlands, a peninsula planed by the weight of the ocean a
scant 23 million years ago. I was physically lost, and culturally an
outsider, and emotionally very, very wary.

Yet I had no good answer to Erika's question, that storm-swept
day. What *did* I want?

Up to that point, knowing what I did *not* want out of my life
had not been too poor a guide to what I *did* want out of life. Not

wanting an office job, or to be enthralled to wealth, status, and stability, I had discovered then embraced the seasonal life of Trails.
Shunning what I perceived as a sort of sedentary cultural malaise,
I had fallen happily into travel, wanderlust. Not wanting the trap-
pings of a conventional relationship, I had helped craft a relationship rooted in ample amounts of personal freedom. Still, in the
long run, fear and loathing are not the most wholesome of guides.
Nor sustainable: even just five years out of high school, my rage-
against-the-System anger had softened, dulled. I had realized that
the System was no more monolithic than the Canyon, that it too
was a complex of independent, interrelated components; that it existed, sure, but that nothing was preordained, nothing was forced;
that opposed to a mass, imposed conspiracy, much arose out of
individual choice and herd mentality, out of the understandable,
occasionally even forgivable faults and fallacies of human nature.
Placing my life in opposition—even slant opposition—to that
complicated beast required a nimbleness, a willowlike flexibility.

My confusion and inability to answer Erika's question wasn't
simply about my conscious or unconscious distaste of certain life
paths, but simply that I had been living my life a few steps at a time,
and as I reckoned it things had been falling into place pretty well. If
I was mindful, and true to myself and my simple needs, and made
the right moves when I needed to, I trusted—certainly naively, but
not without precedent—that new, appealing paths that did not
insult my soul would continue to appear on the horizon. But my
needs were no longer all that mattered. Erika was ambitious in
ways that I was not, focused in ways that I was not. She tended to
look farther into the future than I generally deemed necessary or
helpful, and she was telling me that she was most likely going to
attend the University of Florida, and that she wanted me to come

with her, as I had led her to believe I would. But now that the cold hard decision loomed, a decision that would sever me from the life I was loving in the Canyon, with the sun just then splintering through the rainclouds, its godbeam shafts illuminating a distant cliff face, I hesitated on that threshold.

I *was* tempted to make a life for myself in the Canyon, in the Park Service. But I had not truly committed to that either. During my first summer in the Canyon I had written in my journal, surely as a rejoinder to the mounting temptation, "I can't stay in the Canyon forever." And every time I got laid off for the season I'd think that I was done, ready to move on to something else in my life. But then I'd return home to LA for a visit and realize that my friends there lived vicariously through their idea of me as a healthy, bearded ranger, exuding the smell of pine and fresh air. One said of his girlfriend, "She hates her job. We all do. Except for you. And that's why we hate you"—and I realized how blessed I was to spend my days in the Canyon.

Take the tour I'd worked before my walk in the woods with Erika: we'd been recutting tread on the Nankoweap Trail. The afternoons were so still that I could hear the hiss of the wind in the pines on the rim, two thousand feet above us. A thin scrim of cirrus would gauze the sun as a gift. After work, I'd walk a quarter-mile to a water seep, where a drip fell into our cutout milk jug every four seconds. I'd pour the seepwater into a hardhat, wash my face, neck, arms. Back at our camp, Michael and Ray would be blasting pebbles into the abyss with a busted pick handle. I'd pour myself a few drams of warm whiskey, sit on a cliff edge, and watch the sun fade across the mangled topography of the eastern Canyon. The bats nattered me to sleep. At dawn I'd drink my yerba maté and eat my oats, watching the morning shadows slant the opposite way they had the previous evening. For nine days we'd been submerged in the Canyon's untethered spacetime, a realm in which the thoughts, worries, and responsibilities of bills, deadlines, and debt didn't apply. As Eliot Porter wrote in his elegy for Glen Canyon, *The Place No One Knew*, "In the canyon itself the days flow through your consciousness as the river flows along its course, without a break and with hardly a ripple to disturb their smoothness.... The current becomes the time on which you move. Things happen and days pass.... You glide on into the day unpursued, living, as all good river travelers should, in the present."

Yet we are pursued by death. Time may be a construct, and it may be that the Canyon, of any place I've ever been, revealed and altered this construct, but we do age. Drifting in that great, Buddhist-present eddy of Canyontime was fine, for a while, but the rest of the human-world-river, just on the other side of the eddy fence, just on the rim, flowed ever onward. By that time I was twenty-eight, and I'd worked Trails for most of that crucial, formative decade of my life. I felt that I was nearing the point when I was either going to have to truly commit or truly let go. I was beginning to feel that any dreams I harbored of a life that did not involve the park were slipping past every year. If I was to ever finally fully sever myself from the Park Service and enter the job market, I'd be competing against people whose résumés were already long with references to internships and experiences relevant to, say, teaching creative writing or small-farm agriculture, not drywall masonry and chainsaw field repair. I teetered on the cusp of being too far behind to be able to catch up.

I was also aware that Trails in itself offered a limited future. Yes, if I were dedicated and ambitious I could work my way up the hierarchy, bide my time, and eventually try and land a head-of-

Trails position at a decent park. But I was not ambitious, and that position would essentially be a desk job anyway: dealing with budget, logistics, human resources, and other administrative terrors. Trails as I knew it had spoiled me rotten: it provided what Rainer Maria Rilke called "the deep, simple necessities in which life renews itself." Trails had granted me the knowledge that work could be rewarding, fulfilling, fun, filled with fresh air and laughter; that work and life and place and love could entwine. A supervisory desk job did not supply these necessities.

Of course, I could always consciously stop at whatever highest position I could attain within Trails that allowed me to keep working outside, to continue enjoying the greatest things about trail work, but even that could only last so long—it was difficult to imagine being fifty years old and breaking rock under the summer sun alongside brash twenty-two-year-olds. Already, at the relatively tender age of twenty-eight, my hands and face bore the lines and scars of premature aging, my skin was wind-bitten and sunworn. My joints creaked with the accumulated miles; my liver was surely scarred by the whiskey. I could shift somewhere else within the Maintenance Division—Housing or Roads or Wastewater— but that, too, as signified a loss of almost everything good about my life in the Canyon.

But I wasn't ready to give it up. Though I was loath to once again lapse into the ever-more-difficult together-apart-together-apart cycle that had defined our relationship for so long, I was even more loath to leave the Canyon. I reckoned that we could survive another round of long-distance loving. Though I loved Erika, I feared that the Canyon would not be the only thing that I would be giving up, that leaving the Canyon would set a precedent, some sort of cascading series of sacrifices by which I would subsume my

life to hers. One should be sure of such things before one commits
to them. As I was not, just then, entirely sure, and as I have always
been prone to nostalgia, I feared that I would quit the Canyon and
move to Florida, and whether I worked at Red Lobster or Gator
World or wherever, I would bear it, and tell myself and Erika that
it was worth it, to be living with the woman I loved, but day after
day, month after month, nostalgic remembrance of my Canyon
past—nostalgic remembrances that were *exactly* exercises in dissatisfaction and regression—would seep out of me as poisonous
water drips from so many Canyon springs, and eventually resentment would come flooding out of me, onto Erika, she who *made
me come here.*

My fear in this particular case was bolstered by the cautionary tale
of the life of one who had to that point in my life served as a good
guide: Edward Abbey.

When he first entered the seasonal life, Abbey had convinced
himself that sustaining a family and a seasonal, wilderness-based
life was "within the realm of concrete actuality." At least initially,
though, it seems he underestimated the drawbacks of the seasonal
life: constantly applying and reapplying to jobs, moving every six
months or so, making friends and then leaving them, rarely making much money or receiving benefits. It's a life that necessitates a
certain carefree independence, an unattached regard for a straight
future, a contentment with incertitude, and is thus a life predom-
inantly enjoyed by eighteen- to twenty-five-year-olds. Abbey entered this life as a twenty-nine-year-old with a wife and children.

Three marriages later he admitted, with characteristic candor,
"My wives got sick and tired of the constant moving around and
the poverty level income." Indeed, after two seasons at Arches

(one of which was with his second wife and child, both of whom were—revealingly—edited out of *Desert Solitaire*), his wife had had enough. So in 1962, when Abbey was thirty-four, he followed his wife and by then two children from Albuquerque to Hoboken, New Jersey, at that time the most densely populated city in the United States.

Arriving in Hoboken, Abbey tried teaching writing at New York's New School, hated it, and quit. He tried working as a technical writer for Western Electric, hated it, and quit. He got a job as a caseworker for the New York City Welfare Board, hated it, and managed to keep it for nine months—the longest he had ever worked at one place. Abbey's journal entries during this personal nadir are painful to read—drowning in self-pity, then berating himself for his self-pity, then angry at having to berate himself, then sad again, on and on. In his sad, semiautobiographical novel *The Fool's Progress* he would recall and resolutely forswear those days: "I don't believe in doing work I don't want to do in order to live the way I don't want to live." (He also wrote, in an answer I was tempted to give to Erika, "My life? Do with my life? Why should I do anything with my life? I live my life.") In the midst of his despair he assured himself that if he was living how and where he pleased—working outside, in the Southwest—he would be content. He worked on a never-published book, *City of Dreadful Night*, which featured a group of men sitting around Hoboken dreaming of going back to the Southwest. The desert had become, like the black sun in his later book, "a blinding and terrible beauty which obliterated everything but the image of itself."

I'd love to believe that I could be happy no matter where I am, that happiness wells solely from within. I'd love to believe that I could notice, see, appreciate nature in an urban or semiurban environment as I did in the Canyon; that if I were to move to Gainesville observing the way tree roots heave up sidewalk panels, or the resilience of urban raccoons and coyotes, would suffice. I understand why this is so important. But it's not for me, or for Abbey in Hoboken, who lamented having to watch the "seasons come and go in a small rectangle of walled-in space we called our yard."

What I feared that I would miss most in moving to Florida was not nature constrained or affected, but simply its closeness and ease. Instead of practically effortless access to the wilds, instead of being immersed within them, I'd have to admire them from the periphery, temporarily. For the four or five years that Erika and I would live in Florida (longer than we'd lived anywhere continuously since childhood), we'd have to make pilgrimages, by car, to the last of the wild places, if there even were such places left, a supposition about which, being a western public lands snob, I had my considerable doubts. Sure, I'd be going to Gainesville, Florida, not exactly Hoboken, New Jersey, in terms of population density and concrete-to-grass ratio. There were crystalline springs rife with manatees, coral reefs rich with moray eels, and wetlands boasting giant alligators and roseate spoonbills. But still I knew I'd pine, like Abbey in the welfare office, for the desert, the call of the hermit thrush and canyon wren, the easy access to solitude, the simple days under the naked sun on the naked rock.

I knew that I, too, would fantasize about going back.

Abbey's life was not the sole cautionary note: my own relationship with both Erika and the Canyon had delivered innumerable instances of knotted joy and sorrow, happiness and regret. Take the moment I stood on a broken basalt cliff scouting potential lines through Lava Rapid. Lava may be the most storied rapid in the Grand Canyon. On the one-to-ten scale of rapid difficulty on the Colorado River, Lava, depending on river flows, ranges from an eight to a solid ten. In about a hundred yards the river drops thirty-seven vertical feet, crashing through a maelstrom of jutting rocks, towering waves, and cavernous pour-overs. I was going to run Lava in a nine-foot-long inflatable kayak. I'd never rowed one before this trip, but by the time we reached Lava I had safely run a number of the river's fearsome rapids. I'd been scared, heart-thumping-in-throat scared, but was able to employ the ol' "fuck it" flippancy so useful in getting me to jump off a bridge, swim an ocean wave, or scale a rock cliff. But the calculated carelessness wasn't coming so easily. The run was along river-right, and I could not stop staring at the mass of water surging against the black rock at the bottom of the run, the huge, toothy, scaly lava rock that Blake happily pointed out as "Cheese Grater Rock."

I couldn't stop thinking of Erika.

In ways, our love and the rapid were similar—there was intensity to the two that made me feel alive; within that intensity was a state of calm that completed me. Both involved a release into passion, with only grace and will to keep me afloat. But only one of the two cared about me as I cared about them. Only one returned my love, the one who before I left had made me look her in the eye and promise I'd be careful. "Promise me," she'd said.

She knew that a rapid like Lava represented much that I had shaped my life around. That my feet fell on proving ground after proving ground. I had constructed myself as an insouciant individual, free to throw myself into such lovely risks. Running Lava would require bravery, skill, and wild luck, and for many years being loyal to these challenges, to my own inner fire, was more important than anything in the world.

And yet looking at Lava, for probably the first time in my life, I realized that Erika had eclipsed all that. She'd made me realize that the satisfactions and pride that I derived from such feats were shallow compared to those I found in love. She'd made me realize that life was filled with choices; that whatever I choose to believe, I always had responsibilities, whether to the crew with whom I worked, the love entrusted in me by Erika and kin, the earth on which I subsisted, my unborn child or grandchild: always responsibilities. All too often I was simply choosing to ignore or shirk these responsibilities.

I turned from the rapid, tied my duckie to the back of a raft, boarded the raft, and floated Lava as a passenger.

It was incredibly hard for me to do. I was ashamed to watch Blake run Lava in his own inflatable kayak, alone. My biggest worry, while wavering on the shore, had been that I would always regret not running the rapid. At that point I lived my life so as to never have to look back on a life stratified with regret—regret not so much of mistakes made but of life not lived, of opportunities missed, chances squandered. And I do regret not running Lava that day. Reunited with Erika, I told her, perhaps a little accusingly, of my decision, and she looked me in the eye and thanked me, earnestly, deeply, truly. And that felt good. I felt vindicated; I felt that I had matured, even, in a way, become wiser.

But I still regret it.

It doesn't matter that in the constant reconciliation of the contradictory impulses of adult responsibility and insouciant youth, I've recognized and even occasionally appreciated my development as a person. The pangs of regret I felt were far sharper than such self-congratulatory back-patting. It didn't matter that Erika had eclipsed the wants and needs of my reckless youth: putting Lava aside for her, choosing her over the Canyon, filled me with as much sorrow as it did joy. Thinking about doing this on a much larger scale—moving to Florida—was more terrifying than any rapid.

And so, even though I did not mean it as a final answer, even though I suspected that it was not enough, that it was, ultimately, insufficient for a life, for our life, and that despite its truths it was not even really an answer, it was, finally, all I could find to say: I swept my hand across the Canyon as if to encompass the overcast chasm, the wind across the rock, the raven gurgling among the rain-darkened needles, and said: "This. This is what I want."

SUMMER

When the sun first crested or filled a notch in an eastern ridge, a perfectly straight shaft of light would slant across the sky, then immediately hinge downward into the Canyon. If we were lucky enough to be working on the western side of a ridge, or deep in Bright Angel or Garden Creek Canyon, we could have an hour or so in which to actually enjoy the diaphanous cast of light on the world. The incrementally shortening not-yet-lighted spaces would saturate with a wash of indirect light. Within that wash of light the world became luminous: the cactus spines would glow, the dried grass heads would glow, the redbud or cottonwood leaves would glow, and the iridescent filaments of spiderwebs that streamed from every bush would flicker, and sway, and glow. The gnat motes that hung above the creekbeds would flare like floating stars. As the sun breached that last, blessed rock barrier and finally lay across us, there would be—at least early in the season, and certainly come autumn and early winter, when the high desert air opened itself to the absolute zero of deep space—a few moments when the sun on the skin actually felt good. But as the days approached then slowly passed the summer solstice, these gentle moments became briefer and briefer, the flood of molten light no longer magical but scalding, suffocating, oppressive. Standing in the last of the shade, you could hold your hand inches from the encroaching light and feel its heat as tangibly as open flame. By mid-June on the South Kaibab Trail the sun broke over the distant ridge like the opening of a smelter door. I'd avert myself from it with clothing and hat and sunglasses and sunscreen as if it were some incandescent god, too terrible to behold.

~: :~

The sun slid across me. I sighed, stretched, put down my pick, walked over to my pack, grabbed my shirt, and pulled it over my head. The dirty cotton prickled my sweaty torso. I rummaged around for my sunscreen and slathered it across any and all exposed skin.

We'd been starting work at five in the morning to try and beat the heat. Waking at four was rough, but dawn came quick, and as we had a steep morning commute—1,500 feet in a few miles, from our Phantom Ranch bunkhouse to a stretch of trail below the slumped outcrop of Tapeats sandstone known as Trainwreck—it was good to hike in the cool of dawn. Even so, I'd be wet with sweat long before I grabbed a pick and shovel.

I looked downtrail at Blake, wrestling a liner rock. He was still shirtless, would remain so for much of the day. I noticed he wasn't wearing his heart-rate monitor.

"You're not wearing your monitor," I called out.

He looked up.

"My 'bro'? Fuck that thing. It's chafing my boobs."

"Chafage? Is that what happened to your chest hair? And whatever: you just don't want anybody to know that you don't work very hard."

"Pshhhh. I'm just acclimated."

I grinned, looked around for the NIOSH guy. The National Institute for Occupational Safety and Health, the federal government agency that researches and makes recommendations for preventing work injury, was conducting a study on occupational exposure to hot environments. As part of the study we'd been asked to strap heart-rate monitors across our chests. We'd also been asked to swallow a pill-sized thermometer that would beam out our core body temperatures. Blake had immediately dubbed them "government cyborg fetuses."

Blake's instinctual flair for the dramatic was matched by a wit born from a piercing eye and an intrinsic understanding of irony, pop culture, and human nature. He had a comic's masterly sense of timing, tossing off the instant, cutting quips that for most of us come hours too late. He had a knack for non sequiturs, for improvisation and imitations, for creating hysterical lyrics to silly songs or inventing ridiculous strings of words for everyday objects. I'd look up from my work to see him standing above me, one hand resting on a pionjar (pronounced "poon-jar"; Swedish for "pioneer") and the other holding out a bottle cloudy with citrus-flavored water. "Poon"—he'd say, looking down at the drill, then, switching his carefully neutral gaze to the water bottle—"Tang."

Blake was one of those people it was good to be around, a guy who could lift the people around him. But like all of us he was a gnarl of complexities and contradictions. For all his wit and wonderfulness, he'd lapse into grim moods and dour views wherein he felt persecuted, a pariah. For a while he took to claiming that he was "the guy they don't know what to do with." In a way this was true: the bosses moved him around from laborer to packer to mason. He claimed it was because he didn't "kiss enough ass," but

I always suspected it had more to do with self-fulfilling prophecy, the positive feedback loop within his persecution complexes. It was thus completely in character for him not only immediately to refuse to let the government impregnate him with a cyborg fetus, but also to declare ominously that the studies would be used to "shut down Trails."

Of course, swallowing a strange government radio device that we'd eventually "pass" exceeded most of the crew's notions of civic duty, not to mention a good time. Sara expressed squeamishness about having radio waves so close to her ovaries. Johnny— who, it turns out, had survived that first hike after all, though he'd only work a season before defecting over to a wildland fire crew—mentioned the scene in *The Matrix* when the robot-worm tracker crawled into Keanu Reeves's belly button. I mentioned the Tuskegee Airmen. Evin just glared at the guy. I felt a little bad for him, because in the end only Devin and Patrick volunteered for impregnation.

So for three days the NIOSH man sat at our work site monitoring signals and taking notes on our work. He'd certainly picked a good time and place for heat-work studies: premonsoon June in the Inner Canyon. At least 104 degrees in the shade. The sun nearly vertical in the noon sky. Its light, supposedly already eight minutes old, seeming only seconds removed from its thermonuclear womb. We were working on a section of trail that ran through a long and barren stretch of Hakatai Shale. The brilliant-orange, billion-year-old Hakatai—formed hundreds of millions of years before the first multicellular organisms evolved—seemed a thin membrane under which roiled a magma sea. With its dust hot in my mouth I'd stand upright and take long drinks of water, watching the shadows of refracted heat writhe around my shadow.

The heat would send the antelope ground squirrels into pro-
longed torpors known as aestivation. *Aestus* is Latin for summer.
An obsolete definition is "the taking of a summer holiday." That's
one way of putting it. Generally aestivation involves some sort
of burrowing into the ground. A slowed breath and heart rate.
Lungfish aestivate by burrowing into mud at the top of a dried
lake and secreting a coating of mucus that eventually dries into
a moisture-retaining cocoon. I may have been coated in a pasty
amalgamation of sweat, Hakatai dust, and titanium dioxide
sunscreen, but it didn't exactly retain moisture. During lunch I'd
wedge myself into the diminishing shade of an overhanging rock
and think how incredible it was that I'd once enjoyed the weight of
the sun on the skin, once relaxed in the kind of sunlight to which
my cats offered the whiteness of their bellies.

And Blake? He'd sit bare to the waist in the conflagration of
light, occasionally craning his neck to check the progression of his
shoulder tan. He strove, in his own inimitable words, for a "mocha
latte" tan. I'd tell him he'd be a wrinkled piece of leather by the
time he hit thirty, but he'd shrug it off, saying, "Well, I figure you're
either gonna be old and doughy or old and leathery, and I'd rather
the latter." We let him get away with these things because really,
what were we going to do, it was his body, and he was incredibly
stubborn. But also because he was hilarious. Mocha latte? Who
says that?

And he *was* acclimated. He grew up in the Canyon. His dad
was Trails foreman for fifteen years. Blake joked about having
been conceived at YACC camp, Trails' cloister of trailers in the
South Rim woods. He'd lived other lives in other places—East
Bay, Mount Rainier, Tucson—but those years of his life were not
unlike *rumspringa*, when Amish teenagers leave the community

for a few years to encounter the outside world. Most of the Amish kids find the outside world not to their liking and return to the fold, and Blake returned to the Canyon, likely never to leave. In a way it's too bad neither of us volunteered to host the internal thermometers: I have no doubt that at rest his core body temperature was higher than mine, the salt content of his sweat was lower, and his blood volume may have been greater.

"Acclimated" doesn't capture the whole of it. Like no other person on the crew, or other person I knew of enthralled by the Canyon, Blake formed himself to his Canyon. An impressive number of the crew—especially considering Trails' dearth of "permanent" positions—have made the Canyon their permanent home, have given their lives to the place. But none as thoroughly as Blake: he'd wholly crafted himself around the idea of his presence in the Canyon: doing backflips off cliffs into the river, rallying dune buggies along the forest roads, making love to lonely international girls at the concessionaire. At times I suspected that his passion for the sequestered world of the Canyon—not to mention a lifetime dealing with the stultifying bureaucracy of the federal government—narrowed or encaged his sense of the greater world. But what did the greater world matter?

What fascinated me about Blake's epistemological approach to the Canyon was how much it differed from my own. Very few people I know have spent as much time as he has within the Canyon. He hiked hundreds of miles every year working Trails, and later, when he became a river ranger, he was able to explore those sections of the Canyon to which the river provided easy access. But river work and trail work consistently revisited the same places. He didn't backpack, or climb, or pore over maps in order to explore new areas. He rarely, if ever, struck out on his own, or with a chosen crew. He was content with where he was, what he had, what came to him through the work, what came to him through his particular sense of belonging.

I was not so content.

❧ ❧

At times the gravity of vertical exposure seems to have a greater attraction than that attaching one to terra firma, and sure enough the siren pull of the vast expanses spread beneath Mount Huwethawali arced up and anchored in an expanding hollow between my stomach and sphincter. But I sat comfortably, knees hinged over the edge, feet dangling in open air, having no desire to succumb to the pull, and figuring that it'd require more than my 190 pounds for the deeply weathered summit sandstone to sunder and the rock collapse into the depths.

I'd dedicated my breaks that summer to solo day hikes and climbs off the South Rim. No major backpack trips into the Canyon, just planning the hike the night before on my map, maybe a look in the *Summits Select* guidebook, a morning drive to a trailhead or pull-off, then down off the rim, out to the base of the isolated mountain or temple or castle or butte or plateau, then up, a snack or lunch or howl at the top, a few minutes or hours of silent contemplation, a note and name scribbled in the summit log, then down and back up to the rim, four- to nine-hour days.

Mount Huwethawali was appealing because it was right off the South Bass Trail, there was a clear route up its heavily eroded southern flank, and of the Esplanade's enormous monadnocks it was really the only one that could be easily climbed. The Dome required a technical ascent up decomposing rock, and I considered Mount Sinyella, perhaps the most visually pleasing of all the peaks in the Canyon, a solid, uniform butte with nearly symmetrical alluvial shale skirts rising out of a flat, slickrock mesa, off-limits out of respect for the Havasupai's regard for it as the Center of the Universe.

So I set off one evening and arrived at the South Bass trailhead at sunset. I was the only person there. As individuals, we form our sense of ourselves largely by the way we are reflected by others or our surroundings, and alone in the desert I stretched into the emptiness and came circling back with nothing, or with the sparest of responses, and was thus left, in time, to accept that nothing and weave my sense of myself as a solitary soul more tightly. Yet the high-elevation desert, with the wind ever in the pines, throbs with loneliness, and though much of its beauty and power arises from this severity, the loneliness expands after a while, echoes within itself, reminding us that we are, incurably, social animals. Good company lessens the distance, makes more accessible the ineffable qualities of dimming light on bare rock. Besides, I rarely if ever laughed when I was alone. Sure, I wasn't climbing mountains for comic relief, but nor was I engaged in solemn druidic ritual: I liked to laugh out loud. But my two Canyon climbing partners were otherwise occupied: Kirk off climbing aid routes in Zion and Erika off climbing trees in British Columbia. So in silence I ate my beans and watched the sun slip behind a distant mesa. I unrolled my sleeping pad on the rimrock and slept under the stars. When I started hiking the next morning, I was glad to be alone.

Any attempt to describe the appeal of venturing deep into the Canyon—bushwhacking through hellish thickets of manzanita and locust, scrambling up loose scree slopes, carefully picking your way up rotten rock, stressing about diminishing water supplies—

to attain a distant summit is almost inevitably inadequate. When asked why they climbed, the English climber George Mallory famously replied, "Because it's there"; the American climber Warren Harding replied, "Because we are insane," and my own reasons swung wildly between these two responses. I like what the climber David Roberts wrote in *The Mountain of My Fear*: "At best [I] can hint at what the mountain meant to me; yet if I understood that at all well I would explain it better.... The mountain was beautiful; perhaps that is all that need be said. That, and that it would be very hard to climb."

It's not entirely reductive to say that I climbed for the view. For the access to beauty and solitude. Nor can I avoid the old clichés of escape, exercise, fresh air. But beneath the clichés is this: hiking and climbing were the best ways I knew of engaging the sublime. I'll never truly understand the Canyon, nor will I ever truly understand what it meant to me, but by immersing myself in it in as physical a manner as I could, I could attain a peace with the tumult of awe, mystery, knowledge, and ultimate ignorance it inspired. "No ideas but in things," William Carlos Williams proclaimed, and I understand that, then, there; that sublimity, chaos, time, love, loyalty, passion, and fear are aspects of the Canyon I'd only and ever understand if they burned through me as physically lived experiences: as sweat stinging the eyes, lungs gulping the air, a stone tossed as far as I could into the void, a hand extended to offer help. It wasn't enough to drive to the rim, dangle my legs off the edge, and think long thoughts about my interrelations to the world. Nor was it enough to engage the Canyon through the work, even with all the physical ways of knowing and being that opened for me. I needed the palpatory immediacy of hiking and climbing.

All summer we'd work on one of the same Corridor trails—the

South Kaibab, the North Kaibab, and the Bright Angel—often on no more than two or three different sections of a single trail. Hiking those trails I knew where each foot should fall with every step. I'd focus my footfalls on the resistance of familiar solid objects—check steps, rocks, or roots embedded in the trail—rather than the slight but still significant give of the softer trail tread. Over and over, day after day, for tours on end we'd hike down to our work sites then back up, the months of retreading the same miles like the numbingly repetitive chanting of a Buddhist dharani, the liturgical repetition designed to dissolve the sense of self and move one to Enlightenment.

And as familiar as I became with the trail, as much as I developed peripatetic relationships with its rocks and roots, as much as I knew which trees or boulders provided the best shade or which switchback corner offered the best view, something new always came into focus, and not just a blooming flower or a curious Steller's jay, but, depending on the angle of light or my mood or attention, freshly revealed aspects within stationary objects: a juniper having encased a rock within its stretching trunk; a section of cliff with a weathering scar shaped like the Eye of Horus; a set of reptile tracks adorning an everyday piece of liner rock.

Though I may not have consciously acknowledged it at the time, this recognition of an endless new in the old familiar was an argument *for* sedentism and the rooted life. The opening lines of William Debuys's book *The Walk*, in which he reflects on the same walk he took on his property every day for twenty-seven years, reads: "A species of hope resides in the possibility of seeing one thing, one phenomenon or essence, so cleanly and fully that the light of its understanding illuminates the rest of life." That's how I felt walking the Corridor trails: that my movements were not simply monotonous repetitions of everyday experiences, but an engraining, an invariable and cumulative deepening of my relationship with the desert.

At least that's what I told myself, consigned to working a single trail for an entire summer. And on a greater scale, the Canyon itself was a confinement. The Canyon is, on average, only ten miles wide, and though I could never come close to exhausting that inexhaustible terrain—one would need an obsession spanning multiple lifetimes to do so—over the years I felt that my overlapping hikes were like sutures slowly cinching the place tighter and tighter. As much as I enjoyed coming to know a place; as much as repeating my path was never a true repetition, and as much as I enjoyed exploiting a new break in the Redwall or walking out along a knife-thin ridge to a new viewpoint, each of these acts shrank the Canyon world. I hated the shrinking of the world. So I found myself always in front of my map, seeking out the peaks I hadn't yet summited, the trails and routes and areas I hadn't yet explored.

Like most Canyon neophytes, I'd started hiking in the Canyon along the Corridor trails. But since I hiked them every day for work, and since they were crowded, and since they were redundant in terms of the Canyon regions to which they provided access, I started hiking the "Backcountry Trails"—the Boucher, the Tanner, the Nankoweap—trails far less traveled than the Corridor trails, but still clearly delineated on maps, occasionally maintained, and still hosting thousands of people a year. When I had hiked most of those, I began looking for routes.

A route was essentially any single way of entering, exiting, or moving within large contiguous areas of the Canyon. A route could be anything from an unmaintained but easy path paralleling the river, to a series of Class 4 scrambles up cliffs, to a technical ascent of a remote summit such as Excalibur (5.10+). Some routes were well traveled and marked by cairns and the tread of the sizable community of Canyon hikers; others would peter out into sheep trails or necessitate hideous bushwhacking through brush-choked slopes. Some required vertiginous rappels down cliffs and slot canyon pour-offs, wading through waist-high creeks, or hauling a small inflatable packraft so as to repeatedly cross the river. Many routes were so infrequently traveled or referred to they weren't actually named, but simply referred to as "the route up Fossil Canyon" or "up Outlet." Some routes were once trails strong enough to support stock—like the Old Tanner Trail or the Harry McDonald Route—but a century of vegetation growth and erosion had reduced them to essentially long, painful, and often dangerous ways in or out of the Canyon. There are hundreds of such routes, and thousands of variations one can take depending on where one wants to go, how much time one has, and how well versed one is in Canyon hiking.

These routes did not afford the backcountry ramblings one can enjoy in a place like the High Sierra, where one can see for miles upon miles across the open granite and choose dozens of ways to traverse that distance. The Canyon's enclosed topography offers a bewildering array of ridges and slots, cliffs and terraces. Water was scarce. The sheer cliffs and paucity of water sources funneled hikers toward certain routes—there may be only one break in the massive Redwall cliffs for a span of ten arduous miles. Reaching that break, descending it, and then winding your slow, thorny way through the immense, tortuous, and torturous rock labyrinth to the next water source: that is a route.

There'll be times when the route edges along a two-foot-wide bedrock ledge, a vertical cliff to the right and a precipice to the left, with no other way down, and since you've drunk much of your water there's no retreat, you have to cross the ledge to scramble to the creek below, but no problem, it's a mere twenty-foot-long ledge, scary, sure, but all you have to do is go slow, stand upright, and with every step kick away the rock marbles underfoot to ensure solid footing—totally doable, except for the unfortunate fact that a "Spanish Bayonet" yucca is sprouting out of the middle of the ledge, its three-foot spears occupying the entirety of the space you were hoping to cross. More commonly, when traversing such a ledge, would be a bulge in the cliff wall, so that you'd have to inch along the ledge sideways, hugging the bulge, your backpack out over the abyss, pulling you downward.

Or the way the normally broad Tonto Platform thins to a narrow shelf between the Palisades of the Desert and the Inner Gorge, and, lacking space, has gotten so piled with the accumulated alluvium of the upper cliffs that, even by Grand Canyon standards, it's achieved maximum rubble. Traversing across it, you'll come to the places where the rim lands' drainages spew floods into almost four thousand feet of freefall, and the impact of these cascades shreds the loose conglomerate into dramatic gullies. You must delicately maneuver down the rubble, with car-sized boulders haphazardly held in place by sedimental glue. Picking your way out of that drainage, you top the bank to realize there's a drainage immediately on the other side, the bank you're perched on just a thin fin standing by force of habit alone.

There's the seemingly simple act of navigating the scalloped bays that dominate the western region of the Canyon. From one point of a bay's crescent to another may be three miles to a raven, but we lumbering primates need twelve miles to skirt the deeply incised side canyons that have eaten through the slickrock, some visible only meters from their lip, some stretching only fifty feet across but requiring forty minutes to detour. Once you finally arc around the long rock point that forms the crescent cusp, you immediately enter a new bay, to repeat the process, bay after bay after bay.

There'll be times when there is no trail, no route. The occasional footprint, the occasional cairn, the rare moments when the multiple bighorn sheep paths hatching the red earth converge into one, but then that too dissipates into brush, and again you'll trudge across the sand, breaking through the cryptobiotic crust, weaving through the bushes and cactus. There'll be times you're lost. Dehydrated. Irritable. Wretched. Your vision marred by flashing bars and psychedelic motes. When you're happy to see animal sign, especially sheep shit—where desert bighorn can go, you can go. When you brim with happiness at the sight of a rock stacked on another rock, that little kindness of a stranger letting you know you are on the right path. That you won't die.

Not that I expected disorientation or death while climbing Huwethawali. For one, it's impossible to miss, rising like a stone plug out of the dead center of Darwin Plateau. And since it's so close to the rim, I was able to scout the route the night before with binoculars. The route up was evident, easy: the whole southern portion of the monadnock blown out, its cliffs slumped and ramplike. Still, I'd left Abel—my trailer mate that summer—a note detailing where I was going and when I should return. I'd brought a flashlight, sufficient water, extra food, a warm layer, and a watch to time my "turn back" window, so that I wouldn't be caught out in the dark.

Within two hours of relatively painless hiking and scrambling

I was sitting on the summit, admiring the view. To the north, across the hidden river, were the towering flanks of the Powell Plateau, topped with dark forest; to the west the highly dissected sandstone terraces of "Conquistador Aisle"; to the southwest the snarled geography of the Aztec Amphitheater; and to the far west the dominant horizon of Great Thumb Mesa.

I wasn't alone. The flies had found me, as eager for companionship as always. A pair of ravens coasted past at eye level. A flock of swallows whirled and shrieked. The wind ripped out of the west. My map trembled under the five stones with which I'd weighed it down. Earlier in the season, on the summit of Coronado Butte, a wind gust had punched the map from my hands and lofted it over the abyss. It hovered for a few seconds as perfectly as a kettling buzzard, its edges flapping calmly, five feet out of reach and sixty feet off the ground, then dipped like a falling leaf back into my outstretched palm.

The Canyon winds are a wild and fickle bunch, but subject to certain habits. They'll slosh from rim to river like water in a bathtub: at dawn the katabatic winds surge down the side canyons, knifing into the warm night air pooled in the Inner Gorge, plunging the temperature on the beaches five, ten degrees in minutes. At sunset the wind flips like a switch and rushes frantically up the side canyons, beating the willows, setting the cottonwoods ashimmer. In the heat of the day the thermals shaft out of the depths of the Canyon—I read once that airplanes flying twenty thousand feet above the summer Canyon will rise an additional few hundred feet, just like that, elevated by the great pillows of warm air welling out of the depths.

Watching my map twitch, I wondered if the winds were stronger west of the Grand Scenic Divide; if, less impeded by the eastern

Canyon's long fins of rock, they were free to rip and roam across the broad, scoured shelves of slickrock eponymously known as the Esplanade. The amount of material transported by the winds was almost as impressive as the amount conveyed by the river. I've seen dust storms on the rim lands tower hundreds of feet into the air, blotting the blue sky, scudding for miles across the range, dust devils fractaling off their edges. I've watched individual grains whisk off of the relict, riverside sand dunes into the river. The winds had whittled the juniper on Huwethawali's summit into warped and gnarled shapes: their trunks particularly whorled, the few cords of live cambium braided with dead wood. Their exposed roots clawed across the bare rock, anchoring into available cracks like snakes panicking for holes.

Both the bonsaied junipers and the Canyon's innumerable peaks struck me as resilient individuals, their unique characteristics borne of the vagaries of wind, water, time, and shifting earth. Like tree and rock, I had been shaped by the desert. As I worked to craft it, so too it crafted me. Every spring I returned to the Canyon after a winter away and, mirroring the seasons, my body shifted. My muscles fatigued in spring, tightened in summer, and diminished back toward bone in winter. My neck, forearms, even the webbing between my fingers shifted from white to beige to brown then back to white. My hands and heels blistered, callused, and cracked; my knee skin burned and roughened; my hands grew to the sledge, my feet to the tread, my lungs to the heights. A winter's worth of nostril detritus would clot up and bleed out that first week, but my nosebleeds would stop, my eyes would stop rasping in their sockets, and I'd need to drink less and less water. I'd maneuver rocks onto my tabled thigh before straightening up to carry them; where the rocks had rested, bruises would blossom and fade like mariposa lilies. The fronts of my thighs would be chapped hairless by hiking in denim pants.

Not all the physical effects were so ephemeral. The meniscus in my left knee has worn thin from hauling heavy packs or pionjars or juniper logs. My back has weakened with the bending and lifting and compression. The skin beside my eyes prematurely crinkles into wings. So too the desert had begun to shape my actions, my habits, my modes of thought, so that perhaps it wasn't only the practicality of weight and survival that had me pick and choose what I put in my pack that morning, but a reflection of the desert's own frugality, what the Saharan explorer Wilfred Thesiger described as "everything not a necessity an encumbrance."

This, too, was part of the appeal about hiking: it laid bare the hubris at the heart of so many of our interactions with the world. Picking my way back down Huwethawali, I couldn't help but feel cast in the traditional Western dualism of a hard individual in a hard land: a lone human pausing in his journey to look toward the distant frontier and setting sun. I could almost hear the Ennio Morricone theme music. Yet the intimacies of interdependence were everywhere around me: the wind ripping my desiccated flesh and whirling it into the world, the sun chemically affecting my skin, my skin refracting the light back into sky and onto earth. The water in the barrel cactus was the water within me. My individual feet fell on sand and decomposed rock stitched together by a rich skein of fungus, lichen, and cyanobacteria. I'm an amalgamation of common molecules arranged in a certain way, and, as far as the desert is concerned, no different than a deer, sheep, fish, or fly. If I were to have fallen into a crack and died, never to be found, my body would have decayed so excruciatingly slowly it would have seemed as though the earth was reluctant to accept me. But I'd have dried into dust all the same.

~: :~

Climbing, hiking, and working weren't the only ways of knowing the Canyon. I'd get off work and shuck my clothes in a cloud of dust and enter the shower and the red earth would stream off my arms and legs and swirl around my feet, the melting carapace of sunscreen and sweat and Supai dirt revealing skin, human skin. I'd step out, a new man, and as a new man I'd crack a cold beer and stare at my five-foot-by-three-foot USGS topographical map of the Grand Canyon.

Erika had given me the map my first season in the Canyon. She knew I was becoming attached to the place; that map helped turn attachment into obsession. In time it'd grace the walls of all my Canyon dwellings. That map helped me know the Canyon almost as much as exploring its depths did. Obviously, a cartographical, two-dimensional representation of the Canyon's intricate three-dimensional topography couldn't capture the endless variegations of rock or the contorted realities of physically traveling within the living earth. Eighty-foot contour intervals couldn't truly impart the precipitousness, or magnitude, of those cliffs. That said, though, within the Canyon the endless corrugation of the long, thin ridges that run perpendicular to the river often limit visibility, and the only ways I knew of unfolding that tightness into knowledge was through summit views and maps.

And this map captured, better than any other map I've ever seen, the absolute erosional abandon that conformed the Grand Canyon: its rumpled, ragged-edged rock, the crenulated plateaus and scalloped bays, the chaos of drainages and ridges, the canyons within canyons within canyons. Here, in exacting cartographic detail, was Joseph Wood Krutch's "spectacle too strange to be real... an unbelievable fact." Here was Powell's "wilderness of rocks," Dutton's "sublimest thing on earth," Ellen Meloy's "seemingly irrational geography of space and rock." Here was the stark reality that "Grand Canyon" is a misnomer, or simply an insufficient term, that this canyon, however grand, contains multitudes: rivers, creeks, springs, caves, arches, bridges, peaks, valleys, mountains, capes, plateaus, buttes, mesas, pyramids, castles, towers, temples, shrines, ridges, points, walls, basins, flats, and gorges.

The map helped me grasp the Canyon spatially, objectively. It also revealed something else: stare at it long enough and out of the convoluted madness emerged certain patterns. The fundamental pattern is the bonding between two hydrogen and an oxygen atom, and the resultant molecules' need for rest; a secondary and more personally intriguing pattern is the slashed geometries of faults: how water had exploited the weakened rock so that drainages bared the fault, brought it to the surface. The Canyon's rock is shattered by surface faults—gravity faults, growth faults, reverse faults, thrust faults, anticlines, monoclines; faults that strain, shear, slip, heave, throw; faults that on the map looked like the crazed glass of a broken windshield. The Canyon's faults were formed long before water exposed them to the open sky. Many of the major faults originated in the Precambrian, meaning that the almost vertical mile of rock that makes up the Grand Canyon rests on broken and shaky foundations. Most of the other faults resulted from, or were "reactivated" by, the strain of orogenic uplift—when the Colorado Plateau heaved up out of the surrounding deserts during a massive uplift of the continent some 70 million years ago.

Late at night or in the early morning, back from the bar or a friend's house, slightly or considerably drunk in front of that map, with a fingernail ground down by rock and blackened with grit, I'd trace the faults: Sinyella Fault, Big Springs Fault, Butte Fault, Crazy Jug Fault, Fence Fault, Hance Fault, Mohawk Fault, Hurricane Fault, Bright Angel Fault, Cremation Fault, Hermit Fault. Or the monoclines, where the earth flexed but didn't break as fault: the Grandview, the Crazy Jug, the Monument, or the mighty East Kaibab Monocline, which within some thirty miles upwarps the Kaibab limestone from a height of 3,100 feet at Lees Ferry to 8,800 feet at Point Imperial.

One of the reasons I searched out the surface faults is that these rifts enabled the Canyon's trails and routes. The Canyon's cliff bands afford few opportunities to descend into the Inner Canyon; generally one can pass through the layered rock only where these cliffs are broken by a fault or covered by an apron of erosional debris. For hundreds of thousands of years these cliff breaks were used by cougars, mule deer, Shasta ground sloth, Harrington mountain goat, and dire wolf. At least fifteen thousand years ago Native Americans began using these same routes to pass through the Canyon and, within the last seven hundred years, seasonally migrate between their dwellings on river and rim. These animal and Native American routes didn't become what most now consider a "trail" until the arrival of Anglo miners in the 1850s. As ease of access was imperative for mineral extraction, the miners reinforced some of the aged routes with structures—riprap, walls, water bars—that would support ore-laden pack mules. In time, the miners realized they could earn far more money for far less toil by leading mule strings of tourists down their narrow trails. The major trails of the time—the Grandview, the Bright Angel, the North Kaibab—were thus bolstered for tourists' ease of access, and more closely resembled today's Corridor trails: four feet wide, groomed, and supported by innumerable structures.

Not that my map contained such information. But it did contextualize the place. It aided historical abstractions. For despite our frequent use of pionjar and chainsaw, and our infrequent use of skid steer, mechanized wheelbarrow, and helicopter, our work on those Corridor trails was a continuation of the miner-cum-developers' work: we built trail to allow tourists easier entry into the cracked earth. But on a deeper level we were still enacting the deer's choice of one route across a boulder field as opposed to another, or the ancient Native American nudging a rock off the path to his field. And on an even deeper level we were simply following the strains of our restless earth, following the strains of our restless hearts.

❧ ❧

We talked about girls. We talked about girls and we talked about Brighty the Burro's untimely demise at the hands of hungry miners, about the man who attempted to float the Colorado River in a giant plastic gerbil ball. We talked about different styles of bushwhacking, Henry Butchart, the Great Mule Escape, our daily bowel movements, John Wesley Powell, breasts, beards, beer, bourbon, the official National Park Service expedition to get to the bottom of the Legend of the Canyon's Tiny Horses, *South Park* episodes, mules versus donkeys versus horses, the Anasazi, plate tectonics, whether the Havasupai made fun of the Hualapai for eating chuckwallas or vice versa, ringtail cats, how many people were going to perish in the Canyon that year, mixed martial arts, condors as descended from reptiles, whether all life, even gonorrhea and chlamydia, has a soul, why the overwhelming majority of backpackers are white, ravens, why one should or should not try to smoke prickle poppy seeds, the Bat Cave guano mine, aging, shaving, balding, whether or not to eradicate the bison roaming the North Rim, the generally well-known secret campaign to eradicate the tame ground squirrel population dominating Bright Angel campground, the rez, preferable ways to die, the 1956 midair jetliner collision over the Canyon that killed 128 people, Redwall breaks, the reintroduction of the Mexican wolf, accents, ascents, the Kaibab deer irruption and the subsequent Great Kaibab Deer Dive, how much tougher people used to be, the Pleistocene over-kill, where the Grand Canyon actually begins, our favorite rock layers, scars, knives, marriage, kachinas, our fathers, our mothers, the "Lost World" expedition to Shiva Temple, movies about re-venge, tamarisk beetles, fetishes, what happened to the apostrophe in Lees Ferry, having children, childhood, river rapids, the wars in Iraq and Afghanistan, the old-timers—including Zane Grey—who lassoed cougars on the North Rim.

But mostly we told stories. At times our friendships seemed constructed of nothing but stories, our individual identities, even, inextricably attached to the often-embellished memories that bolstered our opinions of ourselves as proud, passionate, rugged, boisterous, obsessive, carefree, jealous, reckless. The Canyon, to paraphrase Clifford Geertz, was a story we told ourselves about ourselves.

There were the stories of the times we were called on to do something that had nothing to do with trail work but everything to do with the nature of those who worked Trails: when the National Park Service mountain lion biologist died of the pneu-monic plague after performing a necropsy on a dead lion in his garage and, days later, with an eight-hundred-pound elk caught in one of his mountain lion snares, three Trail boys were called in to help tackle and free the beast. Or how, when the poor mules that hauled tourists in and out of the Canyon, day after day, year after year, keeled over and died, right in the middle of the trail, Trails would be called in to drag them over a cliff for the condors and coyotes or, if there was no convenient cliff, to bundle them up in a net for the helicopter to haul. Or when Dee was flown in with rigging gear to extricate a dory that the weight of the river was pinning against a rock in Dubendorff rapids, or Wayne called in to winch out cars that had gone over the rim, or Duke sent down backroads with the backhoe to dig graves for the Havasupai.

There were the endlessly rehashed stories of pranks and shenanigans. The time when, to his everlasting regret and the crew's everlasting delight, the mule packers convinced one poor fool on their crew that the best way to calm a spooked mule was by gently stroking its penis. When Wayne set an alarm clock for two in the morning and hid it under Devin's mattress in the Phantom Ranch bunkhouse. When Blake called me over to the river-camp toilet to catch a chuckwalla and it wasn't until I'd donned a glove and was leaning over it, about to grab it by the neck, that I realized it was made of plastic. (We named the lizard Salvador, and Blake mounted it as a figurehead to the front of his inflatable kayak; years later I'd see it in his backyard in various states of indecency with naked Barbie dolls.)

And there were the stories of John Hiller. John Hiller, an Iowa farm boy with white skin and blue eyes and red hair, was our Pecos Bill, our Paul Bunyan—everything he did was of mythological proportions. John Hiller could devour nine hundred Chips Ahoy cookies and fifteen bags of beef jerky in one sitting. John Hiller could put his head down and dig sixty-two miles of trailside ditch in a single day. When John Hiller was amused he laughed a *huhh-huhh-huhh* chuckle that never fully emerged but burbled within his throat until he found something really funny and it burst out at once and birds flew low for cover thinking, *Thunder.* When John Hiller got tired he got tired all at once: the impressive animating power would drain from his hulking frame and he'd collapse into coma, broken only by violent night fits: thrashings and cursings and punchings of pillow. John Hiller was gigantic—Devin boasted of a bar the crew had built at our bunkhouse at Phantom Ranch by claiming it could withstand Michael body-slamming John Hiller on it, but we all knew that nothing on earth could withstand such an act—that it would rival the bolide that punched the Chicxulub crater and wiped out the dinosaurs.

~: ~

LTB was grunting. He always grunted as he moved stone, just as he muttered as he shaped it, but this was ridiculous. I looked up, annoyed, then awed—he was heaving an oven-sized block of limestone end over end, grunting with every push.

"Jesus, LTB."

"What?"

"That thing's gotta weigh three hundred pounds."

"Yeah," he said happily, looking down at it.

LTB stood for Little Tommy Boyle, though he was little only in a squat, muscular, troglodytic sort of way. Even among all the characters that composed Grand Canyon National Park Service Trail Crew, LTB stood out. He wore a black bandanna headband to keep his stringy-long, sun-blond hair out of his eyes; he braided the rest behind him. He never wore a hat because he feared it would bald him; his hair receded all the same. His moustache overhung much of his upper lip; he trimmed it with his teeth. He wore short shorts that showcased his tanned, trunk-like thighs. He didn't wear underwear. He rarely wore work gloves, begrudgingly pulling them on when a higher-up neared. He preferred his bare hands, his stubby paws, good for grasping a single-jack sledgehammer or breaking apart a mastodon femur to best suck out the marrow. Marie, one of the few long-tenured women on the crew, and an impish raconteur, loved to tell her favorite LTB story: she was walking downtrail for work to find LTB, bare-chested and long hair hanging down, working on a retaining wall. She turned to the hikers behind her and said, in pseudo-ranger voice, "And here we have 'Uugah,' the Grand Canyon's last Neanderthal," and LTB, not catching what she said, rose out of his crouch and half-moaned, half-grunted, "Huhhhhhhhh?" and everybody cracked up laughing.

"Uugah's" block of limestone was to be a foundation stone in the reparation of an old dry-laid retaining wall that supported a section of trail that wound along the lip of the South Rim. Some twenty linear feet of the six-foot-tall wall had sloughed into the abyss of Garden Creek Canyon, taking with it most of the trail. Piñon and juniper roots dangled into the open space once occupied by stone; roots that had wormed between the wall stones and wedged them apart as they fattened with age. Soil spilled from the breach. The Civilian Conservation Corps (CCC) workers who'd built this wall sometime between 1933 and 1942 had used dirt instead of rock as backfill, and that soil, year after year, had been inundated by snowmelt, had frozen, then thawed, then frozen again—the pulsing, sodden earth working against the wall's weakest connections. The wall rose out of a steep declivity of decayed rock; we could see, where the wall still stood, how the slope had slipped from beneath the foundation, undermining the entire structure.

The CCC were generally phenomenal craftsman, but this particular wall was a barely coherent aggregation of unevenly stacked plates and chunks of weathered Kaibab limestone. LTB and I referred to it as a "cowboy wall," as though some cowpoke-turned-miner had thrown it together over a century earlier, as they had on many of the trails that plunged from rim to river. But we also knew that it didn't matter who had built the wall, or even how well it had been built—we'd both looked long enough across the Canyon's expanse of exposed rock to accept the essential futility of our attempts to staunch the greatest active example of erosion in the world.

As to rebuilding the wall, we'd replace the blown-out section of the old wall with a better, burlier wall. We'd replace the flakes and chunks with solid stone blocks. We'd dry-lay the stone so that the wall would weep water, so that it could shift and settle against the slumping earth. We'd use the rock from the not-yet-sundered sections of the old wall as backfill for the new. We'd make sure that each course had at least one "deadman"—a wall stone extending deep into the retained earth, riveting the wall to the slope. We'd position each stone's "batter," or the intrinsic cant of the rock, its unique center of gravity, so that the wall as a whole reclined at an even angle. In this we were unwittingly heeding the *Sakuteiki*, the antique Japanese gardening text, which refers to a stone's "requesting mood": its face, stature, and eventual alignment within the wall and garden. We'd make sure that each stone broke the joint in the two stones it rested on; that the stones of the new wall intertongued with those of the old wall like fingers fitted together in prayer. We'd bless the wall with blood and sweat and curses and laughter.

All of this was routine. Our method of procuring stone for this wall was not. Within the Canyon, where we usually worked, we'd look for loose rocks on slopes above the work site, or split boulders into usable blocks with a rock drill. We'd roll these rocks by hand; occasionally we'd convey them with a rigging system of block and cables, straps and manual winches. Once we had a stone we'd winch it down to those doing the masonry. Or we'd pull up the stone from the wall's previous incarnation to reuse in constructing the latest. Winching rock inch by inch upslope was a pain in the ass, but fitting, too, in that headstrong human way: not for nothing did Robinson Jeffers refer to stonemasons as "fore-defeated challengers of oblivion."

But the cowboy wall was perched on the rim itself, right above the South Rim Village. All we had to do to get stone was drive a stake-bed truck eight miles to the quarry, select good building stone, load it onto the truck with a front-end loader, drive back, roll the stone out of the truck into a pile by the side of the road, then use a rock dolly to roll them the few hundred mostly paved yards to our work site. It was a carbon-intensive process, and almost embarrassingly easy, but we got great stone, and great stone was not easy to come by even in the world-of-stone Canyon.

The majority of the Canyon's rock is choss—friable and rotten, wasted by up to 1.5 billion years of geomorphic activity: supercontinents formed, melded with others, ripped apart; thousands of millions of years' worth of strata laid down and scoured off even before the Canyon's current sedimentary layers were deposited; hundreds of millions of years of strata laid down and scoured off the top of the Canyon's current strata. This ancient, fault-fractured rock has been exposed to the elements for 5 million years; for the past, oh, seven thousand years this rock has suffered the same ele-

ments as it does now—intense heats and bitter colds, heavy winter
snowfalls and heavy summer rainstorms. The weathering of the
rock is as varied in name as in process. There is thermal expansion,
also known as thermal shock, onion-skin weathering, insulation
weathering, exfoliation, spalling. There is chemical weathering—
oxidation, hydrolysis, haloclasty, carbonation. There's slope slump
and creep. Frost wedging and heaving. Spring-sapping and scarp
retreat, which can lead to pressure release, which is also known as
unloading or sheeting. All of this weakening and weathering, this
priming, results in erosion: karst, rockfall, landslide, debris flow,
everything that made—is still making—the Canyon Grand.

The Canyon's rock may have been choss, but the spectacular diversity of that shitty rock was one of the things I loved most about
working Trails in the Canyon. I loved how the material of the stone
structures supporting the trail corresponded to the strata through
which the trail thread—Coconino riprap as I moved through the
Coconino, stacked shale retaining walls as I passed through the
Hermit shale. So when Will, the trail boss, decided to helicopter
some 240,000 pounds of quarried Kaibab limestone into the "Red
and Whites," a steep section of trail ascending a cliff of Redwall
limestone, I shook my head in disgust. I understood the reason-
ing—there wasn't enough available loose rock along the trail to
riprap an entire series of switchbacks—but I disliked the act of flying fifty pallets of rock into the Grand Canyon, not only because of
the astronomical cost, or because it vindicated what I had always
thought was one of the stupider tourist questions (*Where'd you
get the rock?*), but because, aesthetically, it seemed a shame to have
yellow Kaibab limestone inlaying a section of ruddy Redwall cliff.

Further, the helicopter delivery betrayed the artistic pride I
drew out of our work. Though on occasion I'd envy trail crews in

the Sierra Nevada, working that glorious, sectile granite, I agreed
with David James Duncan's paraphrasing of the Mahabharata:
that one sign of a true artist is a willingness to work patiently and
lovingly with even the most inferior materials. Duncan was referring to fly-fishing with a beater pole, but that's how I felt about
working the Canyon's stone, the limestone in particular.

LTB, no longer grunting, was standing next to his block of limestone and looking about, trying to figure out how he was going to
roll his stone around the pile of the old wall's rock that we'd crush
and use as backfill for our wall. I was standing at the foundation
level of the wall; I tossed up a flake, then scrambled after it to help
Tom maneuver his stone. He was staring vacantly at the pile of
white rock, some pieces speckled with lichen and black moss, some
still bearing the marks of a chisel.
    "Yeah, too bad we don't have the rockcrusher down here, huh?"
I asked.
    LTB looked at me, snorted, reached behind his head to adjust
his bandanna.
    "That thing is dumb."
    The rockcrusher was our bosses' latest investment: a 2,200-
pound, six-foot-wide, caboose-shaped rockcrushing machine. It
could digest bowling-ball-sized rocks and spit them out as chunks
and chips. The thing was a monster, so much so that it seemed as
though they'd bought it as an intentionally over-the-top response
to the barely veiled insults we'd receive on a daily basis: the tourists
who'd watched LTB and me roll rocks off the truck by hand and
shouted, "Surely there's a better way"; the ubiquitous "Isn't there a
machine for that?" questions; the snide or incredulous comments
implying that a young man in his prime spinning a sledge in circles

against a rock was not a beautiful act but a crude throwback, a primitive means of production yet to be replaced by progress.

Even if that was their intention in buying the beast, which it certainly wasn't, having more to do with end of the fiscal year budget depletion, LTB was right, it *was* dumb: too wide to drive down trails and too heavy to be flown into the Canyon by the Park Service's helicopters—we'd have to wait until a skycrane flew into the park for one reason or another. The rockcrusher was incredibly loud and incredibly dusty, necessitating a half-face respirator, which in turn necessitated a clean-shaven face, which few of us were in the habit of maintaining.

"Besides," Tommy said, squatting beside his boulder, "I like crushing rock."

I grinned. Of course he did.

I considered many of us craftsmen: we regarded crappy rock-work with the same disdain we reserved for an opponent who wished to play "slop" pool—where any ball hit haphazardly into any pocket counts, rather than the precise, intended shot of a devotee of the game. Trail work mirrored the desert it crafted; it stripped you bare as its own rocks: you couldn't hide shitty work any more than you could hide from the sun, the cold, the wind in the pines. You embraced the work as you dedicated yourself to the Canyon. And after a while the work defined you. This was not limited to my personal physical phenology of muscles waxing and waning and my skin darkening and paling with the seasons. Working trails became the lens through which I viewed the Canyon—came a time I couldn't see a rock without immediately evaluating its batter, couldn't see a reiterating juniper tree without counting how many check steps I could cut from its candelabra trunk, couldn't see a balanced boulder without calculating where the best spot would be to place the rock bar that would tip it over. At times, deep in the backcountry, I'd pass the snout of a rockslide and assume, in the instant before logic set in, that the randomly stacked stones were an old rubble wall.

This last wasn't entirely illogical—again, humanity's spoor, its profound permeations, were everywhere evident and inescapable. Always a mark—the chisel marks in the old wall's stones, the sun creases inscribed on my face. Canyon and crew scathed alike. And we liked that, liked our unique and exclusive relationship, how our work was one of the last ways we could know the Canyon by working the Canyon.

Of course, the reason LTB liked crushing rock had little to do with it being part and process of high craftsmanship or a life-defining activity: he liked it because shattering a rock into separate pieces with a single blow was immensely satisfying to cavemen like Little Tommy Boyle. It was immensely satisfying to us all, for the same reasons, but also because, like most of trail work, even the brute act of crushing rock contained a deliberate rhythm, an intentional calm, an edaphic joy, as Robert Frost put it, in the "grip on earth of outspread feet."

Take carving stone, hewing it to shape so that it fit against another rock like pressing together one's fisted knuckles. Chisel in my left hand, hammer in my right, I exploit the stone's existing seams; shave its ridges and flakes. I angle the chisel in various degrees; at certain angles the grit and fry of the spalling rock peppers my face. I pop off knobs and nubs with single blows or I scour a groove then rain hard, rhythmic blows along the line, the inert rock absorbing blow after blow until cleaving along the intended line.

After a while I'm lost in the work, lulled by the percussive beat.

The periphery of my consciousness flickers with the progress of the rock, but mostly I drift into suspension, islanding occasionally on a stray thought or memory, but then drifting again into the widening stillness. Everything funnels into the particular and specific—a point off here, a nub there, the smell of hammered rock and the ring of hammer in air—and at the same time expands into a greater engagement: I can identify the birds overhead by the way their shadows flit across the ground in front of me: the quick-dart raven, the bent-wing turkey vulture, the darkening of the sun condor. Their sounds too: wind ripping through condor's braced wing feathers; the dull *whup whup whup* of a raven's wingbeats.

The rockcrusher—gigantic, loud, industrial—offered no such moment. It violated such moments. It was a needy machine, and demoted us to the assembly-line auxiliaries we'd always set ourselves against. It reminded me of Thoreau's response to a woman who offered him a mat—"I declined it, preferring to wipe my feet on the sod before my door. It is best to avoid the beginnings of evil." This was stretching it: we were well versed in mechanical evils.

We didn't mind the helicopter long-lining logs to our work sites. We scoffed at the suggestion to use crosscut saws rather than chainsaws in clearing the North Rim's forest trails. As long as they were running smoothly, we adored our rock drills. Some of the same meditative characteristics that flowed from the heft of hammer and dig of chisel also arose out of rock drills and chainsaws. Take felling junipers and limbing them into logs we'd use as check steps: whether it was the earplugs that deadened the world or the risk posed by both saw and tree, I'd enter an almost hypnotic state. The sight of sawdust spitting out the chain, the cloying smell of the exposed pitch, the incrementally widening kerf as the whorled trunk began to hinge, the dusty whump of the anticlimactic crash, all seemed accentuated, distilled. These crystallized moments were not daydreamy epiphanies or catch-the-eye flashes of the unexpected in the otherwise mundane. They didn't arise out of the good work: they *were* the good work. The slivers of shaved metal flashing in the morning sun as I sharpened my chain and the needles shuddered loose from the tree's uppermost branches as it began to fall were aspects as intertwined in our work and life as were the ring, piston, and clip components of the saw.

So perhaps there could have been similar such attunements while manning the rockcrusher. But I doubted it. It was too much. Offensive, even—from no aspect of its use could we derive pride. And, in the end, this pride was all we had.

I know where lies or stands every wall, water bar, switchback corner, section of liner or riprap I've ever lain. If time has passed since I last hiked past, I'll stop and study the structures, how they've shifted and settled, how the Canyon has worn around them. I'll search out individual rocks, and if the anthropomorphic attributes I assigned to the rock as I worked it—the obstinate bastard, the easy beauty—have faded, the pride or shame of the fitting and placement remains.

We couldn't sell what we crafted. We owned only the hours we put into the construction. No, we didn't even own those—we sold them for a bimonthly paycheck. No one profited from the placed stones but in the profits of hiking and experience. These profits— benefits, really—are not to be dismissed. Still, I can't help but feel it's a stretch to think: *I helped people see and experience something greater than themselves, and maybe they will, in some way, come to know it or love it as I have come to know it and love it.*

No, our work was our own, and our most important, reward.

For though we let go of the hours and the product, we were not alienated as Karl Marx may have feared: the loss of our product did not mean a loss of our selves. The work could be monotonous and labor intensive, but Trails was no assembly line. Our work wasn't stretched out across thousands of miles, strangers, machines, and meetings. In working these rocks I was invested in every step of the process. I knew what needed to be done and I did it. I knew what type of rocks I needed, I searched for them, I found them, I rolled them into place, I shaped them to fit one another, I dug them a berth and I placed them, all by hand. When I used a machine—a rock drill or chainsaw—I used the machine, not vice versa. If it broke, I knew enough about it to fix it in the field. So rather than causing loss of the self, the work empowered.

LTB and I grappled his stone to the edge of the trail, then carefully flipped it into its berth. The earth shook as it thudded into place. Marx was right: to be human is to shape the world around us. To be happy as a human is to appreciate that process, to be invested in it as work and art, to embed bits of ourselves in the earth with every rock. Though we knew that in time even the best-built wall will slide into the Canyon, I'd come to see our work in mythological terms, the loss of the wall as sacrifice, an offering celebrating our place in a system, not of the capitalist market or of national parks or even of human endeavors, but one of even greater continuity: order and entropy.

~: ~

The door to the Ranchers' bunkhouse slammed open and out spilled music, laughter, and the flash of colored lights. I slipped in before it closed; it was like stepping into a sauna: hot, humid, and thick with sweat, skin, whiskey, dust, beer, and hormones. A sauna with a flashing disco ball and Prince blaring from the speakers.

There must have been twenty people crammed in the small living room, with more in the loft: Ranchers, Trails, mule packers, trail guides, European volunteers, random peeps, everybody shouting over the music and dancing to the music and carrying on in Independence Day revelry.

Phantom Ranchers are a special breed, not unlike Trails in their love for the Canyon, in the twisted paths that had brought them to live, some for decades, in the reclaimed desert oasis known as Phantom Ranch. Like Trails, they're a wild bunch of hikers and drinkers, though during my years in the Canyon the Ranchers were an artier, more musical, more flamboyant bunch. They reminded me of that famous Jack Kerouac line: "The only people for me are the mad ones, the ones who are mad to live, mad to talk, mad to be saved, desirous of everything at the same time, the ones who never yawn or say a commonplace thing, but burn, burn, burn like fabulous yellow roman candles exploding like spiders across the stars." The room was burning, all right. Barring Burning Man, I've never seen as many bared breasts or casually exposed cocks as I did in that Phantom Ranch bunkhouse. Both were in ample and evident supply that night. As was the bourbon—multiple bottles circled the room, their caps long since discarded.

Squeezing through the crowd, I bumped into Willow. She was wearing a Vegas linedancer-style turkey feather headdress and a small skirt and had coated her bare breasts and belly with some sort of shiny substance, onto which she'd flung indiscriminate handfuls of glitter. Her pupils were as round as new moons and her sense of personal space, always a bit more intimate than mine, had gone the way of her clothing. She was striking, and scary, and after a greasy hug I was eager to escape her gravity. I gravitated instead toward the stack of Tecate twelve-packs towering on the counter.

Aaron was using the same counter to prop himself upright. He'd been that year's Queen of the Parade—was still wearing a slinky cocktail dress—and, considering that he'd been plied with booze to the point of belligerence for the parade at noon, I was impressed he was still standing, nine hours later. I told him so.

"I'm the fucking queen," he slurred, "of 'murica." He released his high-pitched giggle.

"How was the parade?"

"It was...magical," he said, and pretended to break down crying like a teenage pageant winner. "Everything I ever could have wanted." He belched. I'd missed the parade, but it wasn't hard to envision Aaron, slathering drunk, wrapped in Ol' Glory, standing in a gussied-up wheelbarrow "float," waving, calling out to, and occasionally outright insulting the wide-eyed and cheering tourists. He'd have been surrounded by a carousing band of costumed or nearly naked Ranchers singing and playing music and generally prancing along like oreads—grotto nymphs—the whole scene some sort of carnal Gonzo bacchanalia.

A scene I was happy to join, however belatedly. I cracked a Tecate, took off my shirt, grabbed an oversized Huck Finn hat, was gifted a purple feather boa by a flamboyantly gay friend, took a shot of bourbon from a bottle, and commenced celebrating the birth of our nation.

At best I am a deeply ambivalent patriot.

I love America for producing Louis Armstrong, Walt Whitman, Hank Williams, Martin Luther King Jr., Mark Twain, and John Lee Hooker. I like how, in general, Americans are open, independent, affable, honest, direct. I appreciate our easy sense of humor. The thought has occurred to me that the freedom inherent in the life I have chosen to live—like, say, being able to live over three decades without having held a single continuous full-time job for more than a year, and yet having lived in, worked in, enjoyed, and explored some of the most beautiful places in the world without falling into crippling poverty or bottomless debt—may in large part owe to this freedom being inscribed or at least implied in our cultural DNA. And I do appreciate clean water, decent infrastructure, extended life expectancy, nonviolent elections for a constitutional government, passable public education, freedom from religion, and being able to openly air my abundant criticisms without being silenced through censure, prison, or summary execution. But these are the benefits of first-world economies and the civil rights and liberties of liberal democracies—none of which are exclusive to America. No, in my darkest days, I saw America as most exceptional in terms of incarceration rates, per capita energy use, health expenditures, obesity, anxiety disorders, and the obscene amounts of national treasure poured into ingenious ways of simultaneously killing people. I've had citizens with more traditional conceptions of patriotism point to Sudan, North Korea, China, or Russia as examples of places I could live if I didn't like America well enough, but they always failed to point to those objectively happy, healthy, and equitable Scandinavian counties, as if it was either God Bless America or the gulag.

But they're right—I wouldn't want to live anywhere else. Because, despite my abundant criticisms, I have a profound and abiding patriotism, one anchored in the diverse beauties of the American landscape: the forests and rivers and canyons and mountains and deserts. Of these places I am fiercely proud, fiercely protective. The problem with a patriotism so deeply embedded in a love of this unique, rich land is that for the most part we Americans have done and continue to do a fine job at irreparably altering and flat out destroying this unique, rich land. Clear-cuts, tree plantations, dams, GMO monocultures, mountaintop removal, suburban sprawl, dead zones, strip mines, landfills, Superfund sites; the ongoing extinction rate maybe ten thousand times the natural background rate: America is as much this impressive and ongoing litany of degradation and destruction as it is national parks and "purple mountains majesty."

Essentially, I'm patriotic about the last vestiges of the America that existed before European Americans arrived to ruin it.

But we try, here and there, and here and there I have my patriotic moments. One of them welled up a few days before the Phantom Ranch Independence Day bacchanal. Hiking through The Box, the section of narrow canyon upcreek of Phantom, I rounded a corner to find a condor sunning her wings in a shaft of light on a trailside liner rock. Spooked by my approach, she beat heavily upstream—condors are consummate gliders, and watching her work her enormous wings in the narrow confines of the canyon, the deep *thwocking* reverberating against the cliffs, was a rare treat. She didn't fly far, just swooped up to perch amid a thousand-foot-high cliff slab of polished black Vishnu Schist.

The rock generally referred to as Vishnu Schist is really a complex of rocks consisting of all the Canyon's Early Proterozoic crystalline "basement" rocks. Geologists refer to it as the "Vishnu Complex," or even the "Granite Gorge Metamorphic Suite." Regardless, it's the bottommost rock in the Inner Gorge of the Grand Canyon, formed some 1,700 million years ago, when forty thousand feet of ash, lava, mudstone, and siltstone fused together under tremendous heat and pressure. At various times during this metamorphism, the lithic brew of what would become the Vishnu Complex was shot through and through by sills and dikes of plutonic rock we now call Zoroaster Granite. Like the epigenetic deposits that now layer thousands of feet on its foundation, the Vishnu Complex's grains, platey minerals, and quartz and mica crystals are repetitively layered along a plane. Unlike these overlying sedimentary deposits, which are horizontally bedded, the schist's foliation is vertically inclined—the rock stretches toward the sky like interlocking tongues of black flame. Most of the ribbonlike intrusions of Zoroaster Granite parallel this verticality, though others swarm across the thousand-foot-tall cliffs as contorted and discordant veins, their pink and white a marked contrast to the onyx and silver cliffs. There was an apocalyptic glint to this earth marrow rock, like something out of Ragnarök, or akin to the book of Revelation's "sea of glass mingled with fire," and against this fantastical, phantasmal, primordial backdrop the condor had again spread the full glory of her nine-foot wings. She stood into the sun as though crucified. And that, too, was why I was so happy in that moment—it wasn't solely the ecstatic aesthetics, it was that, like some Gymnogyps Jesus, she and her kind had come back from the dead.

In 1987 all twenty-two of the world's last remaining wild California condors were captured and shipped off to breeding centers. Once widespread during the Pleistocene, the genus Gymnogyps had a rough time in the Holocene, contracting until only *Gymnogyps californianus*—California condors—remained. With the end of the ice ages, the relatively sudden lack of mastodon carcasses on which to feed, the introduction of bored, rifle-toting humans, the introduction of these humans' poisonous bullet fragments into otherwise tasty hunting waste, and with their habitat converted into power lines, farmland, and concrete, by 1987 the California condor teetered on the brink of extinction. Perhaps haunted by the memory of poor "Martha," the endling passenger pigeon who died in the Cincinnati Zoo in 1914, the US government captured the last condors and began breeding them in zoos. In 1991 and 1992 young condors were released in California, then again in 1996 in House Rock Valley above Marble Canyon. By June 2014 the California condor population reached 439, with 225 in the wild.

So a few days after my Gymnogyps Jesus experience, Independence Day, I felt good. Downright patriotic. Since the feeling was rare I remember it well, remember the little American flag I found on a picnic table and stuck in my backpack, remember driving out to the trailhead, arm out the window, listening to NPR, and hearing the host discuss with a Pentagon correspondent for the *Los Angeles Times* how American soldiers in Iraq had broken into a civilian family's house, gunned down the parents and their six-year-old daughter, then repeatedly raped the fourteen-year-old daughter before killing her as well.

I left the flag in the van.

Any other day of the year I'd have attempted to absolve my complicity in the war crimes through equal parts open invectives and private grumblings. I'd have spent some time loathing my role as an American. But by my own tradition the Fourth of July was the one damn day of the year I said to myself: I am American, and I will try to own this with as much joy as I have guilt. It was the one day I tried to forgive previous Americans for the spoiled heritage they'd left me—after all, I told myself, these past generations didn't really know what they were doing: it wasn't really until the time of Darwin that we even realized that species could become extinct; we were so ignorant about how the world worked that the first director of the US Geological Survey, in the 1890s, believed that a canyon such as the Grand was formed *before* a river like the Colorado by happenstance began to flow through it. Hell, we didn't even figure out plate tectonics until the 1960s. Independence Day was the one day I could try to forgive myself for the even worse heritage I am leaving my descendants. If I could not quite achieve that, then I could at least attempt to expiate some of the taint by celebrating my idea of America, my American values and ethos, not of unrelenting self-interest, competition, and violence, but of community, solidarity, and profound love of place.

The sweltering heart of the Canyon may have been the best place to celebrate America, and not because the national park was an atonement, but because it provided critical and revelatory context: if the age of our 4.5-billion-year-old earth was compressed into a twenty-four-hour clock, the planet born on midnight, the schist ensconcing us at Phantom Ranch would have come into existence at 2 p.m., the Kaibab limestone that formed the dark rim a mile above us would have chimed in at 10 p.m., and the existence of our human species would have blipped into being only two seconds before midnight. Juxtaposed against that incomprehensible time frame we had our great idea of a country on its 230-year birthday. We had our community of individuals only two, three, four decades old, celebrating not only the blessings of our spark-like, impossibly brief moments amid the ancient rock, but the very idea of belonging: to a tribe, a place, a country, a planet. As an act of resistance, it may ultimately have been shallow and futile, but it was something. It was good, in the moment.

So, having consumed Tecate at the rate of cubic feet per second, and flushed with dancing, hormones, and our individual interpretations of patriotism, a gang of us would stream outside to swim naked in the pool the Ranchers had built in the creek, or down to the boat beach to hurl ourselves in the river, or out to the middle of the Silver Bridge to grab the rails and spread our feet and in unison rock from side to side until the whole 530-foot span of the bridge swayed and rippled like rope. And later, absolutely soused, the planet already having spun the sun back up in the east, the Canyon walls swayed and rippled, and at first the surge of vomit felt good, a purging, and then, surge after surge, it did not feel so good, though this, too, was an atonement.

There are hangovers that you can sense the instant that the long, slow, and disassociated ascension toward consciousness begins. You do not yet actually feel the hangover, and can lie there, still mostly asleep, indeed, to all outwardly appearances in a coma, but you're awake just enough and, unfortunately enough, experienced enough to recognize the situation and dread the actual awakening. Because while asleep, even a sleep disturbed by the first shudders of consciousness, even if that consciousness is capable only of sensing the impending misery and horror, that misery and horror is still a disembodied pain hovering out there like a hawk high in the distant light of day. At this point you may even allow yourself a minor note of congratulation on having made it to your bed, a place you will need to remain for another four or twelve hours, until the shudders subside. But that morning, the fifth of July, I could not sleep another minute for it was midmorning and Blake was shaking me awake because we had to hike out of the bottom of the Grand Canyon.

The hangover descended like a hawk stooping to its prey.

My tongue lay like a dry streambed in the parched gorge of my mouth. My eyes could open, but they struggled to focus. My legs could support the weight of my body, but not strongly. My consciousness seemed to be operating from a distance of about four feet above and behind my body. The Ranchers make the best bacon I've ever eaten, and the cook that morning fixed me eggs to order, but neither the bacon nor the eggs nor the toast nor the pitcher of water nor the coffee nor a plunge in the creek helped staunch the horror. I lay on a rock by the edge of the creek, still drunk, still reeling with the remnants of the night, and looked dumbly at the cicada husks that clung to the willow branches above me. If my brain had been functioning with anything other than the mental capacity of a chuckwalla I might have made some connection with those eclosions, something between those cracked-open cocoons and my condition, something about new beginnings and redemption, something, anything, but my brain was not functioning, and all I could do was watch the husks rattle soundlessly in the down-creek wind.

It was 106 degrees when we began to hike. More accurately, when I began to put one foot in front of the other in hopes that through some miracle these familiar mechanics would convey me out of that great rent in the earth. As my heart began to pump harder, the bourbon, bedded down for the night in my bloodstream, roused up in irritation and anger, and I had to place both hands against the trailside cliff wall to keep from fainting. I was a switchback or two off the bridge, seven miles and 4,700 feet below that insuperable rim, and for the only time in my Canyon life I thought to myself, "I'm not going to make it." Even that first hike I knew I was going to make it because I had pride, something to prove, blisters be damned. That fifth of July I had nothing left to prove. My pride had been burned by the night, retched behind brittlebrush. Still I put one foot in front of the other. Monsoon thunderheads had massed early that morning, cutting the heat but spiking the humidity. I'd replaced my body's liquids with Tecate and Maker's Mark, and then I'd vomited most of those out, replacing them with coffee and a belated few liters of water, and the humidity wrung this out of me as one twists the last moisture from a damp rag.

I could not go on.

Thunder cracked from the clouds. The first spattering of drops vanished on the sunbaked boulders the way breath fades from glass. More thunder, more raindrops, and then the rain fell hard and steady. The aromatic resins of Mormon tea, blackbrush, and sage exhaled from the earth. I stood with my face turned to the sky. The rain began to sheet. The lightning stuttered and flared, staccato; the thunder slurred and pealed, legato. I could hear Blake yelling at me, something about taking shelter beneath the rock formation known as Trainwreck, and I watched him run uptrail, stopping occasionally to kick at clogged water bars—even this he did with theatrical gesture. But still I stood there, my face up, my nausea subsiding, my questionable patriotism something to reexamine next year.

The monsoons had come.

~: :~

Everything about the thunderheads signified rain—their reflective intensity indicating a particular denseness of water molecules; their flat black bellies pressing close to the ground; the updrafting thermals pushing the cloud tops ten, twenty, then thirty thousand feet above their bases.

So when a young family of Belgians hiking through our work site on the Grandview Trail asked us whether the thunder, increasing in frequency and volume, signified an imminent storm, I hesitated.

The clouds that day after day had trundled over our work site were clouds without rain. Or the rain would ease out of them as ten-mile bridal trains of virga, never to grace the parched earth. Or they'd break into rain a hundred miles to the west. The next day nothing. The following day a storm would blot out a plateau five miles to the east, and a side canyon would flash in flood. But nothing overhead but sterile thunder.

It was my first season. I knew nothing about the Southwest's monsoons. I didn't yet understand that the incremental shifting in the weight of the air on the skin signified the arrival of the monsoon season, or what that season entailed. The word "monsoon" is derived from the Arabic *mausim*, meaning "season," a term intimately connected to a shift in the wind. According to author and Arizona monsoon aficionado Craig Childs, the term was brought to Phoenix and Tucson by pilots who had become familiar with the phenomenon in Southeast Asia in the 1950s and '60s. In his exquisite book *The Secret Knowledge of Water,* Childs makes a compelling case that the Southwest monsoons should be called chubascos—an unrelenting stream of convective thunderheads, as opposed to a significant weather front. "Chubasco" is a good word, and may well be more regionally specific, but it doesn't provide quite the same onomatopoeic boom as "monsoon" does when we howled it out across the rain-wet rock as invocations for more. (For even more semantic quibbling, apparently saying "monsoons" as opposed to "monsoon season" or "monsoon thunderclouds" is a meteorological gaffe. But that's what we said, and I liked how a single word—like "Canyon"—could contain the distinctions and complexities of the entire phenomenon.)

Besides, I figured that monsoon is an appropriate enough appropriation for the Four Corners region, whose summer thunderstorms are formed by a seasonal reversal of the wind patterns: in winter the winds flow from the west and northwest, out of the desert; in the summer months the wind blows from the south and southwest, off the ocean. The summer sun radiates off the southwestern deserts like heat off a griddle. Rising hot air is a low front. Air tends to move from high fronts to low fronts, and so the cooler and moister air rising off the Gulf of California and the Gulf of Mexico is sucked inland. The meeting of the colder, moist oceanic air with the hot, arid desert air creates an unstable atmosphere in which spawn monstrous conglomerations of cumulonimbus thunderclouds. The clouds pass over the Sierra Madre Mountains of Mexico, unload on Tucson, load on Phoenix, then barely crest the Mogollon Rim, where the earth between Phoenix and Flagstaff rises 5,700 feet. Around eleven every morning the chubasco thunderclouds in their thousands breached the South Rim and streamed across the whole dome of sky, dwarfing the Canyon below them.

The juxtaposition between stone and cloud was entrancing, the rock solid and to all appearances static, its motion measured in millennia; the clouds mercurial and essentially ephemeral, their motion measured in seconds. I could cloud watch for hours: their continental shadows slipped across the slashed earth like liquid, or the shadows of shoals of fish. In contrast to the earthly grounding of trail work the clouds offered unfettered floatings; in contrast to the preceding sun-blanched weeks the shadows accentuated the Canyon's relief.

But really, at that early point in my Canyon life, the clouds signified little more than a welcome respite from what had been an
indomitable sun. After weeks of bleeding noses and cracking skin
and impossibly arid days, the desert air had grown heavy, sullen.
Yet this meant little to me beyond that it dredged an easier, stick-
ier, muskier sweat. And so, because I was ignorant and young and
cocky, I assured the Belgian family that the approaching storm
was all bark and no bite.

Hopefully they didn't understand the idiom.

An hour later, just as we'd begun our end-of-day hike up to the
rim, a supercell-sized cloud, laden with hundreds of millions of
pounds of water, buoyed only by the miracle of atmospheric ther-
modynamics, suddenly, well, lost its buoyancy.

I've been in storms. A tropical deluge in the upper reaches of
the Amazon that caused a flash flood that nearly killed my parents' only two sons; an unworldly purple and green thunderstorm
that smothered the empty stretches of the Kalahari Desert; a true
monsoon torrent that flooded the streets of Bangkok knee-deep
in foul urban runoff. I've been caught in storms in the Canyon
since that day: thunderstorm downpours that had me scurrying
for shelter under overhangs or hunched miserably under tamarisk,
shivering uncontrollably mere hours after sweating profusely. I've
been engulfed by snowstorms that boiled down side canyons like
avalanches. I've buried my face in my arm as a microburst wind-
storm snapped a half-dozen dead aspens across our work site.

But I've never been in a storm with the thermodynamic violence of that storm that day on the Grandview Trail. All the instability and pyrotechnic turbulence and gigaton nuclear bomb
energy of the mature thunderhead funneled through the conduits

of rain and air and exploded onto rock. Most of the Canyon is steeply sloped rock, and what little soil there is had been baked by the sterile heat of early summer into an impermeable crust. So the oceans of rain pouring out of the sky poured off of the earth. Sediment-tinged water slid in sheets down rock then ripped in hundreds of rills through slopes. The rills gathered into streams, the streams slopped into drainages, the drainages spewed off cliffs into bigger drainages farther below. Through the veil of rain I could see dozens of brown waterfalls sprouting from the Redwall and distant Tapeats cliffs. A surprising number of people believe the Canyon was gutted from the earth as a result of the cataclysmic draining of the waters of Noah's flood; for the first time I sympathized with such nonsense: all the waters of the world were pouring into the depths. I put my head down and began running up the trail.

The rain turned to hail. Some of the hail dwarfed marbles. The ice balls bounced off the rock as high as my knees then bounced frantically downslope. I slipped; the sloppy red earth plastered my hands, calves. A few hundred feet above me lightning stabbed the rim as one stabs a block of ice with an icepick. I could hear the sharp *vitttt* sound of the bolts; I could taste the sour copper of ozone. If some thunder tears slowly across the sky like a metal roof rent by wind, and some thunder booms into the bones, this thunder cracked quick, barely a distinction between lightning strike and thunderclap. In the Epic of Gilgamesh, the gods unleash on the world a flood that so frightens them that they "cowered like dogs lying by the outer wall. Ishtar shrieked like a woman in childbirth." I realized that archetypal fear: after a particularly close flash-boom I ducked, stopped running, and looked around wildly for cover. There was no cover. But for a moment I stood and took it all in.

In the seven more seasons I would spend in the Canyon, I would glean some understanding of how the gorge came into being. Dee and I worked an afternoon building a stone staircase up and over a ten-foot-high by twenty-foot-long rubble pile that blocked a popular trail in the Deer Creek narrows. Two summers later I returned to the spot and neither the stairs nor the mound remained, only the clean sandstone floor, and I doubled back, confused in the strange way that one's assured universe abruptly shifts, but nothing remained, only the creek, the cottonwoods, the corrugated walls—a flood had swept the terrace clean, removed every last trace of rock, rasping away even the scar of impact.

Still, it was rare to witness the actual erosive action, the geologic processes at play. Because of this, most people, trail crew included, tend to view the Canyon as though it were static, as though the processes that sculpted it have stilled. Because our culture tends to regard "nature" as though it were a Sierra Club calendar, it's understandable that we'd see the Canyon as fixed in time, just as it is fixed in those photographs—surely something that so defies our sense of time cannot be subject to change. We tend to see ourselves, or the cicadas, the willows, as the living, dynamic forces; geologic processes seem as stilled in place as raindrops illuminated by a lightning bolt. Every time I discovered a recent rockfall or slide—a microwave-sized rock sitting in the trail or a slide of small rocks and splintered yucca, none of which had been there hours or days previous—I stopped and quizzically stared, as though they had always been there and I had simply failed to notice, as though the frequent clatter of small rocks and the infrequent crack of boulders calving of cliffs were abnormal, freakish occurrences. I'd search the upper slopes and cliffs for the telltale signs: recently exposed roots, lighter patches of unweathered cliff, darker patches of moisture, fresh dirt still clinging to the cliffs.

In *Rough-Hewn Land: A Geologic Journey from California to the Rocky Mountains*, geologist Keith Heyer Meldahl writes of the "lens of human time" as a "perspective that gives the illusion of stability to a world that, over geologic time, is radically mobile." "In human time," he continues, "the continents and ocean basins appear fixed and permanent. To know that the Atlantic Ocean is forty-three feet wider today than when Columbus crossed it lifts, just a little, the veil of our illusion." This storm lifted that veil. It shattered the notion of a static Canyon. The solid earth was melting. The elements were in flux: water in air, water on earth, earth in water, earth in air, earth moving like water. Everything in motion, slipping, sliding, tumbling downward. The Canyon widening around me.

Later, after we'd all safely if soakingly piled in the van and started driving back to headquarters, we saw a debris flow. I'd always wished to see such a thing: part water but mostly soil and sticks and rocks and dead dogs and old tires or whatever else had been flushed into a drainage. The flow, crusted with hailstones and fattening off thousands of rivulets, moved rapidly through the roadside drainage ditch. Eventually we reached the snout of the beast, which pushed before it a bore of duff, pinecones, and sticks. The bore slowed the flood, and the glutted muck behind the bore would build until it was big enough to roll over and absorb the debris. The flow would then pulse faster down the drainage, devouring the earth, the bore again building before it. Eventually, after we had stopped ogling and had driven past, the debris flow swamped the road, fed into a larger drainage, overtopped a four-foot-high pedestrian bridge, and shot off the rim. When it hit Garden Creek, some 2,500 feet below, the flood obliterated a small jungle of vegetation that had grown at the base of the Redwall cliffs. It punched truck-sized boulders aside as though they were toys. The flood roared down Garden Creek, quickly overstuffing the main channel, and then went thrashing about the creek valley like a loose firehose, cutting eight-foot-deep channels twenty feet off the breached main.

If, as I ran uptrail, all the rocks tumbling past me was the active widening of the Canyon, this debris flow was the deepening. Not of the main stem, the Colorado River corridor: that process has been stilled by the Glen Canyon Dam. More on that later. This was the deepening of the venous network of side canyons. The Grand Canyon is not a clean rent, a neat incision in the rim lands, as is Marble Canyon, directly upstream. The massive plateaus that make up the Grand Canyon region—the Kaibab, the Kanab, the Uinkaret, the Coconino, the Shivwits—are lacerated, absolutely ravaged by side canyons. Some 530 tributary drainages merge into the main stem of the Colorado, and every one of the tributaries has its own dendritic network of headwaters. The gutting that these tributary canyons inflict on the rim lands, their incessant removal of incomprehensible quantities of earth, are what have made the Canyon distinct, unique, grand. And so they were doing that day: soon that thrashing flood reentered the course laid before it by previous floods: it compressed itself into the Tapeats Narrows, launched off a three-hundred-foot-tall schist cliff, and then went blasting down the last of Pipe Creek into the Colorado.

Floods like these are why Pipe Creek, like the majority of tributary creeks in the Canyon, enters the Colorado at river level. This
is a remarkable thing. Though Pipe has a small perennial water-
flow, most of the Canyon's tributary canyons do not. Some do not
flow for decades. And yet almost all of them have carved through
the rock as deeply as the main stem of the ever-flowing Colorado.
It's simple mathematics: one inch of rain over one square mile
amounts to 17.38 million gallons of water. Nankoweap Creek,
to take one of the Canyon's larger drainages, drains thirty-three
square miles. The rainstorm I experienced that day could have
dumped two inches of rain. This means 1,147 million gallons of
water could have been ripping through Nankoweap Creek with
that single storm.

Because our Pipe Creek flood had just plunged down the nearly
vertical mile from rim to river, it was flowing very quickly, easily ten miles an hour. For every mile per hour a flow increases,
its carrying capacity is increased to the sixth power, which is to
say, as Wallace Stegner did, "a stream moving two miles an hour
will carry particles sixty-four times as large as the same stream
moving one mile an hour, and that one moving ten miles an hour
will carry particles a million times as great." The flood that ripped
down Garden Creek, into Pipe Creek, and into the Colorado that
afternoon was large, flowing fast, and scouring a creekbed that,
owing to the fracturing and weathering the Bright Angel Fault
had inflicted on the bedrock walls of the Canyon, provided no
small amount of sediment. By the time the flow finally disgorged
into the Colorado it easily could have contained, by volume, 90
percent sediment.

Up and down the length of the Canyon the tributaries dis-
charged their sputum earth into the thickening, darkening river.

ᔇ ᔦ

My settling bag hit the eddy current and inflated like a parachute. I had to use both hands to heave it out of the river and stagger it onto the small beach. The water inside the bag was turbid with suspended sediment. The silt would need a couple of hours to drift to the bottom of the bag, but I'd take what the last hour of daylight gave me—at least the larger grains would subside, and my water filter would last that much longer.

Scrambling up a series of sandstone ledges, I found a nice spot to sit: a bedrock backrest with a view of the wavering line where the waters of the Little Colorado River joined those of the Colorado River. The Little Colorado is usually an opalescent turquoise blue, milk-bright with dissolved travertine and limestone. But the rains from a few days earlier had rusted the color to that of an old ceramic pot, a few shades browner than the gray-green Colorado. The smaller river eased into the Colorado's corridor, but the two rivers didn't immediately merge, they simply ran, side by side, down the course of the Canyon. They'd maintain their distinct flows for a good half-mile before rapids disrupted them into unity. The meeting of any waters is mesmerizing to watch; especially so here, with the Little Colorado's suspended silt mushrooming into the silt-strained Colorado.

Silt-strained. From where I sat at the confluence, I was only sixty-one miles downstream of Glen Canyon Dam. Behind Glen Canyon Dam, the silt-laden, rusted-red Colorado River becomes Lake Powell. At the exact-if-ever-fluctuating spot where river slacks into reservoir the river drops its sediment load, just as the particles of suspended earth were drifting to the bottom of my settling bag. This is a load that wind, water, and humanity has scraped from 108,000 square miles of mostly arid, barren, and highly erodible land. Estimates on the exact annual size of this load range from 45 million tons to nearly 200 million tons, but even the lowest of these estimates is an enormous amount of sediment being deposited into the head of the impounded river. Some 180 miles later, when the dam releases the river from the bottom of the three-hundred-foot deep reservoir, a different river emerges: a green, bitterly cold, enslaved river, its soul having settled down with the silty coagulum burying the drowned contours of Glen Canyon.

The Glen Canyon Dam, completed in 1963, has wreaked havoc on downstream ecology. The seasonal flux of spring flood and winter ebb was replaced by a mechanical, anthropogenic rhythm: the dam now doles out the river in accordance with major metropolitan area's electrical needs. Before the dam, the rise and ebb of floods would deposit and rearrange the river's sediment into ecologically important fluvial formations: sandbars, islands, beaches, backwaters. With the replenishing floods stifled by the dam and the sediment dropped at the top of the reservoir, the beaches and eddy sandbars are slipping away, grain by grain. No longer scoured by floods, the remaining beaches are increasingly impenetrable with tamarisk, Russian olive, and willow. No longer swept aside or rearranged by floods, the debris fans that form at the mouths of tributary canyons constrict the river, forming narrower, bonier rapids. Before the dam, the river could reach a high of eighty-five degrees Fahrenheit; the river is a now a consistently frigid forty-seven degrees—for this alone I hated the dam, how it spoiled one of life's greater pleasures: swimming in a summer-warmed river.

The dam's effects are geological as well as ecological. Before the dam, the melting of the Rocky Mountains' snowpacks sent spring floods raging through the Canyon. The highest recorded flood (in 1884) peaked at 300,000 cubic feet per second, or cfs (the dammed river now fluctuates between 7,000 to 30,000 cfs). And yet even that deluge is dwarfed by floods that ripped through the Canyon within the last 2 million years: the cyclic melting of the Quaternary Ice Ages produced flood after flood—some as large as 1 million cfs. These floods significantly contributed to the downcut topography of the Colorado Plateau; the geologist Wayne Ranney estimates that as much as half of the Grand Canyon's current depth—so, some 2,500 feet—occurred within this time. After all, the Colorado River did not carve the Grand Canyon by the steady rasp of sediment-laden waters abrading bedrock. A thick—in some cases seventy-five-foot-thick—layer of silt, mud, and sediment protects the bedrock from the river's scour. Only when the river swelled in floods big enough to sweep away the sediment, and the giant boulders suspended within the flood hammered the bared bedrock into clasts the flood then whisked away, only then did the Canyon deepen.

No more. The once diluvial Colorado River system is now constrained by more than a hundred dams between headwaters and delta. The once volatile river has been reduced, as the river guide and author Kevin Fedarko has written, to "little more than a giant plumbing system" consigned to slake the thirst of some 30 million people. The river that carved the Grand Canyon in a scant 6 million years has been fettered; the canyon this river carved no longer deepens.

I had crossed the Little Colorado River and walked upstream of the confluence to pump my drinking water, and not just because the river was running thick. The Little Colorado's water is some of the foulest in the Canyon: heavily mineralized, slimy, brackish, stank. Jack Sumner, one of Powell's crewmates on his first trip down the Canyon in 1869, found it "a lothesome little stream, so filthy and muddy that it fairly stinks...as disgusting a stream as there is on the continent...half of its volume and ⅔ of its weight is mud and silt. [It was little but] slime and salt." A hundred years' worth of human effluvia: battery acid, car oil, tires, trash, as well as traces of one of the worst radioactive spills in US history, when 100 million gallons of radioactive water were accidently released into a major tributary in 1979, has done little to improve its flavor.

But honestly, even though it begins as Rocky Mountain snow-melt, by the time it reaches the Canyon, the Colorado River's water isn't all that much more palatable. I pumped a liter and took a sip. Alkaline, almost curdled. The rim of my bottle was gritty; I could feel the grains of rock rasp my tongue, the sand grind my teeth. Despite the dam, the Colorado through the Canyon is by no means devoid of silt. According to Gwendolyn L. Waring, author of *A Natural History of the Intermountain West: Its Ecological and Evolutionary Story*, the river below the dam still conveys some 12 million tons of silt a year. Twelve million tons of silt still makes for a raspy river. Much of the silt comes from the Pariah River, which enters the Colorado hypersaturated with the pink, hema-tite-rich soils of Bryce Canyon. Waring claims that the Pariah, a Paiute word meaning "muddy" or "elk water," has "carried greater concentrations of suspended sediment than any other river in North America; concentrations of up to 2 pounds of sediment per quart." The Little Colorado supplies a significant amount of sediment; the rest comes from the park's hundreds of tributary canyons. And thus a drink of the river, despite the twist of the mouth at the taste, is a desert communion: the dolomites and mudrocks of Nankoweap or Kwagunt basins, having clouding into the Colorado, now billow into my bloodstream.

The Southwest's intense monsoon thunderstorms play an integral role in the conveyance of tributary silt. For those few wet months, floods and debris flows—ranging from 3,500 to 10,600 cfs and, at least once this century as high as 35,314 cfs—race down the tributaries, scorching the river its namesake red. Flush with runoff, again the river moves the wasted continent to the sea. You open your eyes underwater and it's black as a cave. Like being buried alive.

Yet because of repressed river flow, most of this tributary sediment settles to the riverbed shortly downstream of the tributary canyons. Since 1996 the various federal agencies managing the dam and river—mainly the Bureau of Reclamation, US Fish and Wildlife Service, and the National Park Service—have been experimenting with short-duration, high-volume dam releases (aka "high-flow experiments," or HFEs) designed to mobilize these thick mantles of sand and sediment in hopes that when the flood subsides, the mobilized sand will have replenished downstream beaches and riparian areas. As of 2017 they'd conducted six such experiments, with no flood larger than 45,000 cfs. The latest tactic, now part of the Glen Canyon Dam Adaptive Management Program, is to strategically time the high flows with the episodic flooding of tributaries, as when, in a three-month, end-of-monsoon-season span in 2012, the Paria River debouched at least 538,000 metric tons of sand into the Colorado River.

However, according to a 2011 USGS report, the relation "among sand supplied from tributaries, short-term sand enrichment in the Colorado River, sand transport during HFEs, sand transport between HFEs during normal operations, and the resultant sand mass balance" is complex, and delicate, and "uncertainties still remain about downstream impacts of water releases from Glen Canyon Dam." For example, the experimental floods may have had a role in the 800 percent increase in the catch rates of rainbow trout—the endangered humpback chub's main predator—at the confluence between 2007 and 2009. On a wider scale, the question remains whether tributaries even supply enough sand "to provide the elevated suspended-sediment concentrations needed to build and also maintain sandbars." Because of this, environmentalists have urged the Bureau of Reclamation to install a slurry pipe that would inject reservoir sediment back into the river, though the bureau has indicated no more willingness to do this than to install a native-fish-friendly device that pulls warm water from the surface of the reservoir though the penstocks. They have valid reasons: sediment released from Lake Powell will only further reduce the already diminished capacity of Lake Mead, a far more strategic reservoir, and warmer water, while bad for trout, might increase the populations of other voracious warm-water nonnative fishes. Still, the bureau has been historically, notoriously recalcitrant concerning anything other than the Glen Canyon Dam's main purpose as a "cash register" dam, and even getting them to conduct some of the high-flow experiments required litigation.

So it goes with the Colorado River these days; as Marc Reisner put it in his classic book *Cadillac Desert*, "The Colorado's modern notoriety…stems not from its wild rapids and plunging canyons but from the fact that it is the most legislated, most debated, and most litigated river in the entire world." Though there is a great and necessary deal of cooperation over this miracle of a desert river "resource," scarcity and complexity breed conflict, and often enough it's the Bureau of Reclamation versus the National Park

Service versus the Fish and Wildlife Service versus the Navajo Nation versus conservation organizations; urban Phoenicians versus pima cotton farmers versus whitewater rafters; "upper-basin" states versus "lower-basin" states versus the federal government; on and on, all the parties with their own vested interests, competing values, institutional ideologies, and narrative blinders.

And beyond all the tangle of acronyms, abstractions, and differing philosophies is the squat, concrete reality of the dam. So, too, for all the ways our individual and cultural conceptions allow us to see or not see the Grand Canyon, and as much as it may be the most staggering, unknowable, sublime phenomenon that I have ever experienced, the Canyon is still rock, and wind, and river. I was born sixteen years too late to have experienced the Canyon before the dam. I couldn't—can't—see the native fish slipping toward extinction. I haven't yet spent enough years on the river to witness the beaches waning to nothing, the rapids choking with boulders. There is only so much my mind can bear to read about acre-feet allocations, fluvial geomorphology, and adaptive management programs. But every year, as the monsoons waned, I watched brown-green veins more frequently marble the firebrand red until, in time, the entire river flowed that sullen, incarcerated green.

Conversely, during those months when the tributaries are flashing, turning the river brown, or during those rare, brief days of high-flow experiments, one understands that the central miracle of the Grand Canyon is the staggering amount of material that the river is capable of conveying. It's so obvious that it's commonly disregarded, or slips past without notice, but the exposed and spreading rock is not the Grand Canyon: the Canyon is the absence of that rock. The Canyon is a lacuna—a gap, a segment of earth torn from its surroundings, the thousand cubic miles of rock that the river has excavated. And not merely the iconic gorge itself—in what the geologist Clarence Dutton dubbed "the great denudation," strata a mile thick was removed from the *top* of the Grand Canyon region. An entire landscape, gone. The Moenkopi layer, gone. Chinle layer, gone. The Moenave, Kayenta, Navajo, Templecap, Carmel, Dakota, Tropic, Wahweap, Kaiparowits, Wasatch, Brian Head—almost 200 million years' worth of sedimentary deposition—gone. The arterial river flume sluiced the broken landscapes to the Sea of Cortez. Wells sunk along the river's delta have penetrated eighteen thousand feet of alluvial fill without hitting bedrock. Fifty thousand cubic miles of sediment may lie buried under the Gulf of California. In time that material will be subducted and reabsorbed into the hot crust of the earth, and, in even greater scales of time, again rise to the surface as new earth.

And yet, for a geologic gasp, no more sediment disgorges into the gulf. None.

In the fathomless reaches of geologic time, a few centuries' or millennias' lack of silt won't affect the tectonic cycle in the slightest. And that's part of the magic of the Grand Canyon: all I had to do to feel, if not hope, then at least a comforting sense of context, was to look around me, press my bare palms against that unbearably ancient rock, slide my bare feet in that cold, indifferent water. I may mourn that I'll never get to see a 200,000 cfs flood deepening the Canyon, or that I'll never get to sit at the confluence of the free-flowing San Juan River and the free-flowing Colorado River and watch the sediment of one curl like spiral galaxies into the deep space of the other, but I find some small, fatalistic comfort in the fact that the dam is a temporary barrier, that the river, as Robinson Jeffers put it, is a "heart-breaking beauty [that] will remain when there is no heart to break for it."

My water bottles full, I poured the remaining water in my settling bag into the shallows. The force of the water plumed sand into suspension, some of which settled back to the bottom, some of which was whisked away by the eddy. I watched the gauzy ribbons of sediment flow past, allowed myself to fancy that they made the main current to be carried down the river's length to the waters of Lake Mead, where the individual grains will again succumb to their minuscule gravities and fall, slowly, to the bottom.

↜: ↝

Abel placed the old sledge head over the new handle to see how much more wood he needed to rasp off for the head to fit true. A lot more, apparently: the head barely slid down an inch. He looked closely at where head met handle, then into the eyehole of the head, trying to see the contact that impeded the fit. Without taking his eyes off the handle he popped the head off, placed it on the workbench, and with the same hand reached for his rasp. He began scouring vigorously, his brow furrowed in concentration.

I smiled, reminded of the time he was pleading his case to a Navajo Tribal Policeman. Well, not so much pleading as defending his honor, which had been called into question, and in a sequence of flustered, earnest statements, without a hint of braggadocio, he said, "I'm a hardworkin' man!"

Abel was a good ol' boy from the hills of North Carolina. His slow drawl and southern colloquialisms made him a gem to listen to on the Park Service radio. Most of us adopted curt, professional voices, all "Clear!" and "Copy," and Abel did too, but every once in a while he'd get excited and squawk things like: "I just got hit by the squall! It's lightninin' perdy bad!" (Afterward, as the storm would be clearing and the sun would shine through the rain, he'd turn his blue eyes, strong jaw, and hawk nose to the sky and say, happily, "Yup. Devil's beatin' his wife.") He loved to talk politics, read *Newsweek* with his coffee in the morning. A great "geetar" player, though he was shy and didn't know actual songs, just put his head down and jammed blues riffs. Blake called them "songs from the heartland," and Abel thought that Blake was just about the funniest guy he'd ever met in his life. When Blake told stories Abel would slap his knee and let loose a series of short Rebel Yell barks or a single bluegrass falsetto "Ha!" Often he'd be talking and then trail off into muttering, as though accustomed to nobody listening to him, as though so used to talking to himself he would continue doing so among friends. When he was telling a story or had an unexpected audience, he'd spread his legs wider, clasp his hips with his hands, cock his head to the side, stare out into the distance, and talk in measured, almost mock proclamations. At times this pose was clearly a joke, but he adopted it so habitually, in irrelevant or inappropriate situations, that it slipped from joke to refuge. I always suspected these strange mannerisms arose from being raised dirt poor with a strict father. When he'd berate himself for messing up some minor thing I'd have hardly bothered to notice, he'd look as though his father were about to whip him. And he *was* a hardworking man: dedicated, strong as the noonday sun, handled his tools and worked his stone with ease and familiarity.

He knew what he was doing with the sledge shaft. We didn't protect our wood handles with rubber guards, so if I was hammering rebar through a juniper log check and missed by a half-inch, the rebar would shred the handle. Too many missed blows and the handle either splintered outright or become severely compromised. You could feel it, swinging a solid sledge versus one on the verge of cracking. A good helve would shiver and spasm with the blows, tight and muscular. A weakened helve would ring hollow as it hit rock, wouldn't bounce back as smartly. Eventually the handle would break, the wood ligaments still connected but flimsy, folding. On rainy days we'd take off work an hour early and do maintenance on our tools in the barn. Someone would spill a bucket of old sledge heads onto the dirt floor, crack a box of brand new, clean-as-dawn thirty-six-inch hickory wood handles, and we'd get to work.

The new handles were always much fatter than the oval hole in our sledge heads, so we'd have to rasp wood off the top of the handle until the sledge head slid on snug. But you had to be careful not to rasp too much off or the head wouldn't fit faithfully, no matter how the handle widened once you'd corked it with wood and metal wedges. As we rasped, someone on the crew would be sure to point out how much more efficient it'd be to use mechanized wood sanders, but I liked rasping away by hand. So, it seemed, did Abel. He pushed the rasp against the handle with long, powerful strokes; fat-grained sawdust shot onto the floor. He'd rotate the handle rotisserie-style as he worked, he'd check to see how the head fit, then rasp again, then check again.

Abel and I came from different backgrounds and from opposite ends of the country. We had very different ways of being in the world. But we were good buddies. And in a way we were similar. We were both good at trail work because we were strong and had good balance and coordination, and because much of the work came naturally. We also both came to the craft as adults. It is something we learned. Neither of us was like John Hiller or the Luck brothers, who grew up on farms in Iowa, or Jim Bryers, raised by a Mennonite family, also on a farm, or Francis, the Navajo jack-of-all-trades who came up hard on the rez—those guys who knew how to weld, repair tack, mend broken chainsaw links, tie diamond hitches, frame a house, fix a carburetor, all those tricks and tools of the trades that one seems to pick up as a matter of course when growing up on a farm, ranch, or rez.

Me, I grew up in an affluent neighborhood in one of the most urban metropolitan areas in the world. I had to lie to get my first job in the trades: as a carpenter working for Alaska State Parks. I had driven up to Alaska my first summer in college. I didn't have a job lined up and knew only one person in the whole of Alaska— my aunt—but I was wholly taken with the idea of the place, owing to childhood Jack London stories and to a girl I had a crush on in high school telling me of a guy she was probably sleeping with having come back from a summer on a fish boat in Alaska all tan and muscular and bearded. I wanted to be all tan and muscular and bearded and get the girls. When I arrived in Homer, I went down to the docks and asked around for work. A guy asked if I was good at cleaning fish. "Pretty good," I told him, having never cleaned a fish in my life. Later that summer, watching people clean fish on those same docks, I thanked the gods I don't believe in that I hadn't been stupid enough to try and bluff my way into that job—these guys were cleaning four-foot-long king salmon and two-hundred-pound halibut as quickly and efficiently as coring apples. My dumb bluff would have been called quickly, horribly.

Anyway, after a few days of failed searching, my aunt called the local district ranger, and he called a guy and that guy, not all that much older than me but in charge of rebuilding a ranger station in Kachemak Bay State Park, bought my fabrications about my experience on a construction site. I can't remember what specifically

my bullshit consisted of, but I justified it to myself as a necessary
surmounting of the classic catch-22: so often to get a job you need
relevant experience, but usually you can't get this experience without first having had a similar job. Generally this is overcome by a
fair amount of exaggeration on the one hand and a kind person
opening the door for you on the other. I provided the exaggeration;
this kind person opened the door. And what a door: ten-hour days
of honest work and deep camaraderie under the Alaskan summer
sun, with loons crying the sun down and schools of salmon stir-
ring the surface of the lagoon.

I used this experience, along with that from my job on my
college's farm, to get my first job working Trails at Point Reyes
National Seashore. Though to get this job I also lied, this time
about my experience using chainsaws. On the first day of the job,
when the foreman showed us a shed containing about thirty different chainsaws, I asked, "Do you ever use electric saws?" because
back in LA that's what we'd use in the rare instance a eucalyptus
limb would fall across the driveway. And he looked at me like,
"Electric fucking saws? What, we have a ten-mile-long extension
cord, too?" Luckily, before he could dig deeper into what exactly
my experiences with saws had been, the other new guy, a pale, be-
spectacled, skinny kid, was overcome by the oil and gas fumes in
the cramped quarters of the saw shed and fainted. The next day,
continuing my bluff, I simply grabbed a Stihl 440 saw, surreptitiously watched how the others were starting their, fired it up,
and went at a downed redwood. My confidence knew no bounds;
nor, apparently, did my idiocy.

Luckily we spent most of the autumn cutting brush and smaller
deadfalls. My best friend on the crew, a beak-nosed bodybuilder
covered head to toe in tattoos, including one of crucified Jesus that

covered the entirety of his very muscular back, happened to be a wildland fire hotshot during the summers. He babied his saw as if it were his newborn child. He taught me a great deal about cleaning, sharpening, and repairing a saw, the intricacies and physics involved in felling and bucking trees, as Devin was to do about rockwork in the Canyon.

And so, despite having entered the trades through no small amount of bluffing, bullshit, and irrational self-confidence, I became competent, then skilled, at my chosen craft. As had Abel, though surely on more honorable paths. We both felt like we belonged to the work, to the crew, and to the place. Even so, I had my doubts. I didn't know if Trails was something that I could or would want to do indefinitely. I didn't know if I _should_.

During my brief stint as a farmhand in the Pacific Northwest, I worked as a beekeeper for a small honey farm. One of the men on my crew had been born in Mexico—indeed, he had been smuggled through a tunnel under the border when he was a scared-stiff sixteen-year-old—and told me in his broken English about his younger cousin, raised in the States, whose parents had helped pay for him to go to college, but who, with degree in hand, had gone back to work in the fields with his family. My friend said this with scorn; he said this as though I was supposed to laugh in disbelief and shake my head at the idiocy and waste of certain people. Certain people like me. Essentially he was telling me that I had a place and that laboring in the radish seed fields was not that place. That no matter how much I worked to shape myself, no amount of rasping would hone me true to that head.

He had a point: I had graduated from college, perhaps I shouldn't be harvesting honey in a bee suit in the hundred-degree sun for ten hours a day earning ten dollars an hour. A similar thought occurred to me once or twice in the Canyon—that I'd be squandering the incredible good fortune of my birthplace and the rigors and expenses of my education by grubbing ditch in a desert for the rest of my days. After all, I may have been good at swinging a sledge and stacking stone into walls, but what I was really good at? Reading comprehension. What I really liked to do, more than shaping stone and about as much as hiking, was sit in a hammock in the shade on a summer day and read a good book of poetry. I couldn't have been much more than six when my aunt asked me what I wanted to do when I grew up and I said: "A fireman." And even now I think of how that would have been a good job: good tools, good skills, exciting, heroic, a closeness with the elements, part of a brotherhood, an all-around honorable profession. But when she asked me *why* I wanted to be a fireman I said, "So I can lie in a cot and read all day." Even now this rings true.

There was no reason I could not dedicate myself with good conscience to the good work that was Trails, to honing myself in body and mind as I honed a blade or rasped a helve. What laborer work failed to provide monetarily it made up for spiritually. But I had not dedicated myself: I was a fickle dabbler, over and over a novice, going from construction to farming to Trails. And all the while I wrote in my journals; all the while what I really wanted was to do was write.

I had always known this, and I had always buried it. I'd refused to commit to it as I had to anything else. But Trails, and the Canyon, catalyzed that want. Sitting there, that day, watching Abel rasp that helve, I realized that I was paying attention to the details of woodchip and raindrop in that distanced, attentive way a writer watches something he or she will later write about. I realized that I shouldn't ignore the fact that I'd filled hundreds of pages of notes and anecdotes and descriptions of the Canyon. The trove signified that that's what I was doing, anyway: writing.

Reputedly, Hemingway's basic motivations for writing were to find out how fly-fishing and bullfighting worked; I'd been half-heartedly doing the same with Trails. And there were similarities between the crafts of writing and trail work. The quick clack of the keys in the flow of writing was not unlike the sharp ring of the hammer in the rhythm of masonry. Both blank page and gaping hole presented an empty form to fill; be they words in a sentence or stones in a wall, one had to determine the best fit. Writing, like crafting a wall, examines and invests in what is solid, what is satisfying, what matters.

This should have been my answer to the question Erika posed that day on the North Rim. Yes, I wanted the storm-wracked Canyon below us to be part of my life. But I also wanted to write about it. I wanted to create a balance between the worlds of writing and labor, between hard work and proper idleness. Working Trails in the spring, summer, and fall, with a nice winter off-season for writing, was as close to that as I had yet come in my life. I wasn't going to abandon that to move to Florida. I decided, right then, in that barn, what I wanted, what I was going to do: I'd apply to MFA writing programs, continue to work Trails in the summers, and have faith that our relationship could survive the distance.

Abel held the sledge vertically between his legs and tapped the handle end forcibly onto the deck. The boards boomed with each blow. He held the sledge up, looked at it from the top, looked at it from the bottom, slammed it back down against the floor. Looked again. Hefted it, happily. Caught my eye. "Trued," he said.

~: :~

The herd of cow elk ran off the slope so fast I barely had time to gasp before the first, then the second gigantic creature squeaked past the hood of the car, and to duck as Erika punched us broadside into the third elk at fifty-five miles an hour. We hit her right at the knees, so that all eight hundred pounds of ungulate crashed onto the hood and then flipped over the top of the car. My car.

Erika wrenched us over to the side of the road. The car was still running, but the engine squealed and the dashboard flashed red.

"Are you all right?" I asked.

She was crying, shaking, one hand fluttering in agitation, the other death-gripping the steering wheel.

She was all right.

"I've gotta get that elk off the road." Adrenaline had clouded the brain, and I was out of the car and running up the road, barefoot, not bothering to consider how I'd dispatch a mortally wounded elk with my bare hands. But the elk was gone. There was an empty series of tight curves, the cold moonlight on the guardrail, and a mountainous drop into the darkness beyond. I ran back to the car.

Erika was standing there, sobbing. She looked up at my approach.

"I killed your car," she cried.

By all appearances, she had. Fluid was pouring out of the crushed radiator. Shards of headlight lay scattered across the blacktop. The hood bore the cartoonlike impression of an elk: there was the imprint of the legs, there the ass, there the massive belly. There the elk pellets lodged in the windshield wipers.

"Jesus Christ. That thing blew right over the top of the car," I said.

"I killed your car."

"I don't care about the car."

The car was a 1996 Saab convertible, a hand-me-down from my father. It was a nice car, a reliable ride, and I wasn't in any financial position to be turning down gifts of any sort of used vehicle, but it always embarrassed me, driving a teal-green Saab convertible in the southwestern desert. It seemed a slice of LA ostentation that didn't transplant well to the desert, or at least the desert life I was living, or at least the desert rat ego I'd developed. (Did it have California license plates for a while? It may have. All that was missing for total AZ ostracism was a Lakers sticker.) I'd inch it over forty miles of washboard road to a remote trailhead, and in the rare instance anyone else would be out there they'd be getting in their high-clearance, four-wheel-drive vehicle, and would stare at me with what may have been astonishment but which I always assumed was condescension.

But apparently that car was a tank. I had dubbed it Tipitina, in honor of the Professor Longhair song, because it called to my mind a tawdry lady of the night—though I was the whore, for taking it—but the day after Erika plowed it through a full-grown cow elk, after we limped it into a nothing town and it needed just two cans of Radiator Seal-All to stagger another 530 miles to a radiator mechanic, I loved that car a little more, or at least respected her enough to rename her Stagger Lee.

Later Erika visited an old junkyard and bought the same make and model and color of hood. But blowing the literal shit out of an elk had bent Stagger Lee's front frame and the hood didn't fit true. So back on the North Rim, Erika spent a good week putting in new headlights and a grill and jiggering the frame into alignment. The hood never did fit plumb or latch securely, but whatever, it

signaled a good story, especially because if Erika had time to brake
and we'd hit that elk at any slower speed that creature would either
have come through our windshield or flipped atop the ragtop and
crushed us to death.

After work I'd walk to my trailer to find Erika on her back beneath the car, the frame strung between ratchet straps stretched
taut between fir trees. She had received my plan of attending
graduate school, apart from her, calmly, sadly. We didn't discuss
it much, in part because of the possibility that neither of us would
be accepted, and there was no point in shedding unnecessary
tears, but also because it *was* sad, and there was little to say besides
"We'll make it work." This is what we said. As for what would happen once we had received our master's degrees, whether we'd both
come back to work in the Canyon, or I would continue to work in
the Canyon while Erika got her PhD, or I'd pack up and follow her
to Florida, we had no idea. In all honesty, at the time I think I was
less concerned with what would happen years hence than I was
with overcoming my reticence about telling my crewmates that I
was relinquishing a significant amount of time on Trails in order to
study creative writing. Hunching over a computer in an enclosed
space didn't entail quite the same level of manly glory as swinging
a sledge in the open air. If I don't consider myself the platonic ideal
of machismo, this was still an enervation. I'd still be abandoning
a part of my identity: I'd come to regard my scarred arms, tanned
neck, strong grip as though they were birthrights. But the boys
didn't care. They were surprised, sure, but kind of interested, even
admiring of my attempt to break Trails' own particular inertia.

Still, a strong undercurrent of machismo flowed through the
trail crew. Back at the bunkhouse, tossing horseshoes, the boys

on the crew would rag me about having my ol' lady fix my car. I'd shrug, say, "She's the one who wrecked the damn thing," or closer to the truth, "I don't know shit about cars." But the real truth was that I didn't care either way, that for days I'd been caught by another thought: why do things happen? Perhaps the Greeks were right about our threads of fate, or the New Agers right about lines of power crisscrossing the earth, and how we animals go coursing along those preordained lines right into one another to call it chance. If the intersecting currents of elk and car seemed a common enough miracle, the way Erika and I had come crashing together seemed a less common miracle. For unlike the other relationships we'd both been in, we hadn't eventually bounced off one another, back into the proverbial darkness. We had crashed together and wrapped, melded, the imprints one left on the other deep, enduring, and hopefully ongoing.

~: ~

Dee and I were walking to Cape Royal when a four-foot-long, wrist-thick, brilliant-gold and bright-black gopher snake drifted across our path. I followed it, just shy of grabbing it, parting branches to better peer into the desert mahogany in which it took shelter, chattering all the while to Dee until I looked back and realized that he was gone.

I found him at the end of the cape, leaning against the safety rail, looking across the hazy Canyon.

"What happened to you?"

"I'm not supposed to be around snakes."

"Oh."

We looked out at the desert.

"Why?"

"Because I'm Diné."

Years later I sat on a chunk of sandstone amid a field of similar stones, their unblemished surfaces exposed to the elements for the first time in 275 million years. Above me rose the sheer, four-hundred-foot Coconino sandstone cliff from which the slide had originated. I sat there, looking at the cliff, at the slide, wondering how and why it happened, and thinking of Dee shunning that snake.

As to the collapse, which had razed a large section of the Tanner Trail, I considered the cliff itself, formed from an ancient aeolian sea of sand. Perhaps the extensive cross-bedding within the boulders of the slide signified an instability within the dunes that formed this particular section of cliff, and this instability eventually led to this collapse. Perhaps a rare instance of rain fell on the surface of these dunes, then the moistened sand hardened, was covered by dry sand, and this unusually ossified sediment layer proved the weak link. Or, broader still, the fall may owe to how the Tanner Fault—which the trail exploits to descend to the Colorado River—weakened the cliffs to the forces of erosion.

But all of that simply set the stage. More relevant are the processes by which the cliff was primed for the final, violent kinetics. There is scarp retreat: when groundwater percolating through porous sandstone reaches an underlying and impermeable shale layer, it is sluiced out onto the surface. The running water scours the shale; in time the cliff overhangs its undercut bed. When the sapping reaches a vertical joint in the overlying rock, the cliff collapses in landslide. There is frost wedging: when water freezes it expands by 9 percent; thus when snowmelt seeps into a fissured rock and refreezes, it wedges the cracks apart. When the frozen water melts, it penetrates deeper into the expanded cracks, removing particles that helped glue the rock together, further fracturing the rock when frozen again. There is root wedging: the slide contained remnants of an absolutely pulverized piñon; perhaps the tree had shot roots through and through a system of cracks in the cliff, roots that wedged the cracks wider as they fattened. Or perhaps the general seismic activity of the region—the five earthquakes of magnitude 5.0 or bigger since 1900. Or perhaps the fact that when the moon passes especially close to the planet its gravitational pull causes the earth to bulge four to forty inches toward it. Perhaps a particularly strong pulse along an underlying telluric current. Perhaps a sheep hoof, a lizard pushup, a human voice. Perhaps, as the geographer J. B. Jackson put it, "mysteries that fit into no pattern": the shifting of a kachina in sleep, the strict whim of Yahweh.

In the end, I'll never know. Nor does it matter. On a broad scale, no mystery lies in the mechanical processes I sought to interpret: rock erodes and tumbles to rest. But I do believe in fey processes or fluctuations; a minuscule, improbable, powerful event, as with the quintessential chaos theory metaphor of the flapping of butterfly wings in Brazil causing a hurricane in the Gulf of Mexico. It could be that this force, or agent, or whatever, has simply not yet been discovered, as with all the phenomena in the world—germs, neutrinos, tectonic plates—that, before they were empirically verified, were dismissed as unlikely or impossible.

This, then, is why I thought of Dee and the snake.

There is much in this world that we recognize but don't yet understand. Coincidences. Accurate premonitions. *Déjà vu.* How some animals sense earthquakes, or how the fly knows when I have her in my attention and thus evades me. How Erika, from across a crowded room, will feel the touch of my eyes and turn to meet them. How coyote willow seedlings, deposited by floods thirty feet above a creek, unerringly know the exact direction to send their roots toward water. How the light from Betelgeuse affects the cells of an aspen leaf, or a solar flare scrambles the navigational abilities of butterflies. Much of what we will never comprehend is linked to, or gives rise to, superstitions. Yet within the murky waters of superstition are suspended grains of truth.

Take, for example, Dee's belief in not just the snake taboos that accompany his father's Navajo bloodlines, but the animistic beliefs that accompany his mother's Hopi bloodlines: that supernatural power inhabits everything. That not only snakes but also stones, rivers, and clouds possess their own existence. Western physics acknowledges that all these objects contain potential energy, and, in the case of a thunderhead, kinetic energy, but many Native Americans—and indigenous people the world over—go beyond that: they believe that rocks had life. Scientifically, this is false: if living can be defined by cells and the electrical synapses between cells, rocks—inert, cell-less, passive—are, as they say, stone-dead.

I'm a skeptic through and through and, in the case of the Tanner slide, believe in little besides the protean effects of water molecules. But still, I can't wholly dismiss the belief that rocks contain within themselves power or life. For I quite easily accept the fact that water percolates through seemingly impermeable sandstone; that the stone in time saturates with liquid; that the dry air at the stone's open faces draws the water through rock pores to the surface, where it forms a thin film; that this liquid film evaporates and leaves behind crystalloid evidence of calcite, gypsum, halite. To me, the rock's inhalation and exhalation of water resembles breathing, and so the Hopi, if not scientifically correct, are at least poetically accurate—the insensate stone breathes, and what breathes, is, in a way, alive. Or if that stretches belief, put it this way: if one accepts that the mechanical and chemical processes working within a rock, and thus the rock itself, are inextricably threaded into the fabric of what we consider living, breathing life, then to separate the two, to draw distinctions between living and rock, is, in the end, meaningless.

During a Trails off-season, I worked for a few months on the National Park fisheries crew. As part of a native fish reintroduction project, we waded fourteen miles of Bright Angel Creek with backpack electroshockers, culling trout and tagging native fish. Fourteen miles, minus the stretches immediately upstream or downstream of the confluence of Ribbon Falls Creek. For the Zuni tribe believe that they originated from the water cascading from those falls. Out of respect for their beliefs we didn't use our electroshocking backpacks near the confluence. Even so, during one of the meetings between the park and the tribe, the Zunis mentioned how there had been a dramatic increase in "tasing" incidents on the reservation, and hinted that they thought this increase could be attributed to the electroshocking of Bright Angel Creek, hundreds of miles away. As much as I find this hard to believe, even ridiculous, I do believe in the tenets of chaos theory, or the possibility of quantum entanglement—what Einstein described as "spooky action at a distance"—and for that reason I cannot outright dismiss the Zuni's beliefs.

For all the knowledge I have gained through rational, linear thought, through systematic investigation and objective analysis, I also know that these same processes have limited me, distanced me from alternate ways of knowing or being. In his book *One River*, the anthropologist and ethnobotanist Wade Davis relates how shamans of various Amazon basin tribes combine different plants to make entheogenic potions such as ayahuasca. The potions are effective only because of a unique mixture of chemical compounds, yet the range of compounds within the pharmacopoeia of the rainforest is so great that thousands of years of trial-and-error testing cannot explain the shamans' success in discovering the correct combinations. When questioned by Western anthropologists and pharmacologists, the shamans said simply, *The plants sing to us.*

In his poem "When I Heard the Learn'd Astronomer," Walt Whitman writes of becoming "tired and sick" of an astronomer's proofs, figures, charts, and diagrams, and instead glides out into the "mystical moist night-air" to look "up in perfect silence at the stars." (In this he was following the path laid for him by Wordsworth, among others, who claimed that "one impulse from a vernal wood" had taught him more than "all the sages can.") In a way, that's what Dee came to represent for me. Not so much the mystical—the two of us had drunk too much whiskey and watched too much *South Park* together to allow any romantic visions of a modern-day Noble Savage. Nor was he the type to be wholly content with incertitude: he'd riff on Carl Sagan or the latest nature documentary for hours. No, it was something else, his intrinsic capacity for what the poet John Keats called "negative capability": "when a man is capable of being in uncertainties, mysteries, doubts, without any irritable reaching after fact and reason."

Twice we walked forty miles along the river paths of Buckskin Gulch and Pariah Canyon. Twice we tread the same ground but passed through different worlds. If Dee was awed by the beauty, he also accepted it, content as he was with retracing the pathways his ancestors had taken for tens of thousands of years. If I was awed, I was not necessarily content: as a writer I struggled with a lack of words for the beauty, with the way it reduced me to a prelinguistic state: making bird chirps and swooshing sounds, motions with my hand describing waves, ripples, curves. The canyons revealed language as sham, as impotent symbols and structures unable to adequately capture the shifting light on the curved walls, the brilliant green of a young cottonwood's leaves against the red rock. My inarticulateness was no small thing: putting the right words in the right order is how I piece together the world.

Over the eight years I spent in the deserts of the Colorado Plateau, I'd cycle through the ouroboros-like gamut of ways of being and knowing. Sometimes I'd be searching for causes and effects and struggling with words and sentences; other times I'd enter into extended moments of stillness and simple being, of seeing the stars in perfect silence. Many of these more meditative moments pressed into me from my surroundings—sitting in the shade of a rock shelf, stunned into stupor by the heat, or later, at sunset, looking out from the lip of the rim, stilled by the hum of open spaces. There's a wonderful moment in one of Powell's journals when this consummate questioning naturalist writes, simply, "On the summit of the opposite wall of the cañon are rock forms that we do not understand" and leaves it at that.

I have difficulty leaving it at that, or in quieting what Susan Sontag has referred to as a "perennial, never consummated project of interpretation." In her essay "Against Interpretation," Sontag explains that "real art has the capacity to make us nervous. By reducing the work of art to its content and then interpreting that, one tames the work of art. Interpretation makes art manageable, conformable." Obviously, the desert is not a work of art. The

Canyon was created not by a craftsman god, but by the incremental eons. The rasp of water over rock is not trying to "say" anything.
And in the case of the Tanner slide, I wasn't trying to interpret its
subtext, only its physical and historic processes. But still, Sontag
is on to something, and Joseph Wood Krutch echoes the refrain
in *The Desert Year*:

> The fact that I never had stayed long in any part of the monument
> country may be the consequence of a certain defensive reaction.
> There is a kind of beauty—and it is presumably the kind prevailing
> throughout most of the universe—of which man gets thrilling
> glimpses but which is fundamentally alien to him. It is well for him
> to glance occasionally at the stars or to think for a moment about
> eternity. But it is not well to be continuously aware of such things,
> and we must take refuge from them with the small and the familiar.

The Canyon so transcends our accustomed cognitive capacities
that we use any tool at our disposal to cage it into comprehension: analyzing the minute physical processes; using the frames of
"viewfinder" telescopes on the rim; listening to an interpretative
ranger provide statistics designed to subject the Canyon's staggering phenomena into small and familiar frameworks: how many
Rhode Islands can fit into the national park and neighboring national monument, how many Empire State Buildings stacked atop
each other will equal the Canyon's height or span, how many dump
trucks would be filled by a day's worth of transported river-silt.

Dee, and the rest of the trail crew in general, tended to regard
such factoids—and the way of knowing the Canyon from which
they arose—with a good deal of suspicion and scorn. An interpretive ranger's knowledge of the Canyon was dismissed as gleaned

from books and thus shallow—as if you could learn how to run a rapid or recognize the pressings of heat exhaustion by reading a book!—while the crew's deeper knowledge was seen as arising from our hard work, our blood on the rocks. There is truth to this.

But I'm a voracious consumer of Grand Canyon facts and factoids. I love knowing that all the rock layers were laid down long before the North American landmass rammed into the African landmass to form Pangea, or that, as impressive of a geologic record as is the Canyon's rock, 80 percent of the earth's history is lost in the Canyon's unconformities. I like how the detached, disinterested gaze of the interpretive ranger allows one to see the world as a riddle, as a problem to be solved.

Yet I also enjoyed Dee and the crew's immersive and ebulliently subjective way of knowing the Canyon. I, too, place greater trust in the state of suspension and envelopment that arises when I lose myself in wroughting stone, or when I know exactly, easily, how to run the pool table, or when the exact words or sentences complete one another on the page: those heightened, perfect, rare instances of flow. Trusting this instinctive, tacit wisdom is far preferable to my annoyingly persistent postmodern doubts. Furthermore the bite-sized facts and factoids dispensed by the interpretive rangers carried a weight of conclusiveness that seemed suspect, untrued to our understanding of the ever-shifting world of the Canyon, a world offering a continuum of possibility and a web of interrelations, some of whose strands stretched into the fogs of mysticism. As in the case of Ray's statement about "the real world," to take one thing out of that strand and hold it to the light and say "This is this, period," seemed, well, wrong. It wasn't only that the world was mutable: it was ultimately unknowable.

Many in the crew felt that scientific knowledge detracted from

their sovereign experiences, as though knowing the intricacies
of the geologic record or species names for plants or animals removed the object from a general, democratic knowledge and into
the realm of esoteric elitism. As though rigid scientific methods
of objective analysis or the dispassionate pursuit of knowledge
tarnishes the luster of awe, diminishes the great mystery of life
and existence. Far better the direct, personal, sovereign, even naive
experience, objectivity be damned. But I figure that knowledge
gained through the fickle senses is best paired with knowledge
from another, more objective or even empirically verifiable source.
I've never found the pursuit of scientific knowledge to ever detract
from wonder. On a certain level the crew is right: I could admire
that gopher snake without knowing its species (*Pituophis catenifer*).
When hiking with a botanist spouting Latin species names or a
geologist speaking in terms of micritic ooids, I've had to suppress
the urge to throw them into an *Agave americana* rosette or down
an exposed breccia pipe. Discovering through later readings that
the brilliant red shards of the lower Redwall are actually semipre-
cious, gem-quality jasper delivers far less a thrill than the initial
discovery of the jasper by cracking open a stone with a single blow.
And, perhaps in the end, loving without knowing is more important than knowing without loving. But knowing the story behind
the jasper—a story of transgressions and regressions of a primeval
oceanic sea over 15 million years; a sea teeming with life that died
en masse and compressed into rock, in the process of which some
shells morphed into jasper—does nothing but further my appreciation of the gem shining in my palm.

Not everyone on the crew distrusted the scientific worldview;
those who did harbored different reasons for doing so. Dee put

faith in his native traditions. Wayne distrusted that which contradicted the strict Christian beliefs of his upbringing. I always figured Blake didn't appreciate how scientific facts impinged on the imaginative potential of the world, and preferred instead to delight in that moment when a shadow could be a lizard, or a rock spire a giant iguana dick. Some believed in the dichotomy between a cold, rational mind and a warm, intuitive heart, and put their faith in the latter. Many on the crew exhibited little curiosity or interest in the Canyon beyond its role as a place to earn their daily bread. As Anaïs Nin put it, "We don't see things as they are, we see them as we are."

What united the crew's disparate outlooks was a need to ground any and all understanding in self-understanding, in how the perceived world worked through us in action and experience, sensation and emotion. Immersed in the Canyon, day in, day out, for months and years on end, the line between self and surroundings blurred—it was hot, we were hot; it rained, we got wet. Prickly pear glochids that embedded in my skin were eventually absorbed. Moving across the jumbled mass of the Tanner slide, the lines in my palm pressed against the sedimentary lines of ancient slip faces; the finely seamed angles of cross-bedded dunes mirrored the crow's feet beginning to wing my eyes.

Scientific detachment wasn't for us. As Sontag wrote about Marienbad, we fancied ourselves immersed in "the pure, untranslatable, sensuous immediacy" of the irreducible rock, heat, wind. Even now, what I remember and how I remember the Canyon is bound to the sensuous: the shovel's rasping scoop and snickering dig. The way mule's shoes struck sparks against rocks in the early dawn. How a lightning strike would split a ponderosa's bark into a ragged vulva that dripped butterscotch sap where cambium met heartwood. Raindrops plopping into the river and riverdrops rising in perfect synchronicity back up toward sky. Standing wet on a warm rock in the middle of the creek after a swim, the current causing the brilliant pink mats of coyote willow roots to sway above the dark river stones, the water beading like pebbled stars on my bare skin, and nebulae of cottonwood fluff floating slow and steady upcanyon, so that I could stretch my head and have them dissolve on my tongue, the tiny seed cracking between my front teeth.

At the time, I was surprised Dee wouldn't want to grab the snake and note its forked tongue, its overlapping scales, its lidless eye. I was disappointed, too, figuring that someone who loved the Canyon as Dee loved the Canyon should want to know everything about the place he loved, in as fine and visceral detail as he could. But I couldn't hold that against him any more than he could hold against me my pointed if relatively pointless musings about the genesis of the rockslide that wiped out the Tanner Trail. Dee helped me see the Canyon as a richer and more meaningful place, a place of stone and water, superstition and blood.

～ ～

And then the mules escaped.

We'd bought five mules from a breeder in Oregon and locked them in the training facility in the South Rim's woods. Abner, head packer at the time, said that the breeder, in an effort to showcase the mules' agility, had led them through an elaborate obstacle course. If we saw that as perfect for the rigors of hauling loads on the Canyon's steep, winding, and rocky trails, one of the mules saw it as training, and a week into her Arizona stay scrambled up the six-foot rock cliff that formed part of the pen. The mule headed north, back to Oregon, but promptly hit the rim. She stood awhile, admiring the view, then tried to board a tourist bus. The bus driver whipped off his belt and hobbled the mule to a tree.

So we laughed at that, and the packers put a fence across the section of cliff the mule had climbed, but a week later, ten at night, somehow all five of the new mules escaped. They stampeded through a nearby volunteer campsite, the volunteer's flashlights revealing wild green eyes and then black night as the mules vanished into the woods.

The next morning a slew of Trails workers searched the South Rim's endless piñon-juniper forest. By the end of the day they'd recovered one mule nine miles to the west. At the next day's morning meeting, Devin covered a table with maps highlighted in different colors distinguishing boundary fences, fire roads, and water tanks. He immediately started detailing and delineating duties. Abner was there, conferring in low tones with Stan, the Hopi blacksmith. When Devin reached his full head of steam, Abner sidled over, pulling at his cigarette, looking at the maps, silent, impassive, but nodding once or twice, and once even pointing to the map, muttering something to which Devin, pausing, deliberating in that detached way of his, nodded in agreement.

A word about Abner.

Blake's dad, former Trails foreman, told me of how one night on a spike camp, about twenty years before my time in the Canyon, Abner lit into a big bottle of vodka. Later that night, as Blake's dad and an equally bear-sized man were stumbling back to their camp, they heard, down near the creek, a voice call, "Help me." Their flashlights illuminated Abner crumpled up among the boulders. They made their way down the embankment and propped him between them. The whole way up Abner cursed them a blue streak, all "you motherfuckers this, you motherfuckers that," and Blake's dad and the other bear-sized man, struggling over an ingrate drunkard, said, "Fuck this" and dropped him and walked back to camp and went to bed. In the morning Abner hobbled into camp with a shovel as a crutch, complaining about his ankle, asking, "What happened?" Blake's dad didn't want to have to medevac him because of a drunken fall, and made Abner wait it out until they all rode out a few days later. Turns out his ankle was broken in three places.

Little wonder, then, how Abner had weathered: no real teeth, long goatee streaked with gray, the wrinkles on his face like the fault lines on a map, every one a story of wind, sun, rock, heat, dust, leather, cigarettes, whiskey, heartbreak, mule hair, fried chicken and biscuits, three marriages, three divorces. The man could inspire or embody any number of country songs, though Waylon's "Lonesome, Ornery, and Mean" springs quickly to mind. He was a good man, and unfailingly charming to the younger women on the crew, but he was also bitter, bigoted, and an absolute grump. Like most of the crew, Abner mixed stereotypes and categories—he contained a spiritual and pragmatic side, could be sweet-hearted and racist. Take the way he treated the mules: he loved them, certainly, and masterfully worked them, but he'd also fly into a rage: kicking, punching, and cursing at a mule. Though generally gentle of demeanor, he was an absolute wild man behind the joysticks of a skid steer loader, lurching and bucking, spinning around like a dervish. He once spun one so wildly he knocked loose rocks he and Abel had spent the day placing, which sent Abel into a hard-hat-throwing rage, and Abner, still in the Bobcat, cigarette drooping from his mustached lip, just languidly watched him, as though Abel called to mind a rabid dog his papa had to shoot back in his Texas childhood. And the man had style: assorted silver and turquoise bracelets and necklaces, beaded and feathered juju tassels off his flat-brimmed hat. Weathered or not, he looked good. Little wonder that every camera turned from the Canyon to him as he led a mule string downtrail, spurs twinkling, aviator glasses gleaming, chapped hands rolling small cigarillos as he rode, a living, shining relict.

Another thing: he wasn't too fond of Devin. There was a degree of old-blood-versus-new-blood NPS resentment there, and no small amount of fraught personal history between them, and on a whole they were vastly different people, their differences happening to grate harshly on one another, especially as they were differences that, owing to their senior positions on Trails, were not easily avoided. I don't know what Abner thought that morning, watching Devin presiding over his maps like a general at war—I honestly doubt he paid him much mind at all, concerned as he was about his lost mules. The distance between them, the old tensions, was evident, as it always was, but at the same time, for the slightest of moments, came a slackening, a thin but true thread of mutual respect.

Anyway, after the map session, six of the crew went out on mules, two in a six-wheeled Polaris, one on his personal dirt bike. The rest of us went downtrail to work. All day we listened to the search party on the radio as maps in hand they combed the woods, at first sounding professional and organized but by day's end clearly roaming the woods at random—at one point Devin asked LTB's location, and there was a pause in which every single person listening to the Park Service radio could envision LTB looking around at the pressing woods as though seeing for the first time that the hard blue juniper "berries" were actually fused seed cones,

or just then realizing that the unrelenting chatter of birdsong in
the background was an especially large flock of foraging piñon jays,
but then snapping to and coming back on the radio and saying
"Ummmmmmm...in the woods." If it hadn't been so amusing the
whole situation would have been deeply embarrassing.

It *was* deeply embarrassing.

Finally, late that afternoon, Dispatch came over the radio,
reporting a mule in the woods behind Mather Apartments, only
a mile from the pen. Then Dispatch again, with a report from a
UPS man—oh, the laughter from those of us down on the trail at
this—of two mules walking along the side of the highway.

Day three of the Great Mule Escape dawned with four out
of the five mules caught. As the mules cost five thousand bucks
a head, plus the hourly pay of the dozen Trails boys out looking
for them (later, filling out timecards, tragically, hilariously, at-
tributing those hours to "animal caretaking"), plus three hours of
helicopter overflight, and general and specific wear and tear on the
equipment, this last mule had become a rather expensive beast of
burden. Day three and Devin, whose stress was pushing toward
panic, was in the office printing Lost Mule posters to place around
the South Rim Village. Day three, end-of-July hot, the water tanks
in the forest dry.

And finally, after Dee and others slept out by the few tanks that
had water, waiting for the thirsty mule, fearful of the Havasupai's
feral cows, they caught the last one. Except that Stu, our blacksmith and farrier, who had spent his youth roping calves in reservation rodeos, had "borrowed" the law enforcement ranger's horse
for the search, and, in the act of roping the last mule, this horse,
more accustomed to making its way through ice cream–eating
tourist crowds than to chasing after half-wild equines, bucked him

off and bolted. So we had captured the final mule but lost the ranger's horse and saddle—neither of which we had permission to use. As if we weren't already on bad enough terms with the rangers.

This necessitated yet another extensive search, again for a number of days, again embarrassing for Trails, but too farcical to care too much, the radio chatter too classic, too pathetic. Of course, it wasn't really funny—eventually the search was called off, consigning the horse to death by predation or heat exhaustion. We sacrificed the ranger's horse for our mules, we told ourselves, not entirely displeased.

More than a week later the Havasupai found the poor horse: gaunt, lame, its saddle having rubbed gangrenous sores into its parched hide. A year later Abner received the blame for the Great Mule Escape, and wasn't rehired.

~: :~

A search-and-rescue ranger found the man's discarded backpack a little ways off-trail. The following day, a half-mile south, under a large overhanging boulder, another ranger discovered a stash of food, including a can of tuna fish, which the man, as though in a frenzy to drink the juices, had crushed open with a rock. The boulder was between a series of dendritic drainages that merged into a small canyon, which in turn ran less than two miles into the Colorado River.

I figured the hiker was a fool who'd either overestimated his abilities or underestimated the Grand Canyon or both, and if he was dead—which seemed likely, as he was reported missing Tuesday and we flew in Friday—well, then, he had died a fool's death, as had the other five or six a year in my Canyon time.

But then Kirk and I split from the others and slid down several scree slopes, down past the boulder shading the snack cache, down into the narrow canyon, and in the dry stream gravel I saw the first footprint. I followed with my eyes the wavering line of tracks downcanyon, and something settled over me, something that still settles in fits and starts of memory and meaning.

I watched the change take hold of Kirk, as well. Kirk swings between hummingbird-like exuberance and sullen lethargy. When he is down, he is way down, but on this search he was up, way up, his blue eyes sparks above the red earth, his forearms rippling in knots and cords as he scrambled up boulders. When Kirk climbs, he dances along the rock, seemingly more at ease with being alive in the world on vertical rock than on flat ground. Once in the canyon, on the tracks, away from the helicopter and the others, he calmed, became more reflective, as I have often seen him do when high on a route, working through a difficult move.

We followed the tracks. We pushed through branches broken by the man's passage and stepped on boulders still smudged with sand once stuck to his shoes. We'd lose the trail in the boulder fields and move slowly, stopping to scan the walls, the shaded recesses...and then the prints would appear in a sand patch, always downcanyon, always toward the river. The days between our passings had slumped the track's edges into mere pressure spots, indents, nudges.

The heat was staggering. It was easily 105 degrees in the shade, but there was little shade. The heat was not general: in pockets of purple shale or near-black mudstone, it was as though we waded through the heat. I had five liters of water and doubted it would be enough to last the length of the canyon. I tried to breathe through my nose.

I stopped once and called his name. I thought he was dead, but I called out. No echo. The heat, the pressing rock walls, absorbed the call. The natural world is a mirror of moods, reflecting one's joy, claustrophobia, pain. But always, at the core, is indifference. I'd cut my hand on a sharp rock and wiped the blood on my pants, thinking, *unforgiving*, but even as I thought it, I knew the word's little truths had nothing to impart to mute stone or acacia thorn. There is nothing to forgive, nothing to do the forgiving. Every way I turned, every indication from the sere surroundings reinforced what I already knew: life here is hard and not to be taken for granted. Perhaps especially hard for pale, mostly hairless, upright primates, no matter our brain size or will. But hard regardless—I've seen deer and sheep dead before their times in these canyons. I called out again. Silence. A fly would buzz then stop, and the silence hissed in the ears. Kirk called from downcanyon, and I continued following the two pairs of now-intermingled tracks.

Not two weeks before the search, Kirk and a mutual friend on the crew, Luke, attempted to climb a Canyon formation known as Newton Butte. Both Kirk and Luke are highly skilled climbers, and as Newton was not a technical climb, they hadn't brought ropes. They scrambled up a series of natural ramps and small cliff faces but, at a certain point, deemed their chosen route unsafe and turned around. As Luke was navigating a tricky descent, the rock he was using as a handhold peeled off the wall. He plunged twenty feet, bounced off a rock ledge, fell an additional twenty feet, and finally landed on the rocky slopes, shattering one of his feet. They were a few thousand feet below the rim; at least three miles by trail. The sun was setting. Kirk climbed down to Luke, left him with his warm clothes, headlamp, and cigarettes, and set off, up

the dangerously exposed, skinny-as-a-sheep-trail route known as
the Shoshone Point route. He then hiked a mile and a half to the
road, called Dispatch, and within three hours was leading a search-
and-rescue medic back down the route in the dark. The medic later
told me that, on the way down, she felt the wind rising out of the
black night and realized it was coming from four hundred feet
of exposed cliff. They eventually reached Luke, shot him full of
morphine, and, in the morning, attached him, with the medic, to a
line hanging from a helicopter. Kirk, for the fourth time in twelve
hours, made his lonely way along the Shoshone Point route. Later
he would tell me of the "instant and everlasting connection" that
sparked between him and Luke in the seconds Luke plummeted
past him, out of sight, seemingly to his death, before yelling up
that he was alive.

The peculiar realities of this search were stitching such bonds
between Kirk and me, hiking closely together now, just as they
were between us and the man somewhere downcanyon.

Almost immediately, the dry streambed plunged off a rock shelf.
It wasn't a huge drop, maybe thirty feet, but sheer, and I scouted
the steep talus bank to the right of the pour-off. There was sheep
sign and sign of something else, something heavier. I knew it was
his path, because I was looking and because I have traced my own
faint paths back when ledges failed or turned to cliffs. I knew because Trails had familiarized me with the nature of disturbance in
these desert soils: the broken crust, the scuffed rock. We avoided
the pour-off as he had done.

Despite the pressing walls, the heat, the tracks, my eyes were
caught by rocks and shells. In certain sections of the canyon, we
crossed bedrock that had shattered into thousands of crystal-

line shards, all clouded reds and translucent pinks, speckled and marred by intrusive veins of dissimilar rock. I picked them up and held them to the light and pocketed the more brilliant. Dried millipede husks and flat, dime-sized snail shells glinted amid the red shale slopes. I picked them up, they powdered at my touch.

To drill holes into boulders in order to split them into workable blocks we'd use a pionjar, which rattles and chatters, hammering as it drills, necessitating double ear protection—earmuffs over earplugs. The world, suddenly muted, comes alive in unfamiliar ways. I'll notice a single oak leaf, hung from a spider's strand, spinning wildly, without a single other leaf moving. I'll notice, on the flat surface of the rock I am drilling, minute sand grains popping like splattering oil to the vibrations of the drill; the muscle power of a raven's tail feathers angled when banking; the liquid slide of clouds over the canyon's vertical relief. All these phenomena stand out in near silence and acute visual clarity, and strike in me an almost nostalgic chord, like the detached contentment of a lucid dream. So it was then, in that canyon, following those man's tracks, amid the stones and shells. Some ineffable light, glancing off of them, caught me, held me.

Part of the surreal nature of the day, besides the stones and shells, the burning rock walls, the heat and tracks, was that the standard geology of the Grand Canyon was warped and awry. The man had descended a canyon that ran through the heart of the Surprise Valley. Surprise Valley was formed by a series of enormous landslides, perhaps a dozen in all, the biggest landslide complex in the entire Grand Canyon. In total, a two-by-eight-kilometer section of rock and earth broke off the rim of the Esplanade and slumped a half-mile into the river corridor—an event so substantial that geologists refer to it as "bedrock land slippage." We walked through the rubble of these slides. The canyon's distinctive sedimentary layers were present and recognizable, but rather than layered striations, all was rubble, upturned and askew.

The evening was long, but dusk in the confines of a canyon within a canyon is brief. Kirk and I lay our sleeping pads over a stretch of sand broken by the man's footprints and ate our freeze-dried meals in near silence. What we could see of the night sky between the narrow walls was veiled in clouds. We didn't talk about the clouds, about how sleeping in a sandy wash in a narrow canyon in monsoon season was a way of tempting fate. But it was on my mind, and I knew it was on Kirk's. I slept fitfully, in and out of dreams, bothered by the mosquitoes, the heat, the grit on my bare skin. I awoke in predawn to a rising nasal whistle, a *toweeeep* shriek, and only minutes later, hearing the *hoo, hoo-hoo*, did I recognize the owl screech and call. I lay on my pad and watched the bats spasm through the soft spreading light. By the time we were up and hiking, the sun was sliding down the western slope like a guillotine. It was five days after he should have emerged. The first traffic on the Park Service radio concerned flying in a cadaver-sniffing dog.

Within ten minutes of scrambling downcanyon, we came to another pour-off. The bedrock streambed funneled between two cliff walls and abruptly ended, continuing a good 120 vertical feet below. I lay my bare belly on the burnished red floor and inched my head over the drop. The pour-off was overhung—I could look straight down at the rocky streambed below and crane my neck to see the cliff wall concaving beneath me. I suddenly remembered how, the night before we flew in for this search, Luke, with his cast-encased foot propped on a pillow and his eyes alternating between musing vacancy and sparkling intoxication, had told me he'd been praying a lot those last few weeks.

I made my way along the slope to the left of the pour-off, seeing if the man could have avoided the drop and continued downcanyon. If not, there was no point in going over the edge. There was scant space on the steep slope between the sheer cliff above and the sheer cliff below—any misstep and I would have slid over the lip. The only person we knew to have ever hiked this canyon—an affable old canyon ranger—had described the rock as "manky." We didn't know what the word meant, but we didn't have to ask: we well knew the Canyon's rotten rock. I stretched out each foot and scraped the manky scree to form a foothold before stepping into it; the loosened shale skittered into freefall. I stopped every so often and scanned the slope for similar tracks but saw nothing, perhaps because I was so carefully attending to my own footing. I made the traverse—certain the man-boy could have done the same—and returned to the pour-off. Kirk, watching my slow progress, had already pulled out our gear and set up the rappel.

I was accustomed to the heat but was ripe with sweat. The littlest things—fumbling with my climbing harness, a slip of the foot—and the sweat sprang out all at once. I was happy to have it, for I knew there were only so many layers of sweat and that, in time, it would grow thicker, ranker, and eventually stop. I knew sweat was effective only if it evaporated, and I noticed the beads and sheets didn't seem to be evaporating, just runneling down my skin. I also knew the instant irritation at the little nothings that cued some of my sweat flushes signaled the first stages of heat exhaustion.

Kirk rigged an anchor around a large rock perched on the lip of the fall. We clipped ourselves to the rope, and, one after the

other, leaned back into the void and stepped off the edge. Our feet
touched the vertical wall for two steps, then the wall curved away
from us, and we hung, twisting in midair. Kirk zipped down, the
rope whirring through his harness clip. I played the rope slowly
out of mine, enjoying the vertigo that blossomed and pressed my
stomach.

About one hundred yards downstream we found a single footprint in a spill of sand. We sat for a while in the last of the shade
and watched the track change with the rolling sun. The shadows
marking the cupped earth seeped into the sand, and the bleached
track all but disappeared.

The night Luke fell, a number of us had gathered to eat dinner—indeed, Luke's car pulled up, and we cheered, only to have
Kirk rush out and tell us what had happened—and talk turned
to the Canyon and how many of us believed it was, in a way, its
own entity, an eminent or inspirited force with a penchant for
the occasional bitch slap. Most opined that this punishment was
meted out toward those lacking the requisite respect, those who
underestimated or abused the Canyon, but others at the table argued it had more than a little Old Testament retributive wrath,
and would lash even devotees: hence, the handhold that gave on
poor Luke. But I don't believe in a conscious or concerned force, be
it the Canyon or God. Nor do I believe that one can trace an effect
back to a single cause, be it a slight or a mistake.

Nobody knows the exact sequence of events that sparked the
Surprise Valley landslides, or even the time frame in which they
occurred—whether as a sustained and gradual (albeit geologically
quick) slumping or a more typical crash-and-boom collapse. We
know many probable causes: the saturation and lubrication of an

underlying shale strata, the exposure of that shale by the incision of the Colorado River, the significantly wetter climate. But a more exact sequence, a more detailed geomorphic autopsy has yet to emerge, if it ever will.

Nor will we ever know the exact sequence of events that led to this man's journey down this canyon. We know he called his dad before he left and told him when he should return. We know where he parked his car, where he left his backpack, where he ate a snack. We know his brain flooded his skin with sweat, as it flooded his capillaries with blood seeking temperatures cooler than his core. It is likely that his head hurt, a heavy clenching of the mind. Perhaps the strange veil fell across his vision—a sparking of sunspots, his sight marred by floating, psychedelic dust motes. With all his blood pressing against his skin, less blood went to his muscles and brain. His brain had already begun to malfunction—dehydration, like inebriation, allowed bad decisions: abandoning his backpack, leaving the trail, striking off down an unknown canyon. His body, unable to dissipate the heat, began to cramp, stiffen, stumble. His stomach heaved with nausea. His world spun. He tore off his pants. His body became a furnace—at 104 degrees, his life was threatened. At 106 degrees, brain death began. He slipped into a coma.

We know where he died.

After edging past the last pour-off, he hiked downstream. The canyon walls opened into spread-out hills, with an open view of the Colorado River corridor barely a quarter-mile away. The river—water, life—was right there. Perhaps, then, he had hope, though that last pour-off was surely still lodged in his mind like a thorn. And then the open canyon, almost a valley, swung to the south, and the strata shifted into the banded purple-brown

Tapeats sandstone, and there, after all that, so close, so scared, alone, crazed, he scrambled down a series of bedrock ledges, hoping that what he saw wasn't what he saw, and peered off the lip of his life.

On a boulder at the lip of the final, undescendable pour-off was the dead man in the dumb heat. He was draped across the boulder on his belly. He was naked below the waist, and his skin was burnt near black. It was as though he had fallen from a height onto the boulder. It was as though someone or something had placed him on the boulder. There were liquid stains on the boulder and bedrock ledge beneath his head. Maybe he died while bent over the boulder and vomiting; maybe he stood and fainted forward and died, and, in death, his swelling body's liquid ran out of his mouth. What sticks with me, more than the liquid stains, the red-black skin of his bare legs, was the twist in his left knee, the way the muscles and tendons and ligaments skewed and slackened in death.

After some time regarding death, or perhaps in reaction to it, I studied the rock he died on, a water-smoothed boulder of Temple Butte limestone. I thought of how billions of ancient sea organisms died, piled up on the sea floor, were covered by silt and sediment, and, after hundreds of millions of years of pressured weight and heat and uplift and erosion, became this boulder now squatting at this cliff lip, serving as a cradle for death. I thought of how, in a millennium or two, the boulder will be pushed off toward the river, how it will crumble in time and make its way as silt to the ocean floor. As would this man-boy's body, a body like a potsherd in the dust, a ruin, a body to be taken out of this canyon, in a bag attached to a helicopter, and buried in real soil with grass on top. I looked at the body, and I looked up at the implacable face of the distant slopes, the pockets of beauty I had become accustomed to, pockets my ancestors had to learn to find beautiful, and past them, I looked into the white sky, at the spark of the sun in cold space.

·~ :~

After scrambling down the Kaibab cliffs, traversing along the Toroweap, rappelling down the Coconino cliffs, sliding down the Hermit shale, chimneying through the Esplanade sandstone, zigzagging through the remaining Supai terraces, traversing atop the Redwall limestone, after four hours in the August sun, Erika, Kirk, and I arrived at the saddle, stashed our packs in the shade of a scrawny juniper, and were only then ready to begin the true climb, the colossal mass of Vishnu Temple rising another two thousand feet above us.

So back up the same strata we'd scurried down, the patterns of slope/cliff/slope the same as the way down but the threading up them different. Up and up, some tricky moves but we were making great time, which we had to, as the sun hadn't much longer in the sky, and we didn't want to descend in the dark. The last push to the pinnacle-like summit, and there, in the final twenty vertical feet of the entire massif, loomed the most dangerous part of the day: a four-move boulder problem with tremendous exposure on rotten rock.

We fall, we die.

This is not an uncommon occurrence in the Grand Canyon. There are times, many such times, when you do not want to fall. There are times, many such times, when it is not the fall so much as the remoteness of the tortured topography that will kill you. Danger abounded, and we'd all had our close calls. I'd almost stepped on a rattler deep in the backcountry. A lightning bolt struck insanely close to Kirk and me while we sat on the rim watching a thunderstorm. One season the concessionaires hosted an employee party to celebrate the closing of the North Rim lodge: a band played in the lodge's foyer, a bonfire raged in the fireplace on the veranda, and I drank so much bourbon that on the bike ride home, up the hill to our FEMA trailer, I swerved back and forth, and maybe even fell asleep for a moment, because I came to, confused, lying on my back on a steep slope, my bike light shining fifteen feet below me, and a small light that it took me a moment to realize was Erika's headlamp a good twenty feet above me, and Erika's voice, filtering down to me, thick with worry—"Oh, my god, are you okay?"—and it only then occurred to me that I'd biked off the rim of the Grand Canyon. Trying to climb back up the scree with my bike, I kept sliding farther and farther down, and, being drunk, and figuring that I was never going to be able to get out of this Canyon, all I could do was laugh and laugh, and even later, back in our trailer, with Erika scolding me, furious, still all I could do was laugh, because, really, I was alive and unscathed and very drunk, but also because I was not just alive but *living*, the two, in my mind, not synonymous or mutually assured, one associated with breathing, eating, sleeping, shitting, the other associated with drinking, dancing, laughing, and, if so be it, the occasional headlong plummet into the place I'd learned to love like no other.

But I'm not, really, so much a fool. I know that getting hurt, badly hurt, is often the outcome of such endeavors, and that the denial of this inevitably is a crucial component of what I'll readily admit can be an adolescent way of living one's only life—a way I was, perhaps belatedly, learning to forsake. As much as a small, irrational, imbecilic part of me flirted with these touched-by-god experiences—wanted to get tapped by energy five times hotter than the sun, wanted to get recirculated in that chasmal hole in Upset Rapid, wanted to feel the burn of a rattler's poison—the stubborn reality is that the burst of lightning above our head that day made me jump as I've never jumped in my life, the few times I had to swim rapids in the Grand made me never want to repeat the ordeal, and the sight of a rattler spasming in anger underfoot made me spin so quick in panic that I pushed Erika out of the way in my haste to flee.

Nor have I remained entirely unscathed. We once worked sixteen days in a row repairing the Bright Angel Trail after a particularly savage monsoon storm. On the seventeenth day I'd unearthed a huge, obelisk-like rock to use rebuilding a wall, but since it was too long to fit between the rock trail liners to roll down to my work site, I'd used all my strength to stand it on end and then let it flop over downtrail. This worked well for a good fifty feet, but then fatigue set in, or my string of luck frayed, and in the instant the boulder reached its balancing apex I slipped and fell backward and the boulder crashed back down onto my knee, which was pinned against a liner rock. The impact crushed the peroneal nerve in my knee; it was eight months or so before I could fully lift my toes off the earth.

Half an hour into our Vishnu hike, picking her way down a narrow chute in the Toroweap, Erika stepped on a loose, microwave-sized rock. The rock dislodged. She fell forward, the rock rolled over her ankle, and barreled downslope at Kirk and me, who scattered. Her ankle was scraped and bruised, but she wanted to continue the climb. Still, she was shaken, and for the rest of the hike she was cautious and slow. That incident, even the gravest

possible repercussions of that incident, paled in comparison to the
lethal repercussions of those final moves before us.

Kirk, the best climber I've ever known, had danced up the last
twenty feet without a thought, the exposure nothing, the rotten rock nothing, and disappeared from view atop the summit.
Whatever self-congratulatory lines I've written about the way the
Canyon burned through me, Kirk's burning made mine look like
smoldering. When his excitement spiked, which was often, he
burned like a crown fire. The Canyon may have sat closest to his
heart, but the boy was always off crushing climbs in Patagonia,
the Tetons, Zion, Yosemite, the Bugaboos, his phenomenal climbing abilities matched only by his utmost humbleness about them.
Praised for his climbs, he had an utterly disarming response: "I
just like being outside." But that was only half of it. His slight, wiry
frame simmered with the need to be physically active. We'd be at
the base of a cliff, searching for a route up, and I'd look away for an
instant, and when I turned back he'd be halfway up the cliff face.
We'd get off work and I'd shower and collapse into a chair with a
beer and a book; Kirk would go jogging. Or he'd load up his dirt
bike with his camera gear and go roaring down one of the myriad
fire roads scarring the Kaibab Plateau to scout routes or take pictures. He was probably already scribbling in the Vishnu summit
register the end lines of the Jack London quote he'd framed above
his kitchen sink: "The function of man is to live, not to exist. I shall
not waste my days trying to prolong them. I shall use my time."

But Erika and I still stood there, discussing how to prolong
our days. Erika has a catlike tendency to scramble up a cliff or
tree without a care, but when time comes to descend she stiffens,
her eyes deepen into pools, and she starts mewling. She hates

down-climbing—hates having to look into the abyss, hates having to commit herself, however slightly, to the pull of gravity; hates it so much that I know once she summits her jubilation will be tempered by the knowledge that she'll have to make these same four moves in reverse. So we stood there, and Erika cried a bit, and we talked it over, the obvious thing being not to fall, the less obvious thing being not to look down, except at your footholds, and the unspoken thing being: well, do we have to climb up there?

Not the first time we'd faced such a choice.

Once, in South America, Erika and I had already walked something like thirty kilometers in the pouring rain by the time we got to the river. The thing was: there shouldn't have been a river there. At best a creek. But we crested a slight rise in the red clay road and it looked as though the road slid into a lake, and as we got closer it appeared that the middle of the lake was moving, and as we got even closer we saw the road emerging from the riverlake some hundred meters on the other side of the water. We had never before walked the road, only taken the dawn bus—the same bus that had not passed through the village that morning because the rain had disintegrated the roads and, apparently, caused creeks to overtop bridges.

"Is there even a bridge under there?" she asked.

I followed the road into the muddy swell, probing a stick in front of me. The water swifted across my belly button before I'd got a quarter of the way across the river. A log floated past me at a good clip, rolling with the current. I walked back to Erika.

"Well, we either walk back or we swim," I said.

She looked back the way we had come, our tracks like postholes through the ankle-deep mud.

"I don't think I can walk back," she said.

"Yeah."

The road's slick clay mud had necessitated an exhausting toe-gripping gait, and we weren't accustomed to walking so long, especially with packs, and I was barefoot, and my big toe hosted a painful *pique*, a parasitic chigoe flea. So we sat there, watching the water.

And then we waded in.

The river was thick with silt but warm. When the water reached her waist, Erika stopped. She looked unhappy. She muttered, "I can't believe we're doing this." I tried to come up with some encouraging words, failed, and instead offered some lame assurance about how our backpacks should float. We took a few more steps and the ground was no longer beneath us and we were swept downriver. Our backpacks did float, luckily, though towing them made for awkward side swimming. We struggled across, being swept ever farther downstream. Finally we reached a straggly grove of half-submerged trees. We clung to their branches for a while, catching our breath and bobbing in the waves, then pushed off and swam to calmer water within the flooded forest. We pulled ourselves along the overwhelmed branches, getting tangled in underwater vines, until finally we staggered out onto the mud bank and collapsed, panting, happy. After a while we stood, shouldered our bags, and set off farther down the road.

Every risk was different. Every risk had to be respected, sized up as dispassionately as possible, and weighed against the repercussions and rewards. If Erika and I had committed ourselves to some risks together, we had declined many others. The declining was as powerful, perhaps *more* powerful, as the commitment: turning away from Lava Rapid had taught me that restraint, or resisting expectations, demands, glory, whatever, takes its own, and in some ways greater, courage.

So, no, we didn't have to finish the climb.

But I had wanted to climb Vishnu ever since I first saw it dominating the skyline of the eastern Canyon: a titanic pyramid of rock rising out of the depths of the gorge, stunningly detached from the rim. Dutton found it "so admirably designed and so exquisitely decorated that the sight of it must call forth an expression of wonder and delight from the most apathetic beholder." Every different perspective—from atop Coronado peak, directly south; or from Cape Final, to the east, or Duck on a Rock Viewpoint, to the west (this last one with a full inversion layer obscuring almost the entire Canyon except for the tip of Vishnu)—strengthened its pull.

We didn't have to finish the climb.

But we had descended two thousand feet off the rim then ascended another two thousand back up this damn mountain and to turn aside at the last twenty feet would have been almost too cruel. Those last moves were why we climbed in the first place—the potential consequences of our actions cut through all the layers of inattention and distraction inherent in our twenty-first-century lives. Climbing brought about a keen and immediate involvement in the world. The entire world funneled into edges and cracks in rock. For a few vivid minutes seldom recognized minutiae—the presence of desert varnish, the tint of weathering, the texture of lichen—would have amplified, and essential, meanings in my life. Climbing dictates a wholehearted plunge that I'd intentionally avoided making in so many other aspects of my life, including, for the longest time, my relationship with Erika.

Watching Erika compose herself beneath that awful summit I

realized that we'd been committed all along. The risk our recurring separations posed to our relationship was always subsumed to our confidence in ourselves, our trust in one another, our submission to the attractive force that kept pulling us back together. I realized how lucky I was that the girl to whom I would commit was as committed as I was to an outdoor life. I realized that the biggest regret in my life would be to not commit to her, to not abandon my-self to our-selves.

We didn't have to finish the climb.

But at one particularly cuddly point in our relationship, we had decided that, were we ever to marry, we'd ask a dear friend to read Mary Oliver's poem "Spring," the crux of which reads: "There is only one question: / how to love this world."

This is how we loved this world.

Erika stood, smiled, wiped her tears with the back of a dusty hand, and slowly picked her way up the last moves of Vishnu. I followed.

The technical aspects of those last moves were unremarkable; dangerous but not difficult. One of the paradoxes of the intense concentration required in such situations is that it does not, at least for me, seem to employ the same mental circuitry that results in memory: I seldom remember individual moves in a climb unless they were carried out with unusual grace or resulted in a fall. What I do remember, almost always, is the exact moment when my concentrating mind's reduction of the world into tight, distinct moments relaxes and expands into the openness of the summit view, in this case the glory of the eastern Canyon: the burnt, rippled scarp face of the Palisades of the Desert, with Unkar Delta fanning into the main stem of the Colorado, the river muddy with monsoon runoff, and the indomitable horizon line of the Kaibab Plateau already casting a broad shadow on our camp, far below.

What I do remember is how, after having descended those four moves and then safely descended the bulk of Vishnu Temple and then eaten the calzones Erika had prepared the night before, we three spread our sleeping pads on bedrock ledges and lay on them and talked in happy exhaustion as we looked up at the night. I remember how the inky presence of Vishnu blotted the otherwise full flow of the Milky Way. I remember lying there, listening to Erika breathe in sleep beside me, and thinking that nothing mattered as much. Not writing, not Trails, not the Canyon. What were the Neruda lines? "When you surrender you stretch out like the world." I surrendered. It was August, during the Perseids, and green meteors disintegrated across half the sky.

AUTUMN

Much of the work season I measured either broadly or unconsciously: the snow, the melt, the heat, the monsoon, the brisk fall, the snow again. It was easy to recognize the peak of summer in those cloudless stretches of June sun, just as it was easy to acknowledge the nadir of winter in the brief days of January snow. But the incremental transitions between those poles, the finer shiftings of the seasons: the extra minutes of sunlight or stars, the often subtle phenologies of, say, little brown mushroom emergence, or biting blackfly week, or banana yucca bloom, or wild raspberry ripeness, those exact, ancient ways of marking the planet's rotation, were easy to overlook and even easier to miss completely, as so many of them flared and disappeared in just the five days we'd be out of the Canyon on break. So at certain points, especially near the end of summer, especially on the North Rim, its eight-thousand-foot elevation acting like a latitude adjustment, a northering, my consciousness seemed to lurch forward into the seasonal present, and I'd catch myself staring wistfully at the low slant of afternoon light on the translucent grass.

Eventually autumn became too obvious to ignore, its timbre

revealed in color on every scale and form: the Oregon grape and epazote reddening like wildfire; the bracken fern yellowing in the hollows; the richly textured trunk of the oldest ponderosas kindling incandescent orange in the alpenglow evenings. The softer light and the longer shadows made the color of the Canyon's walls seem to emanate intrinsically, as if from weird processes within the rock itself, just as the aspen's chlorophyll was draining from leaf to root. By October the summer green of the Kaibab Plateau's long meadows seemed but a brilliant and all-too-brief dream—lost to brown by September, gray by October.

The world resonated with that bone deep, bittersweet seasonal paradox of gathering and releasing. The Uinta chipmunks bounded between trees in last mad rushes to collect and store food. I'd sit in the booth in my trailer or cabin in the morning, drinking my maté and writing in my journal, watching the same deer I had watched in spring, the fawns having lost their spots, the yearlings shagged with the first mantle of a winter coat, all of them half-heartedly nuzzling the tawny, frost-limned grass.

Something so nostalgic, sentimental, and rich woven through that waning light of autumn. Something sad. The Canyon's rock was a structure outside of seasons, and thus offered solace of sorts. So too did the fact that, for most of my Canyon years, Trails had enough money to employ "seasonals" during the winter months. Still, even without a looming off-season, the world ached with what the Japanese called *mono-no-ware*, the beautiful sadness of temporality. I suspected the most confident and carefree among us harbored doubts about their decisions to remain out of the mainstream life. In autumn these doubts coalesced; with age they deepened.

What I was most susceptible to, in terms of *mono-no-ware*, was not simple transience: I did not mourn change in and of itself. Nor did I mourn that which I did not value. But I valued Trails: the work, the friendships. And over and over we faced the knowledge that, though our work helped people flow along the ancient pathways, in five hundred or five thousand years our maintained trails—like the ruined granaries, the potsherds in the dust, the abandoned asbestos mines, the dam at the head of the Canyon, our names on the land—would disintegrate and be forgotten, reclaimed by the earth of which they were made. We could respect, even celebrate, that the eventual collapse of our trails is the continuing creation of the Canyon, but deeper still—and I think this twined round my need to ferret out new routes to hike—is a sadness. That we live, as Augustine said, "in time already gone." That my crew would soon peel off into other lives, one by one, or in atomizing rushes. That I too would leave the Canyon, and, in time, crumble into dust myself. That all trails end.

ᴖ: ᴐ

Earth had rolled on its ellipses onto the celestial equator, strung us halfway between the solstices, and, as if to give credence to the discredited theory of an equinoctial storm, a ferocious thunderstorm enveloped the Canyon. The following morning Michael and I were hiking down the soggy North Kaibab to our work site when a man hiking uptrail paused and took note of my uniform and radio.

"You a ranger?"

"No. Do you need one?"

"Yeah, I need some help. Well, not me"—and with this he nodded over his shoulder—"him."

Behind him stood a man, his head down, his arm outstretched onto a trekking pole that the first guy extended behind him. This man was essentially being towed out of the Canyon. Apparently he'd been so exhausted by his hike or so terrified by the storm (or both) that he had spent the night beneath a rocky overhang, shivering through the storm. Which would explain the mud and leaves matted in his hair and ear.

"He's okay," continued the Good Samaritan. "But I think his family will want to know he's making it out."

"Yeah, of course. I'll call Dispatch. A ranger will probably meet you at the trailhead."

"Thanks."

They continued uptrail. The bedraggled man hadn't said a word. I don't think he'd even raised his head.

I waited until I was done calling Dispatch before I dared a glance at Michael.

He was looking uptrail at the pair, grinning his half-grin.

"Did you see the pine needles stuck in that guy's hair?" he said.

The Canyon, I told Michael as we continued on downtrail, re-minded me of India.

In my travels I'd been struck by how many of us tourists and travelers seemed to experience the places we were passing through as though we had never left home. To a degree, everybody, no mat-ter where they go, remains tethered to the places they are from and the people they were in those places. But this was more than the reflexive spasms of self-identity: this was a form of protection. Certain circumstances may have allowed us or forced us to emerge from our shells of self and culture and into the "Other," into the place we were physically passing through, but then the dislocations of travel almost inevitably caused us to retreat into our shells.

Which was unfortunate. Travel offered the opportunity to step outside oneself, to challenge and expand and destroy what that self was accustomed to, what it knew or expected or perceived. For all the ways new cultures, languages, and landscapes enlarge one's understanding of the greater world, perhaps the greatest thing about travel is in T. S. Eliot's old adage—"the end of all our exploring / will be to arrive where we started / and know the place for the first time." But not just "place": self. I believed in the paradox that one knows the Self only in relation to the Other, yet the best—perhaps only—way to know that Other is through the (temporary and nonphysiological) annihilation of the Self.

Some tourists are better at or more interested in emerging out of their shells and becoming immersed into the Other, and some places more than others press against or penetrate that shell, and India, like no other place I've been, took a sledgehammer to that shell. You could not escape. Every instinctual act of mental evasion or refuge was interrupted and overcome by the place's sights and sounds and smells and general, inescapable overwhelm.

As we walked, I told Michael of how, our first day in Kolkata, Erika and I walked to Khalighat, the great Kali Temple for which Kolkata was named. Outside the Temple were hundreds of aged, begging widows, some too feeble to raise their alms bowls, some literally dying on the street. Inside the temple a Brahmin in unblemished white robes raised a scimitar and with a single stroke beheaded a goat. The carcass was flung on a huge pile of other decapitated goats—they'd kill hundreds by the end of day—which were being skinned by Dalit tanners. Supplicants approached the chopping block and dipped their hands and marked their foreheads with goat blood. Another priest slung a bucket of blood on the black-faced idol of Kali; a thousand flies rose in a momentary cloud. A dramatic scene, to be sure, but the thickness of it—the incense and crowd and blood and heat and humidity—seemed to me emblematic of the way India itself pressed against you.

Like India, the Canyon demanded attention. A single misplaced step could shatter your ankle or send you hurtling over a cliff to your death. Like India, the Canyon overwhelmed; there was a pressing immediacy to its physical and conceptual bombardment. Both India and Canyon were sensuous in ways not synonymous with sex or pleasure, as how the tourist mules would repeatedly gush milky-green piss in the same spots on the trail, which in short time became stagnant cesspools of constantly evaporating and repuddling urine, the hoofprints filling with sludgy, brown-yellow liquid, the overpowering ammonia matched only by the orgy of flies that rushed up from the fresh green shit scattered twenty yards downtrail. After weeks in the sun, the mule-piss spots turned tar black, curling on the edges like rotting flesh.

Like India, the Canyon both clarified and obliterated the old Cartesian dualities between observer/observed, human/nature, heart/mind. The Canyon's heat, cold, storms, and aridity destroyed the notion of apartness, as this poor hiker had learned as he sheltered from the elements of darkness and equinoctial storm. I wish, now, that after he had showered and slept, I could have sat with him in the saloon, bought him a drink, and asked about his close encounter with the night, if in the howling storm he could have believed that the lightning cobwebbing the sky and the thunder guttering the night were the acts of the kachina. If in the darkest hours he felt the touch of Kali, the black one beyond time. I wondered, too, if beneath his distress and fear endured a genetic acceptance, a cellular-level remembrance of millions of years of similar such miseries.

I wonder because, despite many close calls, I have never been in his situation. For all my time in the wild—including some desperate times—I've always made it back to camp, or had the gear to pitch camp where circumstances dictated. For all my drunken revelry, I've never blacked out or failed to make it to my sleeping place. For all my psychoactive escapades I've never, not once, truly lost myself. As far down the entheogenic rabbit hole I've tripped, I've always, quite unconsciously, employed a sort of cognitive lifeline that allowed me to retain just enough rational self to keep me from truly plumbing oblivion. This disappointments me. Much of the reason I've thrown myself into travel, or danger, or hallucinogens, was in hopes of easing if not abandoning entirely that acute sense of—and tight grip—on self. I suppose I should be thankful for this resiliency. But in the end it has kept me, I believe, from knowing the self as I wanted to know the Canyon: as it is known by snake and sagebrush.

A half-mile farther downtrail, Michael and I were still chuckling about the mud caked in the dude's ear when LTB came charging down the trail. When LTB gets excited, his eyes widen and he pants.

"Rockslide! Just on the radio! Mules can't get through! Jasper Falls!" he blurted.

He paused for a moment, searching our faces for corresponding exultation. Apparently finding an insufficient amount, he snorted and resumed running downtrail. Michael and I looked at each other, grinned, shrugged, and continued walking, moving a bit faster, excited by the possibilities of the slide, but now laughing at Tom Boyle rather than the guy who'd had to curl under a rock.

We decided we knew the exact location of the slide. Some years prior a large section of Muav limestone had sheared off the wall near Jasper Falls, and even then it was obvious that much more remained to fall. Sure enough, the storm had caused another huge section of the broken cliff to calve. The trail in that section was essentially a ledge blasted into a sheer cliff—indeed, the cliff wall was collapsing exactly *because* the trail had undermined it—so much of the debris had plummeted into the canyon below. What remained occupied the whole of the trail ledge. Within a few hours the three of us had trundled and raked enough of the debris to allow the mule-train of tourists stuck on the downhill side to pass through. But a few massive slabs remained, so the following day Michael and I humped a pionjar and set of feathers and wedges down from our work site, a good mile uptrail, and began to split the slabs.

Something mystical resided in those remaining slabs of 500-million-year-old rock: what Robert Hass dubbed the "powerful, directionless, hungry, theatrical, terrifying, beautiful, and incessant play of the energies of transformation." The compressed, thinly bedded, gray-green Muav limestone made me sympathize with LTB's aversion to gloves. Watching him run his bare hands over the bare rock made me think of the voice of God in the burning bush telling Moses, "Remove the sandals from your feet, for the place where you stand is holy ground." Who was LTB—who were any of us—to place a dirty work glove between calloused skin and sacred stone?

I've never needed to equate sacredness with divinity—the feelings that I receive as sacred do not arise as revelations from some meddling god. They are born of me and a particular place, of me in that place, that place in me, and all entailed by that entanglement. A beautiful tension lay between the opposing pulls of work and place: for all the ways the Canyon drew you toward it or hammered on your shell of self, trail work had its own magnetism, its

own ways of working into you, claiming you. Splitting those slabs
that day, I felt that sacredness. That Khalighat-like ritual.

I used a small rock to scratch the intended split lines onto the
slab, quartering or halving the rock, sometimes merely marking
the dross to remove in order to form a more perfect face. All the
while I paid attention to the rock's natural grain, searching for the
seams, weaknesses, or stresses that might affect the split. Much
of Muav is mudstone, with layered, flat-plate minerals tending to
break off in ugly sheets. But I'd impose my intended split line regardless, figuring to compensate by drilling an extra few holes to
assure a clean break.

With the pionjar I'd drill three to five deep and evenly distrib-
uted holes across the length of the rock. The dust from the drilled
rock would powder my inner calves white, and the oil from the
pionjar would pox the white dust black. Into the holes I'd place the
feathers and wedges. A wedge is just that—a foot-long, tapered
steel wedge. Feathers resemble wedges, but are generally shorter,
don't taper to an edge, and bend outward at the ends. Two feathers
into each hole, the crack between them aligned with the intended
split of the rock. Between the feathers go the wedges, tapped down
until tight.

With a single-jack or double-jack, I slowly and evenly hammer
on the wedges. With each blow the wedges enter deeper into the
rock, pushing the feathers apart. With each blow the resistance
increases. With increased resistance the pitch of hammer head on
wedge head rises, as though ascending the bars of a xylophone:
tong tong, teng teng, ting ting. Eventually the wedges seem stuck,
incapable of farther descent. I'd wait, listening. Nothing. One
more blow. Listen. Another blow. And then I'd hear it: a dry, crin-
kling sound coming from the weakening rock. The stone, singing.

The heat and sun or cold and wind faded, Canyon and self were reduced, forgotten: all was song. Another blow, casual now, the popping noises sustained, louder, like ice cubes dropped in warm water, the stone molecules shearing with the strain. A final blow and the crack opens along the intended line, a black sliver through the white dust of the split rock.

The rock would crack and I'd look up and out at my surroundings: the achingly blue sky, the burnt red walls, Michael and LTB joyously heaving debris into the depths of Roaring Springs Canyon. My focus would take a second to expand again so wide, and again I'd be struck by the immensity, again the Canyon would come rushing onto me, and again I'd turn to the pionjar to drill more holes in that sacred rock, and again the work would swallow my attention, that oscillation the essence of Trails: the rubble at my feet the exhaustion of form, the work and world a welcome exhaustion of self.

~: ~

Walter and I were paid overtime by the interpretive rangers to install signs on the South Rim. The signs' placards were inscribed with an icon of a ringing cell phone and a series of numbers, so that one could dial the number, punch in the code, and listen as a recorded voice recited factoids about fossiliferous limestone or John Wesley Powell or whatever. Or so we assumed—we never actually called, figuring that the signs were yet another automated and thus cheaper alternative to hiring living and breathing humans to interact with tourists.

Not that Walter necessarily cared about real breathing people. Interacting with tourists was the last thing he wanted to do. Walter was one of the most misanthropic people I've ever met. Intelligent,

opinionated, and capable of a bitter intellectual cruelty, he held
some edgy views about, among others, capital punishment (mainly,
kill them all) and paying his taxes (mainly, not). He was fiercely
loyal to his friends, and sweet as a lamb to his girlfriend, but didn't
give a damn about strangers. Especially if they were fat. He hated
fat people. As it so happened, having to place twenty-two posts in
the heart of the South Rim in the thick of the Labor Day tourist
season, we were surrounded by some serious corpulence. We were
surrounded by a lot of people, period.

The legislation that established the National Park Service in
1916 declared its purpose to "conserve the scenery and the natural
historic objects and the wild life therein and to provide for the
enjoyment of the same in such manner and by such means as will
leave them unimpaired for the enjoyment of future generations."
But it seemed to me that the park administration paid far more
attention and contributed far more resources to the mandate of
"provide for the enjoyment" than they did that of "conserve." This
was nothing new—as Richard West Sellars writes in *Preserving
Nature in the National Parks*, "Nature preservation—especially
that requiring a thorough scientific understanding of the resources intended for preservation—is an aspect of park operations
in which the Service has advanced in a reluctant, vacillating way."
From the beginning, the Park Service, largely as a matter of necessity, constructed itself as a tourist-based industry. The incipient
bureau lacked a strong political base (unlike the young Forest
Service's ranching, mining, and timber industry allies) and thus
turned to the most powerful ally it could: the railroads, who were
already promoting recreational sightseeing. It's not hyperbole to
say that the Atchison, Topeka & Santa Fe Railway and the Fred
Harvey Company almost wholly created what we now know as the

South Rim Village. Almost a century later tourism has become the major source of revenue in the West, and the National Park Service has long put emphasis, at times overriding emphasis, on tourism development.

Every once and awhile I'd catch snippets of the mini-lectures that interpretive rangers gave as they led groups of hikers down the South Kaibab or as they roamed the South Rim's promenade. In one of their go-to speeches they would quote Joseph Ives, who in 1857 explored the western reaches of the Grand Canyon. "The region," they would recite, "is, of course, altogether valueless.... Ours has been the first and will doubtless be the last, party of whites to visit this profitless locality. It seems intended by nature that the Colorado River, along the greater portion of its lonely and majestic way, shall be forever unvisited and undisturbed." The crowd of tourists would chuckle and shake their heads—man, wasn't that guy a fool.

Poor Ives—to be remembered more for uttering one dead-wrong opinion than he ever will be for the adventures of his expedition or later life. How could he have known what the Canyon would become? That he himself was able to appreciate the scenery—pausing in "wondering delight, surveying this stupendous formation"—might have been a clue, but his was one of the first generations in Anglo-American history to be able to see the desert as an object worthy of aesthetic contemplation. Even the old miners—the Bill Basses and Pete Berrys—shrewd enough to build hotels and tourist camps on the rim rather than mines in the Canyon could hardly have imagined that in a century's time nearly 6 million visitors from all over the world would stream into the Canyon every year; or that, in 2013, when the cycle came anew for private companies to bid on the contract to run the hotels and restaurants and mule rides, the National Park Service estimated the combined gross revenue from these concessions to be almost $100 million a year, or $1.5 billion over the life of the fifteen-year contract.

I knew this. I knew that tourism was part of the park's mandate. I knew that Trails, by providing tourists access to the sublime, was essentially a service industry; that much of our pay derived from the fees tourists paid to enter the park. Yet I was disgusted by much of what Abbey had decried as "industrial tourism." I hated the traffic of the South Rim, the crowds, the noise, the inevitable effects; hated how the park administrators and their congressional superiors seemed more concerned with the Canyon as a catered source of enjoyment for humans than as a functioning and fragile ecosystem.

Some of this was out of management's control: they were simply responding with what little resources they had to a dramatic increase in visitation. In my time at Grand Canyon, visitation rose 25 percent; 5.5 million people passed through the gates in 2015. During peak weekends, we're talking an estimated 40,000 people *a day* clogging the campgrounds, roads, trails, restaurants, and parking spaces of the South Rim. Yes, half the mission of the Park Service is to welcome visitation to public lands, and yes, people are more likely to support and cherish—maybe even contribute to the protection of—places they have visited. But the saying is true: we're "loving the parks to death." The campgrounds are full every day for eight months, the most popular sunset photo viewpoints are dozens of people thick, the intense competition for securing a private river trip during the more temperate months renders success nearly impossible.

At the same time that visitation began skyrocketing in the late

2000s, annual appropriations from Congress, which make up nearly 88 percent of the National Park Service budget, declined 8 percent. Little wonder, then, that as of 2016 there was a backlog on service-wide maintenance of $11.9 billion—almost twice as much as Congress annually appropriates for the NPS. In 2016 Grand Canyon National Park accounted for $371,589,415 million of that deferred maintenance, largely owing to the need for a new $24.5 million wastewater treatment plant and at least a $160 million upgrade to the park's antiquated trans-canyon water pipeline. All this with the park's 2015 annual operating budget only some $20 million.

In some ways, the deferred maintenance is a less troubling facet of the pressures affecting the park than the unrelenting pursuit of profit by private industries: those seeking to allow mountain bikes in the wilderness areas, or to build a gondola to the confluence of the Little Colorado and the Colorado. Or the aviation-based sight-seeing industries operating near the South Rim Village and the Hualapai reservation in the western reaches of the Canyon. The Hualapai, for some reason unconstrained by FAA regulations, run unlimited air tours along a twenty-two-mile stretch of river corridor. A National Geographic team hiking that stretch in 2015 counted 262 flights in five hours, and claimed that busy days can see 450 or more. The chatter and buzz of low-flying helicopters, minute to minute, hour to hour, sunrise to sunset, mar a place once as rich in natural quiet as anywhere in the world. There has been no shortage of complaints over the past thirty years, and to its credit the Park Service tried to impose tougher noise standards on the 400,000-people-a-year overflights based off the South Rim. In 2012, after decades of planning and studies, and at the eventual taxpayer-funded cost of $6 million, Grand Canyon National Park completed a Final Environmental Impact Statement aiming to let 70 percent of the park experience "substantial natural quiet." This didn't entail pristine quiet—in fact, the plan would have allowed *more* annual tourist flights than had ever occurred—but even so, the $120-million-a-year air tour industry wasn't taking any chances and successfully lobbied Arizona and Nevada congresspeople into inserting a rider into the 2012 transportation bill that blocked the Park Service's ability to restrict overflights.

And so there I was with Walter the Misanthrope, about to install a sign into the lower patio of Lookout Studio, the beating heart of the industrial tourism beast. Having worked on the Corridor trails for six years, I'd have figured that I was accustomed to tourists. After all, most of the trail degradation, and thus most of the reason for our jobs, could be laid, literally, at the feet of the fifty thousand people a year hiking the trails. After ten years, solid sandstone riprap wore down so thoroughly under foot and hoof that it bowed in the middle like a canoe. At times, repairing sections of trail on the first few miles of the Bright Angel Trail, I'd spend far more time waiting patiently for tourists to pass than I would swinging a pick or planting a shovel. I didn't always mind—Teddy Roosevelt observed that the preservation of nature was "essentially a democratic movement," and sure enough, the democratic masses offered superb people-watching.

Dutch, German, Spanish, Italian, Chinese, a dozen dialects of English: a microcosm world flowed downtrail. There were white women with no bras and breasts hanging to their waists or petite Asian women with elbow-length gloves carrying Wal-Mart plastic bags with twelve ounces of water in the hundred-degree sun. Girls in prairie dresses, bonnets and hiking boots, or Indians in saris and velvet sandals, or sorority girls with faux cowboy hats and slivers of butt cheek peeping out beneath booty shorts. There were men with legs too spindly for their bellies and voices too loud for their words, draped in garish pastels or Hawaiian shirts with cargo shorts. Athletic men in brand new hiking gear and expensive cameras aimed at turkey vultures they'd mistaken for condors. Strange survival freaks in head-to-toe camo with old-school metal canteens and huge serrated knives strapped to their thighs. Sinewy, gazelle-like rim-to-rim-to-rimmers in wraparound sunglasses and spandex.

And the shoes! Tevas or Chacos or Jesus sandals, sandals with socks, sandals with toilet paper stuffed under the straps to stop the blisters. Crocs, Vibram Five Fingers, Desert Storm combat boots, cowboy boots, biker boots, heels, dress shoes, Italian designer shoes, deck shoes, no shoes at all.

And the comments! The sincere thanks: "Thank you for your hard work" or "You're doing a great job." The convict jokes: "What crime did you commit?" or "A chain-gang, huh?" The escalator jokes: "You building an escalator?" or "When is the elevator going to be finished?" The questions: "How far is it to _____?" or "What are you doing?" or "Are you volunteers?" (This last consistently followed by "Well, they can't pay you enough for this.") The wise guy comments: "The US government is trying to fill the Grand Canyon!" or "So that's how the Canyon was built!" The insults: "See, son, this is what happens when you don't get into college." The bigot comments: "Y'all need to get some Mexicans to do this work." The spiritual comments: "That's a strange way to serve the Lord" or "The Ancient Ones left a lot of energy here." The Captain Oblivious comments: "You guys have a problem with erosion here?" The random comments: "Is

Phantom Ranch in a different time zone?" or "That's a good place
to commit suicide."

Easy to belittle how unbearably unsuited to the sere surroundings were these tourists. Easy to take offense at their condescension
or scoff at their stupidity. Easy to reflect ourselves against them,
to pit our often-inflated notions of belonging and knowing, our
opinions of ourselves as stewards and proprietors, against their in-
experience and inadequacy and ignorance. But that was when we
were on the trail, in our element. On the South Rim with Walter,
with the crowds surging along the promenade above us, the din of
their voices drowning out the sound of the wind on the rock, we
were the ones out of our element.

"Look at these fucking people," Walter said, not bothering to
lower his voice. He was rolling a cigarette without looking down at
it, his eyes sliding from one oversized belly to the next.

"I know it. The rim world. Let's see if we can close off this patio."

I only had a single small orange safety cone to close off access
to the patio, but figured the noise and dust would keep the tourist
hordes at bay. We needed to drive the posts at least ten inches deep
into the Kaibab limestone that caprocked the rim. The steel post
was wider than any of our drill bits, so for each post we had to
drill four holes in as tight a pattern as possible then chisel out the
remnant arcs of stone to make a single hole. It took almost thirty
minutes to drill each post. We'd switch off, one of us drilling the
holes, the other watching, relaxing—in Walter's case smoking—
until it was time to prep the "mud" and set the pole.

Walter fired up the pionjar and placed the spinning bit between
his steel-toes to control the initial bore. As the bit sank into the
stone the pulverized rock milled up as a thick, rich, yellow powder,
part turmeric, part cream. I reached forward to scoop some of the

powdered rock and idly rub it between my palms. I was watching the powdered ancient sea life and sand sift into the wind when something made me look up.

Above us, on the promenade, stood a man and his son. Both looked past us, into the Canyon. Something about the open expressions on their faces, the careful way the man rested his hand on the boy's shoulder, made me turn to follow their gaze. A California condor soared about ten vertical feet above and thirty horizontal feet from us. Within seconds another giant, primordial bird rose out of the Canyon to join the first. Then another. All three rose in tight circles until they coursed directly above our heads. Walter, with his ear protection on and his head wreathed in rock dust, hadn't noticed the birds. I threw a pebble past his sightline and he looked up at me. I pointed. He glanced up, did a double take, and with his head still craned back he turned off the pionjar. The roar of the machine died, replaced by the sound of the wind ripping through the condors' fretted feathers. It was easily the closest I had come to a condor—eye level, then a dozen feet above me— close enough to almost stretch out and touch.

For all the glory of their nine-foot wingspan, I'd long since come to the reluctant conclusion that condors are hideous-looking creatures. Their necks, bare to better shove into ground sloth carcasses, are pimpled, uneven, translucent-pink, resembling a sausage swollen in the sun. Their hatchet head crooks at an indignant, prudish angle on their distended neck, both neck and head looking as if they'd been randomly grafted onto the powerful black body. A hole for an ear. A bald slant of a forehead, stretched taut across the skull, mottled with black marks, slanting down into the twisted, overbit black beak, and all that acceptable, quite raptor-like, but then the horrible swollen cheeks, at times folded

into jowls, other times sagging like a dentureless grandma. And
their eyes! Stern, red, glaring eyes. Unlike ravens, there wasn't a
damn thing playful about the way they'd stare down at you with
those reptilian eyes, focusing on one thing: the unfortunate fact
that you're still alive.

But that day was different. That day it seemed as though their
release into the wild after captive breeding had made the world
new and exciting, that if not exactly playful they were certainly
curious about the pionjar's unusual chattering.

I glanced back at the man and his son. They had been joined
by dozens of other tourists, all pressed up against the railing, all
murmuring and smiling and pointing fingers and cameras, all their
faces lit by wonder and awe at what essentially felt like getting
buzzed by pterodactyls. I suddenly loved them for their happiness
at those ugly birds. I looked at Walter, and loved him for the way
he watched those ugly birds. I loved the Park Service for the care
and compassion they'd shown these ugly birds. The geographer
Yi-Fu Tuan defined "places" (as opposed to "spaces") as "centers of
felt value," and right then I, we, were feeling that value.

Eventually the condors coasted elsewhere. The crowd on the
railing dispersed. A few still stood looking out at the Canyon. I
stood looking at them. I looked over at Walter. He shrugged. He
fired the drill and again the air shuddered with vibrations and
clouded with dust. I brushed the last of the powder from my palms,
looked at the tourists, looked into the empty sky, then walked up
the stairs to mix the mud.

ᔌ ᔌ

"—you should be listening to the goddamn canyon wrens. Would
you even recognize a hermit thrush?"

I'm haranguing Walter and Ken about wearing their iPods when hiking.

"You should be paying attention, not immersing yourself in some insular bubble, listening to, to,"—fumbling—"fucking Jack Johnson."

They look at me.

"You don't like Jack Johnson?" Walter asks.

"No, I like Jack Johnson. That's not the poi—"

"Brodie doesn't like Jack Johnson," Walter tells Ken.

"That's 'cause he just listens to weird jungle music."

"Yeah. I think Jack Johnson's pretty good."

I know they're only getting started, so I shake my head and shoulder my pack and start uptrail. Behind me their conversation turns from Jack Johnson to Hawaii to surfing, then their breath picks up tempo with the ascent, their conversation stops, and in the silence I can hear from out of Ken's earbuds the tinny but unmistakable power chords to Billy Idol's "Rebel Yell."

As much as I can wax philosophical about the engraining nature of our daily hiking, we were not in a constant state of transcendentalist rapture. Exhausted by the work, we were too tired to attend to the Canyon every minute. Thoreau's "What business have I in the woods, if I am thinking of something out of the woods?" is a good line, to be sure, but the ol' hermit wasn't hiking in and out of the Canyon every single day for years on end. Hiking the same trail we'd hiked a thousand times got old, even boring, and at times we needed to turn ourselves inward as we trudged. In general, working Trails wasn't like those old Maoist propaganda posters showing happy socialist workers singing while tightening giant lug nuts. It wasn't like that at all. We bitched and moaned about the heat and the cold and the tourists and the rangers and the bosses and each other. The work could be dissatisfying, un-rewarding; it could be excruciatingly mundane, futile drudgery. It wasn't all trundling rockslide debris or blowing up boulders or hanging in harnesses, repairing blown-out retaining walls. We dug a lot of inglorious ditch. We raked down the shitcones in the backcountry composting toilets.

We all chose to be there, to work Trails. But some worked for the money, or because they were local, or because that's all they knew how to do. We weren't all climbers or conservationists or neopagan Lost Boys. We were conservatives and bigots. New England aristocrats and white trash roustabouts. Drifters and dirtbags and dropouts. Not all of us professed to a spiritual love of the Canyon, and even if we did, this didn't occlude the occasional act of aggression toward innocent pine trees. One kid worked on the crew for years even though he didn't like to hike.

So I knew I couldn't expect the crew to abide my self-righteous hectoring about receptivity to birdsong and river sound. Besides, I understand the appeal of the iPod: I know how the beat in the ears helps propel the feet up the trail. I know how music casts a cinematic shade on the world, so that one seems to move as a protagonist—a Rebel Yell hero, damnit—through a narrative that one controls with a push of a button. I know that it is in no way useful to first realize then eventually know that the wind sounds differently when sifting through needles of fir as opposed to pine. The ability to differentiate between wren, junco, and jay call does not make me a better person. Still, I like knowing the theory of biophony: that animals, by altering frequency and time shifting, evolved their calls so that they'd occupy their own unique sonic niche, so that their particular vocal territory is not masked by other beasties' bandwidths. I like thinking that beneath this exquisitely precise biophony are the slower rhythms of geophony: the cadence of drum sand, slab crack, slope creep. Beneath that the interminable rasp of fault shift and plate tectonics, and deeper still, within the earth's mantle, the howl and whine of isotope decay. I like considering how our bodies respond to these inaudible rhythms. Idle thought, of course. Borderline nonsense. But if you're in the right spot, and quick, and lucky, and not listening to Norwegian black metal, you can spot rocks as they clatter and erode downslope…*there*: a single fist-sized stone representing the whole aeonial process bounding down the cliffs, a single stone in a practical universe of stone, and all of it slipping, breaking, falling down, slab by slab, stone by stone, grain by grain.

There are doors of perception only open to the silent, and one of the reasons we spoke of our time in the Canyon as submergence—and, conversely, our "emergence" into, onto, the surface world—owed to the desert's literal and metaphysical silence. The silence of the Canyon seemed more than the lack of sound. There was texture to the way it blanketed stone; at times it seemed to seethe, hiss, hum; other times it had an underwater, womb-like, or vacuumed quality, as though the universe was holding its breath. One could seek out places and moments of absolute silence, but in general the Canyon offered too much rock for the wind to rub against. The river sings too loudly through the heart of it. There's the ubiquitous buzz of blackflies. The drone of airplanes descending into Las Vegas. The sudden whirr of a tarantula hawk. The clatter of rockfall. The scuff of foot. The air dispelled from lungs. And yet these ambient sounds are accents to the silence, minor perturbations to what was, really, a greater *stillness*.

This stillness was incessantly disrupted, most blatantly by the

annual intrusion of 6 million people (and their associated cars, bus-
ses, motorcycles, motorhomes, cell phones, radios, and larynxes).
Sometime around 2005 a cell phone tower was installed on the South
Rim. Within days of its operation, hikers were passing through our
work site, miles off the rim, talking on their cell phones (the most
common overheard snippet being, predictably, "You'd never believe
where I am"). If you are able to escape the crowds on the rim by
driving out to some remote spot, or the crowds on the Corridor
trails by hiking a backcountry trail, you're still often within audio
range of the incessant sightseeing helicopter overflights.

Obviously, human voices and helicopters weren't the only intrusions on the near-silent ambient hum of wind and river. But I felt
differently about corvid scream and cicada shrill. These instances
of nonhuman sound were still encompassed within "natural
quiet"—the Park Service's generally quixotic term for the absence
of man-made sounds.

But we live in an entwined, contested world: a Canyon of birds
and copters, larynx and syrinx, wind in the pines and iPods in the
ears. Take, for example, watching the sunset on one of the crowded
rim points, and the accompanying if unspoken code of conduct
that demands reverent silence. Again, I understand: silence is such
a rare phenomenon in our modern world, who wants a loud voice
blathering on about petty bullshit when one is watching a star be
spun out of view behind a distant horizon? I will state here, now,
that I believe the objectively best way of being in the Canyon is
sitting, preferably with a loved one, above or amid the rock, and
simply and silently listening. But the expectation of silence when
in a crowd thirty people deep seems contrived, a studied solemnity. This plotted piousness is why Mencken quipped that nature
is a place to throw beer cans on Sunday afternoons.

If I like to pay attention to the aural ways of the world for no other reason than avoiding a rattlesnake; if I wanted to bitch to my hiking companions about attentiveness, or fire off the occasional angry letter to those US senators blocking more-stringent over-flight regulations, I wasn't going to be tendentious with my crew. Not just because it was pointless: I knew well enough, by then, how we all become entrapped in our ways of seeing and knowing and being in the world.

∻ ∻

It was a crisp autumnal morning after a rainstorm, and water still dripped from leaves and pooled within rocks, and every drop and pool reflected the first light of the sun so that everything was the glint and twinkle of crystal. The last of the rainclouds within the Canyon were dissipating into scarves of drifting mist that alternately obscured then revealed an ashen ridge, a ghostly pair of pines. I was hiking, slowly, alone, down the North Kaibab Trail to the work site and was so moved by the beauty that I said to the first hiker I saw: "Isn't this amazing?"

She looked at me and then out at the Canyon. She shrugged. "But you can't see anything."

Years later, watching the sunset from the patio of the North Rim lodge, I heard a man say into his cell phone, "Well, you can't see the *actual* Grand Canyon from here," and I looked at him then back to the sweeping view of Deva, Brahma, and Zoroaster Temples, and I wondered what Grand Canyon he was expecting to see.

How we see the Grand Canyon—and thus a significant part of what we know of the Canyon—is influenced by expectations and anticipations formed long before we ever actually lay eyes on it:

the place as portrayed by a lifetime's worth of billboards, adver-
tisements, stamps, cartoons, calendars, postcards, TV shows, and
movies. This inundation of images—and the preconceived expectations they create—form what Walker Percy called the "symbolic
complex" of the Grand Canyon. This is powerful enough, Percy argues, that when one finally stands at the rim and looks at the abyss
he measures "his satisfaction by the degree to which the canyon
conforms to the preformed complex." This is the case whether the
Canyon measures up satisfactorily—say, with a perfectly photo-
genic thunderstorm sunset—or not, as was the case with the lone
hiker's clouded view.

The complex is an accretion of both culturally imposed expectations and those that arise out of personal needs, wants, and
worldviews. After all, the one person we know of in the enviable
position to appreciate the Canyon without the weight of previous
knowledge and expectation, indeed, a man whose utter lack of
previous experience or even possible conception of such a titanic
geologic phenomenon led him to believe that the Colorado River
was a mere six feet wide, didn't appreciate the place at all. García
López de Cárdenas, the Spanish conquistador searching for the
mythical cities of gold in 1540, was led by a Hopi guide to a place
on the South Rim "elevated and full of low twisted pines, very
cold, and lying open to the north." Looking across the ten-mile-
wide gorge, he saw the Canyon as nothing more than a significant
impediment to travel.

Hundreds of years after Cárdenas, few visitors have had all that
much more physical exposure to as singular a place as the Canyon
as Cárdenas had. The Canyon so defies perspective, its distances,
volume, and especially the timescale implicit in its rock stretch so
far beyond the limits of our conceptual framework that it's little

wonder so many accept the creationist viewpoint: rather than an alien time frame of 2.7 billion years, the Church offers a far more graspable and comforting time frame of six thousand years.

The Canyon that is conveyed through the Creationists' complex is, of course, a flawed construct, but we all have our filters. If the lone hiker's disappointment revealed her expectation to see the Canyon washed in the usual sunlight, my excitement at the change in that scene revealed as much of an expectation of the sunlit vistas as hers. We both had something at stake—she wanted to see far and wide on her rare trip to the Grand Canyon, while I focused more narrowly on the cloudy weather as perfect working conditions. Still, in my experience the unexpected and unforeseeable occurrences are often the best ways of breaking through the symbolic complex and seeing the world as more sovereign individuals: the impeded views of a cloudy day force us to look more closely at the microcosms of wildflowers; the flat tire provides a knees-on-the-ground opportunity to discover the Kaibab limestone's chert nodules or crinoid fossils.

Still, such spontaneous breakdowns are all too rare, and I walked through the Canyon with a tremendous amount of cultural and personal baggage. The first time I looked down on the great curve of the Colorado at Horseshoe Bend and the first time I scrambled into that oasitic grotto of Elves Chasm were influenced by having had their pictures on my wall for years in high school. I can't help but suspect I would have had different, or better, or—if such things exist—more *authentic* experiences had I not at each spot had the distinct thought: "Yup. Looks like the pictures."

I had my tricks. My means of even momentarily parting the scrim of complex and seeing the Canyon unfiltered and raw. Take running the river. Sitting in my inflatable kayak that first time down the river, I drifted toward Crystal Rapid, one of the most famous rapids in the West. I had heard its murmur resonating up the curving walls from a quarter-mile upstream. The murmur steadily increased to a roar as I floated around the last corner and saw Crystal. Except I didn't see it. All I could see from river level was an abrupt line where the river descends the rapid, a line punctuated at times by upthrusts of whitewater splash and the *whump whump* of the bigger waves collapsing on themselves. The boats in front of me disappeared one by one over the drop-off line, and all I could hear was the wild roar of the water and the wild thumping of my heart, and then for one last moment I was perched at the lip of the rapid, the whole sublime course of waves and holes and rocks spread out before me, the smooth tongue of river quickening into white, and I was in.

In the same way that exhaustion dulls aesthetic appreciation, terror-tinged exhilaration demands a presence in the moment. I was obviously far removed from J. W. Powell descending an unknown river, with unknown rapids around each bend. I'd heard rumors of Crystal for years, and surely the anticipation both augmented and flattened the experience. Regardless, few things equal the rush of adrenaline in making an experience personal and immediate, in shattering any anticipation of what it "should" feel like. One cannot adequately prepare for that feeling, and I have sought it again and again in my life.

Of course, the adrenaline artifice only goes so far. A certain degree of youthful arrogance is inherent in the assumption that the way to achieve deep, meaningful, or even life-changing experiences is best brought about by brushing up against death or matching the hot spark of yourself against the cold, unforgiving rock. (Or, for that matter, in the assumption that what one wants out of life is deep, meaningful, or even life-changing experiences.) And in time these tricks accrete into their own complexes. In time many of them become part of the greater cultural complex, the things that one must do to have "best" experienced the Canyon.

But one of the reasons I so love the Canyon is that even if I lacked the tingling of discovery I might have enjoyed if I'd had no previous conception of Horseshoe Bend and Elves Chasm, I was still awed by what I saw. For all the weight of the symbolic complex, the Canyon still delivers a dramatic blow. Expectations can't capture the smell of hot rock, the way grit in wind rasps the skin, the way maidenhair ferns tremble in time to the wash of water on rock. These are phenomena, and there are innumerable such, that slip through the cracks in the assembled constructs. Somewhere within we suspect this; this is why, instead of staying at home watching nature documentaries, we still bother to visit—we need to experience the details of the world for ourselves.

In the end, all one could do—all I could do—is try and be attentive: to what my personal complex entailed, to the tricks and tools I used to break through it. Given time, these individual moments of attention accrue into a deeper, unconscious attentiveness to the Canyon as *it* is: apart, mantled in snow, or clouds, or unadulterated sunlight; in torrid summer heat and bitter winter cold; with the river as bottom-of-the-reservoir blue and monsoon runoff-induced red; with the aspens bare, budded, greened, yellowed, then bare again.

⁖ ⁖

After twenty miles and unrelenting oceans of sun, Michael, John Hiller, Jeff, and I were shambling across the parched earth. No streams ran through that section of Canyon. The Esplanade's slickrock sandstone is pockmarked with millions of potholes, and we'd been counting on rains to fill those holes, and the rainwater in those holes to sustain us until we reached a spring, twenty miles away. But it had not rained in weeks. Longer. Every hole was dry.

My head bowed to the yoke of heat and thirst, the thought occurred that if not for the hot oxygen in the lungs we could well have been walking across the surface of an alien planet. Where wind had piled soil between open slickrock and gnarled mounds of cryptobiotic soil-crust, the earth erupted with writhing creosote tendrils, flaccid prickly pear, unnecessarily aggressive yucca. The ruddy slickrock sopped the heat. The sun sapped the strength. Hiking beneath it was courting disaster. But we had little choice. The nights were moonless and the days long. We'd start hiking early so as to cover miles in the dawn and in the long slants of morning shade along the eastern ridges, but there were too many hours of daylight and too many miles to hike. So we hiked in the sun. Occasionally the four of us folded into any available shade and waited for the weight of light on the skin to stop smoldering toward bone. But the shade slipped through the sand like liquid. The line of sun would touch our feet, then creep up our legs, knees, and crotch, and when it finally lay fully upon us we'd move into another irregularly shaped spot of shade or we'd sigh and shoulder out packs and step back into the sun to whittle off more miles from the hike.

The heat fogged the mind. Reeling, I thought, "Oh, a cicada singing," but John Hiller was veering away from me, and some numb warning song of my own was sounding, and my body, on its own primal accord, was also swerving, and only then did my dull mind snag on the possibility of serpent, my head turning in time to see it rattling toward the deeper shade of a juniper.

No matter the season, no matter the hike, if you spend enough time in Canyon backcountry you'll come to understand thirst.

How a lack can weigh heavier and heavier on your consciousness. You'll come to understand desperation. Craving. As I hiked my mind twitched—a dowser—toward signs and traces of past water: the evaporate minerals visible in the limestone cliffs, the ghost of ancient waters in the limestone itself, the raindrops and mud-cracks preserved in the surrounding shale, the millions of years of runoff that had shred the terrace underfoot into thousands of now dry drainages. Every so often the Esplanade platform would split and reveal, three thousand feet below, the green-brown river. Reportedly only one route ran from rim to river on our hike, and we weren't sure where it lay.

For a pale urban American living in postwar England, T. S. Eliot ably captured the heavy cadence of water deprivation: the throbbing brain in the tight skull, the cruelly diminishing efficiency of footfalls, the fear crouched in the recesses of the mind.

> If there were water
> And no rock
> If there were rock
> And also water
> And Water
> A spring ·
> A pool among the rock
> If there were the sound of water only
> Not the cicada
> And dry grass singing
> But sound of water over rock
> Where the hermit thrush sings in the pine trees
> Drip drop drip drop drop drop drop
> But there is no water

There was no water. With every step I could hear the last quarter-liter of my water sloshing in my Nalgene bottle. "The sound of life," I thought as I walked. Even less remained in my Camelback, and I feared at any moment to hear the gurgle-suck of an empty reservoir, the sound of a closer death. In fear of that sound I took timid sips through the tube, sips that seemed to absorb through the shriveled linings of my mouth without necessitating a swallow.

Finally, we tromped down a slope into the canyon rumored to have water and saw two small pools shining in the sun. Few things in my life have ever seemed so precious, pure, perfect, as those two small puddles of water. John Hiller chortled a deep bovine moan, made a half-motion to hug me, then made a full motion to the side, lurching down into the narrow canyon, heedless of the heights.

"Water," he said. "Water."

~ ~

Erika would have hated that trip.

Driving through the Great Basin, Erika, in a moment of unguarded musing, referred to the barren expanse as "ugly." She glanced at me to see if I'd taken offense. Earlier I'd remarked that Nevada might be the most beautiful state in the Union, and she'd answered: "Yeah, until you take about ten steps outside the air-conditioned car." But I could forgive her: she grew up in Seattle and prefers the mist, greenery, and giant trees of the Pacific Northwest to the dust, brownery, and stunted shrubs of the inland Southwest. It's not that she didn't love the Canyon, or think the desert was beautiful, she just avidly disliked the sun. Hated the desiccating wind. And she was terrified of running out of water.

"Are you sure we have enough water?" she asked, for the second time, as we shouldered our considerable packs for a descent into the Canyon.

"We have *seventeen* liters of water between us, Erika. More than enough to get us to Deer Creek."

"Yeah," she said, not entirely convinced.

Still, I kept an eye on her. She'd take huge gulps of water through her Camelback, but I also knew she'd always keep some in reserve, just in case, a seemingly wise strategy, but one that might keep her from consuming as much as she needed. Sure enough, by the time we were trudging across the Esplanade slickrock, the sun had tightened the air like a vise, and though she still found it in her to crouch in fascination over old-growth colonies of fruiting microbiotic soil-crust, she was beginning to stumble and wilt. We dropped off the rim of the Esplanade and descended into the inferno of the Surprise Valley, stopping in the only scrap of shade we could find in the whole of those land-slipped, sun-ravaged wastes. Erika looked across the desert.

"I'm really kind of a slug, you know," Erika said.

"No," I said, sarcastically, having heard this one before.

"Yeah. I'm not really...evolved...for this climate."

"No, you're not."

"Nope."

She was silent.

Then: "Burrowing under some wet moss sounds really good right about now." She stood and poured a half-liter of water over the top of her head and asked, "Are we going to do this or what?"

Mary Austin, in *Land of Little Rain*, wrote: "For all the toil the desert takes of a man, it gives compensations, deep breath, deep sleep, and the communion of the stars." And this: water blossoming from rock. For a mile and a half later the trail brought us level with Deer Springs, where a fully formed creek thundered from a cleft in the Muav limestone, fell thirty feet, crashed against the spring-sapped slabs below, then reorganized itself as an open creek sliding gently on a bed of shale through banks of green willows toward the river, less than a mile away.

Of all the names placed atop the parched rock of the Grand Canyon, the most reverently spoken are those that denote a source of water: the perennial creeks like Flint or Monument, the perennial seeps like Kwagunt or Horn, the ephemeral springs like Cheyava Falls or San Magee Spring, and, of course, "Colorado," that muscular ribbon of red water flowing through thousands of miles of desert, the central miracle of the entire Southwest.

But nothing compared to crossing the desert and beholding Thunder River or Dutton Springs or Tapeats Spring or Vasey's Paradise or any other of those "gushet" springs bursting forth from solid rock. Their emergence was epiphanic: who knows how many hundreds of square miles worth of desert snowmelt and rainwater drained through the thousands of feet of sand, sandstone, and limestone, reached an impermeable shale layer, accrued into subterranean streams, and slanted toward this one narrow cleft of emergence to fall in open air and baptize our faces and quench our thirst?

A slow, occasionally overt violence underlay much of the Canyon: the scalding rock, the gouged earth, the incessant degradation, the inexorable grinding away of form. And yet these springs were peace, solace, tranquility. Rare, tender places enfolded within the severe rock. They plunged as showers to stand under or stilled as pools to swim in; they flowed through lush Edens of moss and fern and wildflowers. The ambient temperature in the springs' direct vicinity was usually a good ten to twenty degrees lower than that of the surrounding desert—many of the plants in these hanging gardens were endemic relicts from the colder climate of the Pleistocene.

In 2005 the USGS conducted a study of springs emanating from the South Rim. They discovered that some springs' water was less than fifty years old, while others' was thirty-four hundred years old. Sometimes a single spring would produce a mixture of young and ancient water, two separate watercourses having merged miles underground. They also found that "the water chemistry of each spring was distinct from that of all other springs and creeks." For example, Lonetree Spring was "unusual in that it has much higher concentrations of the rare earth elements than the other springs." Monument Spring had a much higher concentration of nitrates than any other spring, probably because it emerges a few thousand feet below the South Rim wastewater treatment plant. Salt Creek Spring had "high concentrations of uranium and selenium, and had a high gross alpha radioactivity, and anomalously high concentrations (relative to the other springs) of magnesium, potassium, sulfate, lithium, bromide, molybdenum, and rhenium," probably because it emerges a few thousand feet below a shuttered uranium mine. Grapevine Main Spring, Pumphouse Spring, Hawaii Spring, Hermit Spring, and Boucher East Spring have, "in general, a similar chemistry—derived, no doubt, from the same aquifer," but each also has "its own particular chemistry that is dependent on its geological and spatial location."

In short, each spring is unique, and many of them—most of them—after percolating through (up to) seven thousand feet of desert soils are unpalatable. Others are fetid, poisonous cesspools. Pumpkin Spring, a large orange bulb of hollowed-out travertine overflowing into the Colorado, offers a lukewarm brew of arsenic.

The usually dry orifice of Hell Spring, ringed by bright mineral precipitate, only occasionally oozes an odious liquid. Miner's Spring, which I once relied on for two straight days, is now, according to the National Park Service, "not recommended due to high radioactive radium concentrations." But sometimes you have no choice: on our hike across the parched Esplanade we found those pools of water, and we drank and drank, and we were saved worry and misery and perhaps worse, but the water flowed from a diarrheic swamp, and John Hiller shat seven times the next day, Michael six. The legendary Canyon hiker George Steck spoke of a hike around Powell Plateau in which the river "looked just ghastly. If it hadn't been for the dam, I'm sure there would have been dead cows floating downstream. There probably were dead beavers, we just didn't see them. So we went along on the Tonto a little ways and found a small pool with water that looked almost as bad as the river, grungy stuff, but we boiled it. You know boiling that kind of water produces a scum, a kind of a revolting scum, but you skim it off and the water is the better for it."

But Deer Springs was a delectation. Erika and I stripped naked and turned our heat-flushed, salt-encrusted faces to the falling water like supplicants receiving benediction. We reclined naked on the great slabs of rock that previous hikers had with no small effort placed together into thrones. Again we stood under the waterfall, holding our water bottles in the air to fill them. After some time we reluctantly dressed and continued downstream, stopping to look at an archaeological site.

Though tributary streams occupy only 0.003 percent of the area of Grand Canyon, they attract five hundred times more species—many of them rare and endemic—than does the surrounding desert. They certainly attracted humans: at the ruins Erika pointed out thick-leaved ground cherry and prickly pear, both important food sources, both plants likely descendants of those grown in the Anasazi's garden plot. Somewhere in the area were Grand Canyon agaves, an unusual agave in that it reproduces vegetatively, though cloning, meaning someone brought it to the Canyon, most likely as a trade item from Mexico, to be planted and tended. We dropped our bags and walked along the terrace through the Deer Creek narrows, where the incised creek serpentines through the purple-banded sandstone. There, too, was sign of human presence: an ancient handprint stenciled with red dust onto bare rock.

Deer Creek slides for a few hundred feet through its slot in the narrows before plummeting off a cliff, virtually into the Colorado River. Deer Creek Falls is one of the most spectacular sights along the entire spectacular river corridor, in part because it's so unusual. Nearly all the Colorado River's tributary canyons enter the main passage at the same level—not from a 130-foot cascade. The difference can be attributed to the disruption of the Surprise Valley landslides, which buried both the original Deer Creek Canyon and the Colorado's original course. The Colorado eventually cut a new channel through the debris (though this channel is still the narrowest section of river in the entire corridor: seventy feet across and some eighty feet deep). At some point, relatively recently, Deer Spring worked its way through its joint in the Muav, and Deer Creek began working its way through the fill, trying to reestablish its grossly disturbed equilibrium gradient with the Colorado River. The erosional knickpoint that is Deer Creek Falls represents that disturbed equilibrium.

Erika and I swam in the frigid plunge pool at the base of the falls, then lay warming ourselves on the beach above the confluence of creek and river. There was a large baccharis bush nearby, alight with rosy-white flowers. A sizable aura of bugs and gnats enveloped the bush, and whirling around and into the bug cloud was a dervish of bats. I tried to watch the bats, note any distinguishing characteristics, but there are twenty-two species of bat in the park, and they spun almost too fast to follow. I looked at Erika instead, now standing in the bush's embrace, in the center of the bat gyre, her red-flecked, brown-green eyes bright, radiant. After a few minutes she saw me watching her and said, as happy as I've ever heard her, "I like dem bats!"

The springs and their descendant creeks, like the endemic animal and plant species that so often cluster around them, are the true children of the Canyon. As a National Park Service pamphlet describes in surprisingly poetic terms, "Although the Colorado River flows through Grand Canyon's very heart, it is not of this place. The waters are exotic; the headwaters far off in the Never Summer Mountains of north-central Colorado. Precipitation falling on the Coconino (South Rim) and Kaibab (North Rim) Plateaus creates Grand Canyon's only native waters—waters derived in place." Neither Erika nor I was of this place. Like the waters of the Colorado, we'd come from elsewhere and would soon leave. I idly searched the beach for rounded pebbles, sent them skittering across the water. I looked again at Erika, the bats, the waterfall. Thomas Cole, the founder of the Hudson River School, found waterfalls a "beautiful, but apparently incongruous idea, of fixedness and motion—a single existence in which we perceive unceasing change and everlasting duration."

Not unlike my relationship with Erika.

I'd once hiked down Red Canyon and slept on a narrow strip of sand above Hance Rapid. That night I'd wake to the splash and dash of the river, the bass *whump* of the collapsing waves, and I'd lie in my sleeping bag and look up at the river of stars above me until I slipped back into sleep. Waking again, and again, I tracked the progression of the night by the way the sextillion stars wheeled between the confines of the Canyon walls. Change and duration. The stationary Canyon walls I'd used to track the stars that night also tracked our relationship for almost a decade. There had been changes: Erika's blond hair had darkened with age, her almost baby-fleshed face had slimmed into womanhood, her confidence and ambition had deepened and widened. And so too there was duration: we were still together, still strong in love.

That season, Erika worked for the NPS Vegetation Program on the South Rim. I worked off the North Rim, and thus the chasm separated us, but we'd talk on the phone most nights, and during our breaks we'd hike the twenty-one miles across the Canyon, or drive the 211 miles around the Canyon. Certain mornings, days after she'd left, hours after waking, I'd pull her golden hairs out of my beard, their long thin strength tugging my face. And often, after dinner, when the sun was setting or had long since set, I'd step out the trailer and look down the long expanse of Transept Canyon, at the dusk gathering in the great folds of the earth, the blue haze of dust and distance dissolving into the blackness of night. The whole of Scorpius would still be splayed in the south-western sky, but every night the constellation would drift lower, to be swallowed by the horizon come November. I'd look across the gulf at the constellation of lights of the South Rim Village, and I'd imagine Erika there, also looking across the gulf, and think of how we could each start signal fires on some promontory on the rim, or use spotlights to flash Morse-code love haikus to each other, or arc the lone firework up into the night, or something, or nothing, our two selves reaching across the river and rock, across the darkness and distance, to one another, as we'd have to do across the continent for the coming two years.

For at the end of the summer I'd once again pack my car with my worldly belongings and drive down to find a place in Tucson, where I'd pursue a master's of fine arts. Erika was already packing her gear to head across country to Gainesville, to begin her own master's program. This was to be out last trip together in the Canyon for eighteen months. A time of its own thirst. A time when the lack of one another weighed heavier and heavier on our consciousness. The compensations were worth it. So after skipping one last stone across the river, after hiking back up toward our camp, past the wavy laminations of stromatolites, through the flood-smoothed sandstone in the narrows, under the canopy of cottonwoods, we once again plunged into those native waters, and in those waters I took to one knee and asked her to be my wife.

ᕀ ᕀ

Years after we'd left the Canyon, Erika and I spent a summer in a cabin above Oregon's Rogue River. Black bear abounded. Out of the stillness of the heat-struck summer evenings in the old orchard would come the sound of claws scratching up tree trunks, then the distinctive crunch of apple mastication. In spring the trails around the meadow were adorned with globular bear poos consisting entirely of partially digested green apples. Other trails bore torn apart logs, or tree bark adorned with bear fur. The owner of the cabin regaled me with stories of bears having to be snared and shot, of bears meeting cougars on the trail, of bears ripping though the wall of the cabin, maddened by the smell of a rusted-through tin of oysters.

Once, back in the late 1970s, a huge black bear plagued the

cabin, becoming, according to the owner, "too familiar and too fearless." Finally, they saw him in the orchard meadow and shot him. Wounded, he ran downhill. They tracked him to his lair in a dense section of the conifer, oak, and madrone forest, and then shot him again, and again, and again he ran downhill. He proved impossible to track this second time, which may have been for the best, as they were wary of hounding a mortally wounded bear. Instead, they poked about his lair under the fallen snag of a giant tree not more than 150 yards below the meadow. Around the lair lay a mess of deer bones, turkey feathers, and bear fur; from every direction trails honed into the den like spokes on a wheel.

I had once come across a bear's den like this. Two friends and I were bushwhacking off of Numa Peak in Glacier National Park, cutting straight downslope to Bowman Lake. Scrambling down a rock outcrop we came upon a cave. A bear cave. There, too, were bones, and fur, and the thick must of bear. You could feel the bear in your bones. The cave was large, and in the dim forest the opening yawed black and impenetrable to the eye. I wanted to go into the cave. We had been intentionally making a lot of noise, so there was no way the bear was in that cave. I wanted to find gris-gris and juju. I wanted to tap that darkness. But I could not enter that cave. In preschool—this is one of my earliest memories—a friend had dared me to shove my finger in a tree hole into which he had seen an earwig slither. Even at that age I was not one to refuse a dare. Yet I was paralyzed by fear. I could not put my finger in that dark hole. I remember this vividly. I could not enter that dark cave.

That familiar and fearless bear raided my mind for months after I had heard that story. A creature that had absorbed bullet after bullet after bullet and still vanished into the forest. Mostly I thought of that lair. That lair became for me a well of wildness, of duende, magic, and myth. In it, all the bears of the world were spawned. It represented all those chthonic places of emergence— the Hopi sipapu, or Chicomoztoc, the mythological cave of emergence for the Aztec and Toltec—or those archetypal portals into the underworld that Orpheus or Aeneas or Gilgamesh had entered. I sought that lair. Tromped through the dog-hair pine thickets, slipped over and over on the slick madrone leaves matting the steep slopes. Bear sign everywhere. But no lair. Again I looked and again I found only standing trees, ravaged logs. In retrospect I am happy for it: the lair is better left unfound. I doubt I'd have found anything that would have gripped my psyche as did the idea of that lair, or that bear's cave in Glacier, or that earwig's hole, those places I could not enter.

I did enter such a place in the Canyon once, a place marked in my mind not by fear or myth but by anticipation. Cleaning out an old storage closet, Doc discovered a two-foot-long laminated scroll mapping the labyrinthine inner passageways of a cave etched into existence by one of the Canyon's larger springs. According to our reading of the map, the source of the spring, a mile into the earth, and some 1,500 feet below the surface of the earth, appeared to be an underground lake. That lake seemed to me an impossible wonder, as much a place of magic and mystery as would become, years later, that bear's lair. Perhaps we need these sort of places to attach our dreams, to beat back the irony and shallow materialism and inevitable, countless disappointments of our daily lives. Perhaps I'm an incurable romantic, a neotenous dreamer having read too much mythology. But Blake, Lake, and I searched for the opening of that cave as we'd have searched for pirate treasure.

An entire rock face humming. A darkness—an opening—

throbbing with the roar of pressured water. We entered the darkness. Almost immediately we came to where the roof of the passage had collapsed. But we were able to inch on our bellies under and through the rubble pile, and on the other side of the collapse the cave opened to where a crystalline stream cut through the karst in a narrow slot.

We waded up the knee-high water or walked above it on shale ledges. The brittle ledges often broke underfoot, plunging us into the frigid water. The ceiling, walls—entire hallways—glittered with calcium carbonate stalactites and smooth white crystal formations. As we walked these walls narrowed or widened, ran straight or angled; the roof, dripping with condensation, rose and fell, ten feet high, then twenty, then ten again. Grikes and clints running with water merged and split from our passage: one side channel merged as a solemn waterfall, and I found something terrible in a waterfall burbling to the silence of the earth, the utter black snuffing what would in the sun be whitewater. At one confluence the creek slowed and pooled, forcing a swim, the water as cold as the cave was dark. Our skin, speckled with goosebumps, glowed white in the headlamps. There, at the confluence, we saw the only other sign of life in the subterranean world: a hairlike wisp of a spider. Then, after more than an hour, having picked our slow way along two miles, we turned a final corner and reached the source.

It was not a lake but a cavern. In the middle of the cavern a mound of fallen slabs stretched to the upper reaches of a great domed ceiling. Beneath the rubble the spring siphoned out. In the immense darkness of the dome, our headlights merely pinpricks, it was hard to tell if the slab mound was three or ten stories tall. My sense of place was off-kilter: the humid dark, the crystalloid walls, the hypothermic waters, the albino spider, the black waterfall—all

were of a different world, a Canyon of which I had no conception
or knowledge. The disorientation stayed with me long after re-
emerging into the bright heat of the sagebrush slopes.

I will remember that final cavern until the day I die. And yet
the impossibility of a lake suspended within desert rock was, in
a way, better than the actual cavern, the anticipation more delicious than the reality. By knowing the world, we lose something
of the world, and a part of me wishes that I had not made it back
to that cavern, that I still believed in a black lake beneath a mile
of stone. It's an interesting paradox, one that Thoreau, that old
sage, recognized: "At the same time that we are earnest to explore
and learn all things, we require that all things be mysterious and
unexplorable, that land and sea be indefinitely wild, unsurveyed
and unfathomed by us because unfathomable. We can never have
enough of nature." Writing about the Canyon, John C. Van Dyke
acknowledged this same tension: "It is too big for us to do more
than creep along the rim and wonder over it"—which is, of course,
ridiculous, blasphemous, even pathetic (coming as it does from a
man who so promoted his desert caliber). But he continued, to
my mind rightly: "Perhaps that is not cause for lamentation. Some
things should be beyond us—aspired to but never attained."

We're a restless species; always grasping for what's just out of
reach, what we dream about, covet, desire, even if, in the end, the
attainment is disappointing, or unfulfilling. Faced with such disappointments, we simply ignore them, or forget them, and set off
again. Hiking in the open granite of the High Sierra, or the rid-
geline topography of the Cascades, what kept me going, mile after
mile, ridge after ridge, was the anticipation of the view beyond the
next horizon. Always just one more ridge, one more rise, one more

viewshed, the anticipation and curiosity bordering on spiritual yearning. It was everything I loved about the North Rim opener: a world alive and endless with possibilities.

This restlessness and hope urged my Canyon exploration. I'd always longed for the world for which I'd been born too late, when one could come upon the Canyon with no warning, or be the first to discover Modred Abyss Cave or Royal Arch, or see the sand floor of Redwall Cavern unbroken by footprints, or run the river without knowing what lay around the next bend; hell, run it before it the dam choked it tame. Obviously, those days are long gone. The Grand Canyon is hardly an undiscovered and unnamed world. Everywhere I went in the Canyon I'd find signs of previous presence: footprints, cairns, trash, pictographs, petroglyphs, potsherds, tailings, ore carts, granaries, long-buried retaining walls, agave-roasting pits, axe-hewn check steps, a battered moonshine still. The historical sites and debris from the times of the miners and first cattlemen struck me all too often as the familiar crass litter of my own culture, but I was fascinated by the native archaeological sites. They were as intriguing as they were ubiquitous. Though only 6 percent of the park has been intensively surveyed for archaeological "resources"—granaries, dwellings, agave pits, and such—nearly 4,300 have been discovered in that small fraction. After all, according to a Park Service brochure, "archeological evidence from the following culture groups is found in Grand Canyon National Park: Paleo-Indian, Archaic, Basketmaker, Ancestral Puebloan (Kayenta and Virgin branches), Cohonina, Cerbat, Pai, Southern Paiute, Zuni, Hopi, Navajo, and Euro-American." According to the author and former interpretative ranger Susan Lamb, "Statistical projections estimate that there may be sixty thousand (archaeological) sites in the park altogether." Native sign has been found in some of the most remote and seemingly inaccessible parts of the park, including many of the Canyon's summits. The much-heralded 1937 "Lost World" expedition to the top of Shiva Temple found, to their quiet dismay, that natives had already climbed Shiva and roasted the sweet hearts of agave at the top. The same expedition found similar evidence on the summit of Wotan's Throne. There are archaeological sites on Nankoweap Mesa, Sky Island, Elaine Castle, Guinevere Castle, and many more.

Some of the Canyon's archaeological sites are striking. Take the "Anasazi Bridge," a set of 1,100-year-old driftwood poles bridging a collapsed section of a cliff. Or Shaman's Gallery, a stunning panel of pictographs whose richly detailed polychrome animals, supernatural anthropomorphs, and six-foot-tall spectral figures bear great resemblance to Australian aboriginal art; they're thought to have been painted by Archaic hunter-gatherers anywhere between 8000 and 2000 BCE. Archaic hunters also crafted some of the Canyon's oldest and most justly famous artifacts: the split-twig figurines, single willow twigs folded into effigies of deer or bighorn sheep, many of them ritualistically impaled by another stick, a "spear." The figurines, ranging from an inch to a foot tall, were buried in nearly inaccessible caves in the Redwall limestone, with a flat stone or cairn of stones atop them. More than five hundred of these talismans have been discovered.

That Shaman's Galley was not discovered until 1986, that surely within the Canyon are yet undiscovered pictograph or petroglyph panels, or unearthed split-twig figurines, or intact granary complexes—all of it kindled the old boyish longings for exploration and discovery that had me scrambling over ridge after ridge. And even if so many of those things *had* been previously discovered, they were still imbued with a deep and abiding aura of mystery. They were at least new to me. Abbey, as usual, nailed it: "Wilderness offers a taste of adventure, a chance for the rediscovery of our ancient, preagricultural, preindustrial freedom. Forest and desert; mountain and river, when ventured upon in primitive terms, allow us a sort of Proustian recapture, however superficial and brief, of the rich sensations of our former existence, our basic heritage of a million years of hunting, gathering, wandering."

Faced with the fact that the world is known, that the Canyon is well known, I basically had two options. I could enter the Canyon without a map or other guide, determined to unlock its secrets on my own accord, just like, in Alaska, Chris McCandless, the young nomad immortalized in Jon Krakauer's *Into the Wild*. McCandless's untimely demise is stark evidence of the dangers of this plan, but those dangers are no small part of the adventure. Responding to people's criticism of McCandless, Krakauer said: "People don't get it. 'He didn't even have a fuckin' map; what kind of idiot?' That was the point. There's no blank spots on the map anymore, anywhere on earth. If you want a blank spot on the map, you gotta leave the map behind."

Leaving the map behind is part of a tradition of intentionally losing oneself, of putting oneself in situations designed to make one "at home in the unknown," in Rebecca Solnit's phrase. In *A Field Guide to Getting Lost*, she writes, "To be lost is to be fully present, and to be fully present is to be capable of being in uncertainty choice, a chosen surrender, a psychic state achievable through geography. That thing the nature of which is totally unknown to you is usually what you need to find, and finding it is a matter of getting lost."

Unfortunately, intentionally getting lost is not in my nature.

Intentionally getting lost in the Canyon could quickly become suicidal, and I was not suicidal. No, I veered wholly in the other direction. I needed to know everything. I'd pore over maps, I'd talk to
friends, I'd read online accounts, I'd mine nuggets of information
from George Steck's and Harvey Butchart's guidebooks. Hours
of my life have been consumed by the digital replica of Butchart's
topo map, the map on which he traced his Canyon explorations.
Same with Google Earth: I'll zoom in and out at all scales, scouting
potential beaches for camps, trying to determine if the scrambled
pixels betray a possible break in the cliffs. The mapping and stories
of those before me allowed me to experience the Canyon the way
I did—I'd have seen far less and had far harder experiences had I
not known the location of cliff breaks and water sources.

But after a while this approach was a bit depressing. You realize how much information is out there about your special place.
How many people are also caught by its spell. Obsessed. Some of
these people become legend, like Harvey Butchart, a small, wiry
man who in the span of forty-two years spent a thousand days
in the Canyon, wound twelve thousand miles through its rock,
climbed eighty-three summits (twenty-eight of them first ascents),
and recorded 116 routes from rim to river. He was the first person
we know of to walk the length of the park below the rim (though
he did it in increments, linking the length through dozens if not
hundreds of different trips), and his "beta" enabled Colin Fletcher
to make the journey he memorialized in his book *The Man Who
Walked through Time*. Perhaps most remarkably, Butchart didn't
even see the Canyon until he was thirty-eight, when he moved to
Flagstaff. Thereafter it consumed his life.

Or take Robert Benson Eschka. Eschka fell so deeply under
the spell of the Canyon that he completed what Tom Myers, au-

thor and yet another Canyon aficionado, called "likely the most astounding hiking feat in southwest canyoneering history": in 1982 Eschka followed the Green River through Canyonlands National Park to its confluence with the Colorado, then followed the course of the Colorado all the way through Cataract Canyon, around Lake Powell—whose shoreline is rumored to be longer than the western coast of the United States—and through the Grand Canyon to Lake Mead. He recuperated for a few months, then began walking upstream, this time on the south side of the river, all the way back to Moab, Utah, a 2,800-mile megahike that took him a year, break included.

Or take Bill Beer, who with a friend in 1955 swam the length of the Canyon in rubber shirts and wool long johns. Beer wrote of how "the Canyon becomes a mind-altering drug, the canyoneer an addict. He wonders if ordinary people can understand what he's experienced; he becomes 'born again,' sharing a bond only with others of the same persuasion. It becomes 'his' or 'her' canyon. Only the initiated can truly understand the power of this fanatic possessiveness."

Butchart, Eschka, Beer, the Steck brothers, the Kolb brothers, Georgie White, Kenton Grua, these were Canyon legends, a breed apart in their obsession and dedication. But there are literally thousands of people fixated on the Canyon, and in a jealous, absurd, but surely not wholly unusual way, I found the fact that so many others were so similarly ensnared by the place ultimately deflating. Thoreau had nailed it: at the same time I was eager to explore the Canyon I wanted it to be unexplorable, to always contain in its depths the dark, inaccessible mysteries of that bear lair.

Again, a large part of the inexhaustible glory of the place is that it rendered ridiculous petty desires, claims, jealousies. The

Canyon gave the impression, as strongly as any place I have ever
been in my life, that it was apart, absolute, independent from hu-
mankind and its strange, possessive, passionate, and self-defeating
desires. But Butchart's map, with its bold delineations of his past
presence, reminded me of those maps of the Anthropocene that
detail Earth awash with human impact: roads, flight patterns,
ship lanes, electrical grids; the whole world, barring the deepest
wastes of sand and ice, swarming and stained with our presence. It
wasn't hard, looking at Butchart's map, to imagine a similar map
in which every hiker's and boater's path in the Canyon was tracked
over a year and traced on a map: the steady streams of boaters
would turn the river solid red, the paths that the tens of thousands
of hikers followed within the Canyon would lace thick across it,
solid on the trails, funneling toward cliff breaks and water sources
in the backcountry.

Envisioning such a map sent me right back to thinking that
maybe McCandless was on to something, intentionally setting off
into a world unknown to him; that it might have been best had
we left one place on the earth unexplored, set aside tracts of land,
as the Brazilian government has done, in hopes that indigenous
tribes can live without ever being contacted—destroyed—by
"modern" humans. Envisioning such a map sent me right back to
restlessness. Made me realize I could leave.

~: ~

Erika was practically immobilized. Her hair, clothing, and backpack were independently ensnared in a giant bramble of wild rose.
Her face was streaked with dirt, sweat, and blood, and further
marked by determination, exhaustion, and touches of anger. She
reached both arms upward as far as she could, wrapped one bare

hand around a New Mexican locust, the other around a mountain mahogany, and attempted to pull herself out of the briar and up the cliff. She managing to thrust herself a foot or two upward, only to balance precariously on a bent-over branch of the mahogany. She looked up at me, and I was tempted to make a crack about this being the honeymoon she'd always dreamed of, but as I was close to tears with frustration myself, I smiled at her, shook my head in commiseration, and turned and reached through the thickage to try and haul myself a few feet farther.

All had been going well on this last day of our honeymoon in the depths of the Shinamu Amphitheater, Harvey Butchart described as "perfect and total wilderness." We'd started hiking before dawn, worked our way up an unnamed fault canyon, and easily routed through the breaks in the Esplanade and Redwall cliffs, and by the time we rested on the saddle between Lancelot Point and Elaine Castle it wasn't yet ten in the morning, we still had over a gallon of water between us, and only the Coconino and Kaibab cliffs and a flat seven-mile rim hike separated us from the car.

We sat there, happy in the shade, finishing our peanut M&Ms, looking up at Elaine Castle, a fine pyramid of a peak, just a few hundred yards away, and as I sat there I knew that I'd likely never again be so close, and though the route was out of sight I knew the ascent was easy, and that I'd likely need less than an hour to summit, and that there were Anasazi granaries somewhere near the top, and that the view would be spectacular—the deep gorges of the amphitheater spread out below, Holy Grail Temple directly to the west, the monolith known as Excalibur rising out of a ridge to the south.

Of course I wanted to climb it. So did Erika, and even if she hadn't wanted to climb it she would have said, as she had before, "You go. I'll nap here in the shade. It's fine"—and I'd have chosen to believe her, as I had before, and I would have gone up alone.

And yet we didn't climb Elaine.

Easy now to cite laziness, or exhaustion, or that particular eagerness to finish a trip, no matter how good it had been. Certainly we were concerned about the wildfire on the rim above us, a fire that, as indicated by the increasing amount of smoke billowing into the Canyon, was not only growing in size but consuming the exact portion of forest that lay between our exit route and our car. But I like to think that intuition held us back—that we knew that we'd be fools to take anything for granted.

Already that trip we'd run out of water and I'd seen the look of animal panic slip into Erika's eyes. I'd dropped my pack and gone ahead and come to a slot canyon where past floods had cut through the rock. Leaning over the incision, I could hear falling water, and spied a steep way down, and so we were saved, that day. And already that trip I'd been a half-step from stepping on a big pink rattlesnake that had been lying sluggish on the cold morning rock, but which exploded into rattling and lunging at our panicked retreat.

We *would* have been fools to climb Elaine, for the following seven hours were straight out of Exodus 14:3: we were "entangled in the land, the wilderness hath shut us in." From the Elaine Saddle we needed five hours to traverse a hellish mile and a half. The shrub forest of Gambel oaks and desert mahogany was taller than we were and sprouting horizontally out of the steep Hermit Shale slope. I thrashed through, berserker-like, beating at the bushes with my hiking poles. Erika crept through, elf-like, ducking and weaving her own path. Eventually she found it far easier to follow my blazed passage, though far enough behind me to avoid the bush shrapnel. We worked our way upslope to the base of the Coconino cliff, hoping to find the narrow, flat, and relatively bare shelf that often exists between the cliffs and slopes. There was such a shelf, one evidently used by sheep and deer, but our relief was short-lived, as we quickly faced the first of many places where floods had cascaded off the cliff above and gouged deep, steeply exposed rents into the shale. Hating to descend and reascend hundreds of feet merely to more safely cross a hundred or so feet of slope, we edged our way across the first of the fissures. I'd kick a foot-sized shelf into the unstable shale, then, with exquisite precision, place my foot sideways into the foothold, turn my knee in-slope, and move my weight onto the angled, outer blade of my foot, all the while trying to ignore the crumbled rock bouncing faster and unstoppably faster down the two-hundred-foot slide. Erika followed, but once safely across we agreed not to do it again. So for all the other fissures we'd descend hundreds of feet through the overhead brush to the less steeply inclined sections, cross, then reascend the slope, through the brush, back to the cliff base. In 1898 the traveloguer John Stoddard declared: "A descent into the Canyon is essential for a proper estimate of its details, and one can never realize the enormity of certain valleys, till he has crawled like a maimed insect at their base and looked thence upward to the narrowed sky." "Maimed insect" had always struck me as a peculiar phrase, but it aptly captured our progress across the Hermit Shale that day.

We slowly traversed the base of the Coconino, looking upward for a break in the uniform cliffs, a break I swore I'd heard about or read about once, though as we inched along my doubts grew. I kept them to myself. Just as I was really beginning to worry that we'd have to retrace our steps all the miserable way back to the saddle, where we'd seen a break but for some reason not taken it, we finally, luckily, blessedly, found a split in the cliffs.

But climbing up that chute was like swimming up a thicket avalanche. The chute was so steep—1,500 feet of elevation in a half-mile—that, had there been no bushes, nothing but bare ground, I could have leaned my head oh-so-slightly forward and buried my face in the duff, and, being tired, perhaps have taken a brief upright nap. But since there were bushes, a lot of bushes, a damn near close to impenetrable amount of bushes, the only way we could squirm upward was by wiggling our feet into awkward perches on bent-over branches then reaching through the mass to grab a bush to heave ourselves another half-body-length upward. Seeing Erika immobilized I recalled how, before the trip, I'd told the backcountry ranger with some degree of sarcasm: "I know, a four-day, off-trail backpacking honeymoon in the Inner Canyon in the beginning of July—how romantic," and how he'd replied, in all honesty, "I hope to marry a woman who will want to do the same thing." I was pleased by his comments, but then, entangled in the land, I swore that the next time I saw him I'd tell him, for the love of God, head to a beach in Mexico.

Erika could handle it, though. She was way tougher than me. When finally we topped out of that horrible chute and collapsed on the rim and ate the last of our cheese and crackers in an exultant daze I said, "That was the worst bushwhacking of my life."

She nodded and shrugged. "I've done worse."

"What? No. When?"

"Climbing trees in the Coast Range, down by the Siskiyou. I had a fifty-pound pack, plus my big crossbow, and I had to wade through all this tan oak—you know how it grows all close together and gnarly in some of those old coastal clear-cuts? It was, like, ninety degrees and I was pouring sweat and I was completely coated in that carcinogenic yellow powder that comes off the leaves: it was burning my skin and I could barely breath, my throat was closing, and I still had all these trees to climb."

Erika was always one-upping me with her tree-climbing experiences. Once, in Oregon, I returned from a hike in which a large black bear descended a slope to the creek I was swimming in. I was downwind, and the sound of the creek filled the narrow canyon, so I pulled on my shorts and stalked the bear upcanyon for a few hundred yards. I peered around boulders to see it nosing at an old log; I climbed a windfall to get better views of its slow progress. But then I rounded a corner and couldn't see the bear, though it should have been right in front of me, and since the canyon had opened a little I feared it may have gotten behind me. I didn't want to press my luck, so I turned back downstream. Later, when I told Erika this, I mentioned that I had grabbed a pointy stick, you know, just in case. She snorted in derision.

"Pointy sticks wiped out the Pleistocene megafauna!" I exclaimed.

"A black bear won't attack you."

"It was a big black bear. And I was following it. What if it had cubs and I poked my head around a boulder and it was right there and its cub was on one side and it was on the other and"— here I imitated an enraged mama bear.

"They'd still run away. One time, climbing trees, I came across a mama with cubs and they bolted." And then she proceeded to tell me all her encounters with black bears when tromping through the woods climbing old-growth trees, including the one where she had started ascending her rope, wasn't but eight feet off the ground, when out of a nearby huckleberry bush reared a bear, standing on its hind legs and sniffing the air.

I didn't mind the one-upmanship. Found it endearing, actually. She didn't realize that she was doing it, for one; and two, Jesus, that tan oak sounded awful; and three, already her canopy work had legended within her, as Trails had within me. And four, well, I was happy to be reminded that I'd married a badass. Traditionally, most if not all western movies and literature depict females as intrusive forces come to civilize and tame the hard-bitten men, to lure them out of the wilderness and soften them up for tea parties and baby coddling or whatever, but that wasn't Erika, not by a long shot. We sat there, eating the last of our food, watching the sun arc toward evening.

"Only seven more miles," I told Erika.

"And…a wildfire," she replied.

The smoke from the fire blanketed the forest. She was right. It looked to be exactly where we'd left our car.

So we stumbled along, spooking a pair of baby deer, tripping over logs, until we reached a dirt road. We trudged along the road until it branched onto the Swamp Ridge Road, which dead-ended at the trailhead at which we'd started our journey. In the middle of this road stood a barricade that had not been there when we drove through four days earlier. The sign on the barricade read: ROAD CLOSED! FIRE!

We stood there.

I stole a glance at Erika. Though she'd been living in my cabin on the North Rim for a few months, hiking and climbing (and planning and preparing the wedding), she'd always been slow to acclimate to the high desert, and she was filthy, bloody, and obviously exhausted.

"No reason we should both walk all the way down there," I said. "I'll go."

"Are you sure?" said Erika. "We could rock, paper, scissors."

Rock, paper, scissors was how we decided who would undertake most of the more unpleasant chores in our relationship. Unfortunately for my sake, Erika was preternaturally gifted at the game. You had to win two out of three games, and we played each game fast, so there wasn't time for thinking about one's next throw, it was just *bam, bam, bam, show,* and in that quick flow Erika read me like a book. At one point in our relationship she must have been on a thirty-game winning streak. It was unbelievable. I'd ask her what her trick was and she'd scoff: "I'm not going to tell you!" and then, sweetly, saucily: "You're just so predictable." But no, this was our honeymoon, and I had blazed the trail and kicked the steps in the shale, and gallant fool that I was, I was going to walk through the fire.

I left her at the sign with our gear and took our last half-liter of water and set off down the road. After three days of off-trail walking, usually up flowing streams and boulder-choked streambeds, not to mention clawing our way up that insanity of a chute, walking down an open, level road was a pleasure, even if I was beginning to stumble with fatigue. I swung my arms as I walked, trying to remember more of the scarecrow's song than "If I only had a brain." As I walked I considered the odds that the fire would still be burning across the road, and decided, somewhat uncharacteristically, that it would not be burning because we were out of water, virtually out of food, and we'd packed for Inner Canyon nights in the nineties, not North Rim nights in the fifties, and thus had no tent and only one sleeping bag between us, and so having to spend a hungry, thirsty, and cold night after a twelve-

mile, fifteen-hour day would have been too shitty a way for our
honeymoon to end. Less optimistically, I figured that if the fire
were still burning across the road, as seemed likely, as the smoke
was only thickening the farther I went, well, maybe I could skirt
alongside it to a thin spot, wrap my tattered shirt over my face, and
sprint through.

The fire *was* still burning across the road. Flames snarled amid
bushes, grass clumps flared, ponderosa snags candled into flame.
Patches of burning bark plummeted out of the canopy. Everything
was either smoke or flames or ember or char. There's no way in
living hell I would have ventured through that inferno on foot,
tattered T-shirt mask or not. Luckily by then I'd run into a convoy
of wildland fire engines leaving the fire for the day, and they'd radioed a crew staying on the opposite side of the fire to come get me
and drive me to my car. I sat in the back of the engine's cab, wide-
eyed at the fire, occasionally having to move away from the window
as the heat from the flames pressed through the glass. The smoke
was so blinding that, to stay on the road, the engine boss had to
peer up at where the parted forest canopy revealed the road cut.

He dropped me at my car, and then, in a gesture that made
me reconsider my opinion of wildland firefighters as overpaid,
ego-swollen, military-industrial-styled douchebags, he drove back
through the fire so that I could follow his lead. Wreathed in smoke,
I followed inches from his bumper, occasionally swinging off the
road to avoid the more intense flames. At the edge of the fire I
waved him thanks and continued into the darkness. I drove down
the single-lane dirt road like a madman. To pass over the earth
without moving my legs! As I crested a small hill, my headlights
settled on Erika, and of all the images seared into my memory
from that trip—the last of the sun kindling the Holy Grail rock

formation; the river of mystical, gray-blue water pouring out of the cave within Modred's Abyss; the yellow flowers of flame in the forest—I remember most fondly, resonantly, the sight of Erika in the middle of the road, her sleeping bag over her shoulders, hopping up and down with joy.

And you know what? Screw the beach honeymoon. The whole experience mirrored our relationship: hard yet rewarding, tough but wholesome, a journey of perseverance and reward, guided by no small degree of faith, trust, intuition, and luck. After all, if we had climbed Elaine we would have missed the firemen leaving the fire, and I would have come up on the blaze and turned around, and we'd have spent the night in the cold forest and not, as we did, indulging in hot showers, omelets, leftover wedding cake, and a bottle of champagne. If my foot had fallen on that slack muscle of snake and it had whipped about and bit me, I would have suffered greatly and possibly died in the depths of the remote Canyon. And if we hadn't found that arduous, atrocious break in the Coconino cliffs, we might have had to turn around, and if so would likely have run out of water, and then again missed the fireman, and been in even worse straits for the night.

As it was it all worked out, even if Erika refers to it, neither unkindly nor jokingly, as the Honeymoon Death March.

᭜ ᭜

And then one day, barely October, I'm walking back to the North Rim bunkhouse at workday's end and Salty Dave says, "Hey, it's snowing," and I stop and look up at the glittering gold fines floating through the ranked pines and firs, and I say, "No, it's ponderosa pollen," and Dave, the drunk mule-rider pirate and cranky solar-panel wizard, hoarder of guns, gold, and art, who was to die

too young of cancer in Great Basin National Park only a few years
after that day, laughs his smoker's rasp of a laugh and says, "Pollen?
Are you on acid, Brodie?" and I can only stand there, watching the
tiny ice grains sift through the golden light of an achingly cold
North Rim autumn to settle and melt on my upturned face.

That night I'd press my forehead against the cold window of my
cabin and watch the snow fall out of the low night clouds, watch it
hit the black duff and melt as though it were passing through a porous earth, pulling with it the last of summer. I'm unaccustomed
to the sight of falling snow, and to this day find it entrancing, won-
drous, especially the slow and steady drift of big flakes, as though
the single snowflake eyed amid the flurried millions mirrors my
own singular and limited moment, looking out at the meadow and
the snow and the night.

I only worked one winter on Trails. We have our seasons, and winter is not my season. The five-thirty morning alarm was never so
unwelcome, the barely dawned workday dark and cold; the shadows, by the end of work, having stretched back to darkness. Even
at midday the bleak sun arced so low across the southern sky that
the tightly enclosed or north-facing sections of trail received sunlight for at best an hour or two a day. For most of that winter we
lived down at Phantom, where it rarely drops below forty degrees,
but our work sites on the South Kaibab were relatively exposed,
and that high-desert winter wind cut like a blade where coat met
pants or collar met hat. The frozen steel of our tools stuck and
burned the bare grip. We'd fight over who got to run the pionjar
so as to press parasitically close to its warmth. Our sweat turned
clammy and cold as soon as we stopped working, and on break I'd
add another layer, wedge my numb digits deeper into my pockets,

and think of how incredible it was to have once shied from sunlight, to have once feared its life-giving warmth. While I shoveled snow from the South Rim's viewpoints the cold would wick into my bones, and once, shivering, I confessed to Dee that the coldest it ever got in my childhood was one morning when our birdbath had a thin layer of ice—and that was *cold*. He looked at me, shook his head.

Not that it wasn't good to know the Canyon in winter: the way the snow softened the edges of rock, or how the pale, low-angled light illuminated the Redwall cliffs. The spoor of animals in the snow, the way their individual trails became visible, distinct, intersecting, braided. The reduced crowds. Thick, lush moss on the Vishnu schist; thick, lush fur on the coyote. Water brimming from a thousand potholes on the Esplanade: a thousand round mirrors of reflected sky. Watching the last yellow cottonwood leaves come swirling down at Phantom Ranch, with snow laid across the Canyon's slopes from rim to Redwall.

But my body ached. The work of spring and summer and fall took its toll, and I craved tropical beaches, or eating pancakes at my parent's place in LA, or sitting by an adobe fireplace, sipping whiskey and watching the snow fall past the window. My soul, sunflower-like, seemed to orient itself to the southward-slipping sun. A part of me wondered if these weren't just pathetic, southern-California-boy excuses designed to hide the fact that I wasn't running from winter but from commitment, responsibility, stability, the sedentary life. Maybe so. But I justified it to myself by thinking that, because I so frequently left, I never got burned out from the work or tired of looking at the Canyon. My return each spring was a renewal, a rediscovery of the Canyon and my love for it, a love that then burned hot, the way I liked it, rather than the long and slow burn of those who stayed year-round, or the smoldering ashes of those who'd worked too continuously long. Or so I told myself. So I tell myself now, resigned to an even more infrequent relationship with the Canyon.

~: ~

Every fall I'd make a pilgrimage to Ed Abbey's fire tower. I'd park my car at his old cabin by the North Rim's entrance gate and walk up the dirt road, just as Abbey had done for two of the three seasons he worked on the North Rim. Abbey described the walk in an essay: "To get to my job I walked for a mile and a half each morning up a trail through a dense grove of quaking aspens. I called this grove 'the crooked wood' because the trees there, nearly all of them, have been curiously deformed. The trunks are bent in whimsical shapes: dog legs, S curves, elbows, knees." On Trails we called them "dancing aspen," their funky dance moves the result of the deforming weight of snow and the trees' subsequent contortions toward whatever varied direction the sun happened to seep through the snow that year.

I'd walk in silence. The mottled, chalky-white trunks and the last boughs of still-green leaves accentuated the hypnotic, shimmering radiance of that yellow and orange and red canopy. The writer Scott Thybony wrote, "In rain country the organic cycle of growth and decay shapes the sense of duration. But here in the arid West it's different. Time is more geologic than biologic." This is certainly the case within the Canyon and in the lowlands, but nearing nine thousand feet on the Kaibab Plateau, immersed in old-growth groves of ponderosa, fir, and aspen, one is blessed by both senses of time. And looks can be deceiving—though the aspen forest seemed young, the trees not the thickest aspen

I've ever seen, the individual trees are actually ephemeral, clonal suckers off what may be an ancient rootmass. A couple hundred miles north of here, on the western edge of the Colorado Plateau, a hundred-acre aspen grove has been estimated to be at least eighty thousand years old. I found it comforting that beneath these dancing trunks are ancient roots, and beneath these ancient roots are the even more ancient rocks of the Canyon. As I walked the aspen thinned into fir, and the fir thinned into an opening, and in the opening stood the tower.

I poked my head into the ruins of the small cabin at the foot of the tower, where Abbey lived one of his seasons. The pile of decomposed porcupine was still there, reduced by the years. I'd encountered this porcupine, alive, clinging to the beams in the cabin, bristling at my approach. I paid my silent respects to the remains of porcupine and prickly writer's cabin alike, and climbed up the tower's sixty feet of stairs. I used my government key to open the trapdoor in the floor, and climbed up the ladder into the small, six-by-six-foot room. I fiddled with the old azimuth and studied the decaying table map, but mainly I leaned against the windows and looked out across the swath of treetops and communed with a ghost.

Of all Abbey's national park and forest positions—from ranger to fee collector to bus driver—the fire lookout position best exemplified Abbey's desire to live "far out on the very verge of things, on the edge of the abyss, where this world falls off into the depths of another." His fire lookout positions were essentially extended writer's residencies; Abbey admitted his position was "ideal for reading and writing…all you have to do is get up and have a good look around every 15 minutes or so." Little wonder he eventually wrote atop seven different lookout towers. In a sign of his happiness with the position, he remarked, "A man or woman could hardly ask for a better way to make a living than as a seasonal ranger or naturalist for the National Park Service." The problems with this life, as Abbey discovered in his Arches-to-Hoboken ordeal, arose in living it while maintaining a family. He had some difficulty with that, and these difficulties lay on my mind this last pilgrimage.

For years after Erika had taken a chance toward commitment and followed me to the Canyon, and even more years after we had again separated to attend different universities, I was quitting Trails, leaving the Canyon, following her to Oregon, where she'd start work on a doctoral degree. And this time, finally, I was content with this decision.

When I'd contemplated following Erika to Florida, I'd feared that I wouldn't be able to let go: that the Canyon wouldn't let go of *me*. Anthropologist Keith Basso studied language and storytelling among the Western Apache. "If we go far away from here to some big city," one informant told him, "places around here keep stalking us.... They keep on stalking you, even if you go across oceans.... They make you remember how to live right, so you want to replace yourself again." That's how I feared that lodestone rock would work on me: it'd stalk me. If not physically, at least in how it would arise unbidden in the small, spare moments of the day. How it would recur in my dreams, sometimes for three or four consecutive nights. How I'd find myself telling stories about it, sometimes the same stories to the same people.

Abbey's life, struggles, sacrifices, they *were* a cautionary tale. Having followed his wife to Hoboken, he lasted only a few miserable and tormented years before abandoning wife and children and heading back to "exile in the desert." Like the desert prophet before him, he was willing to sacrifice his children, wives, and even what he would admit was a significant amount of happiness to his deep and uncompromising love of place, his idea of "how to live a full, meaningful, joyous life."

The struggle wasn't—isn't—Abbey's alone. The Canyon demands sacrifices from its devotees; the truer the devotee the greater the sacrifice. Harvey Butchart's obsession with the Canyon put tremendous, almost irreparable strains on his marriage and family life; his son doesn't remember him attending a single one of his baseball games. Georgie White, the legendary river runner, admitted: "I made no bones about it. I put the Canyon first: I put it before anything." Everett Ruess, a promising young artist and unquenchable romantic, sacrificed his own life in pursuit of desert beauty. I admire all of those fanatics; indeed, I find their passion worthy of emulation, their belief that one should not compromise what one holds most dear; that if one truly holds it so dear, one cannot compromise it.

But I could not compromise what Erika and I had wrought. However I once may have felt about the romance of those other's sacrifices, I had softened. I no longer needed to whet the edge of obsession and test it against my own skin. Perhaps I never burned as Abbey burned, or raged as he raged, or chafed quite as he chafed, all the qualities that made him a great writer. But I would not admit, as Abbey did, that "I've not been a very good family man or father." I would not edit Erika out of my book or my life.

Still, in that tower, looking out over that sea of trees, I couldn't wholly say what had changed, why I was content to leave. It helped, certainly, that the crew had begun to scatter. Michael had moved to Chicago, John Hiller had transferred over to Wastewater

Facilities, Blake over to River Operations, Sara over to Vegetation, then on to nursing school, then a job in the Flagstaff hospital. Ray had been moving from park to park. As was Devin, ever ascending the hierarchy. Marie had moved down to Saguaro National Park. Shortly after I left, Abel would leave for the Great Smokies, and Dee would badly herniate his back and be unable to pass a physical to remain on Trails. Wayne would stay, as would Doc, and some others, and of course others would replace those who'd left, but for better or worse Trails had changed: YACC camp had been destroyed, and the crew no longer lived together on the rim, no longer spent off days together on river trips or climbing expeditions or Canyon backpacks as they had in my heyday. On a twenty-day trip down the Colorado through the Canyon, a friend told me. "River trips are about the people." My initial reaction was to argue, "What? No, they're about the river, and the canyons those rivers have carved." But he was right, and the same applied to working Trails: as much as the work served as a conduit between me and the Canyon, it was ultimately about the people, those people who'd begun scattering to the winds.

That was part of it. As was that dead boy in the canyon. That dervish of bats. Vishnu. As was the simple fact that Erika was leaving and Erika was my wife and I was going to live my life with my wife. Maybe, like certain desert annual wildflowers, which only sprout when specific and exact temporal conditions of sunlight, temperature, and moisture have been met, my conditions of age, experience, passion, and the lessons learned from walking the trails woven between desert and heart had, finally, been met. The familiar stirrings of wanderlust, the tingle and thrill of threshold I felt were now bolstered with the knowledge that, as the Apaches warned, I could replace myself again and again and carry the

Canyon with me. Not as a curse but as a blessing: it would remind me how to live right.

From the trees beneath the tower rose the melancholy trill of the hermit thrush. The call broke my reverie, and I shivered. Autumn. A fading sun. Time to leave. I climbed back down the ladder, swung the trapdoor and locked it behind me, and slowly descended the tower. I squatted in the thin litter that wind had pushed into the ruined shack and gathered the last intact porcupine quills. I threaded them through my backpack. I walked back down through that dancing aspen forest, the golden leaves showering loose in the wind and carpeting the trail before me.

NOTES

Epigraph: William Stafford, "Bi-Focal," in *The Way It Is: New and Selected Poems* (Graywolf Press, 1998).

PAGE 12: *best possible state of your soul*   See Plato, *The Apology.*

PAGE 12: *something nebulous / silent / isolated / unchanging and alone / eternal*   Lao Tzu, *Tao Te Ching*, as found in Peter Matthiessen, *The Snow Leopard* (Penguin Classics, 2008), 65.

PAGE 21: *One great thing about fly fishing...about fly fishing*   John Maclean, *A River Runs Through It and Other Stories* (University of Chicago Press, 2001), 18.

PAGE 26: *California condors, badgers, and foxes*   Information about predator eradication on the Kaibab Plateau is from Michael Anderson, *Living at the Edge: Explorers, Exploiters and Settlers of the Grand Canyon Region* (Grand Canyon Association Press, 2007), and Christian C. Young, *In the Absence of Predators: Conservation and Controversy on the Kaibab Plateau* (University of Nebraska Press, 2002).

PAGE 31: *gap in the world...slim yellow mountain lion!*   D. H. Lawrence, *Birds, Beasts and Flowers!* (Godine, 2007), 189.

PAGE 32: *smog blown in from...China*   See "Smog in the Western U.S.: Blame China?," *Greenspace* (blog), *Los Angeles Times*, January 20, 2010, http://latimesblogs.latimes.com/greenspace/2010/01/ozone-smog-air-pollution-greenhouse-gases-china-pollution-owen-r-cooper-kathy-law.html.

PAGE 33: *irradiated, hot with tritium from decades of nearby nuclear weapons testing*   See Craig Childs, *The Secret Knowledge of Water* (Backbay Books, 2000).

PAGE 33: *what Leo Marx dubbed the "technological sublime"*   Leo Marx, *The Machine in the Garden: Technology and the Pastoral Ideal in America* (Oxford University Press, 2000).

PAGE 33: *If we are to forge…the extinction of experience*   Robert Michael Pyle, *The Thunder Tree: Lessons from an Urban Wildland* (Lyons Press, 1998), 152.

PAGE 34: *whittled so fine / the fleet limbs of the antelope*   Robinson Jeffers, "The Bloody Sire," in *The Selected Poetry of Robinson Jeffers*, ed. Tim Hunt (Stanford University Press, 2002).

PAGE 35: *ignorance and hostility…exploiting fellow humans*   Gary Snyder, "Exhortations for Baby Tigers," in *A Place in Space: Ethics, Aesthetics, and Watersheds* (Counterpoint, 1995), 211.

PAGES 35–36: *on the exploits of individual lives…*   Daniel Justin Herman, *Hunting and the American Imagination* (Smithsonian, 2001).

PAGE 36: *We must become believers in the world*   Robert Michael Pyle, *The Thunder Tree: Lessons from an Urban Wildland* (Lyons Press, 1998), 152.

PAGE 38: *knew how to burn…their own longing*   Mary Szybist, "The Troubadours Etc.," in *Incarnadine* (Graywolf Press, 2013), 3.

PAGE 43: *Apparently Tebeaux was a martial arts instructor*   See William Finnegan, "The Last Tour," *New Yorker*, September 29, 2008.

PAGE 48: *I am alive in the world…reduced to my irreducible self*   Wendell Berry, "An Entrance to the Woods," in *The Art of the Personal Essay*, ed. Philip Lopate (Anchor Press, 1994), 671.

PAGE 48: *leading to the most amazing view*   Edward Abbey, preface to *Desert Solitaire: A Season in the Wilderness* (University of Arizona Press, 1988), xiii.

PAGE 48: *clamor and filth and confusion of the cultural apparatus*   Edward Abbey, preface to *Desert Solitaire: A Season in the Wilderness* (University of Arizona Press, 1988), 6.

PAGE 48: *explore the forests…run the rivers*   From a speech Abbey gave to environmentalists in Missoula, Montana, and in Colorado, published in *High Country News*, September 24, 1976, under the title "Joy, Shipmates, Joy!," as quoted in Reed F. Noss, Allen Y. Cooperrider, and Rodger Schlickeisen, *Saving Nature's Legacy: Protecting and Restoring Biodiversity* (Island Press, 1994), 338.

PAGES 48–49: *the old true world* Edward Abbey, *Beyond the Wall* (Holt Paperbacks, 1984), xvi.

PAGE 49: *Dedicated urbanites "know"…Both worlds are real* Colin Fletcher, *River* (Vintage, 1998), 191.

PAGE 49: *I believe that … many people live* Robert Michael Pyle, *The Thunder Tree: Lessons from an Urban Wildland* (Lyons Press, 1998), 145.

PAGE 49: *But the wilderness world…certainly last longer* Colin Fletcher, *River* (Vintage, 1998), 192.

PAGE 51: *lower upper middle class* George Orwell, *The Road to Wigan Pier*, part 2, chapter 8.

PAGE 52: *We do not receive wisdom…at last to regard the world* Marcel Proust, *Remembrance of Things Past*, vol. 1 (Vintage, 1982), 922.

PAGE 55: *fulfilling their intended function* Gaston Rebuffat, *Starlight and Storm* (Modern Library, 1999), 56.

PAGE 56: *We have learned…rapids and falls* John Wesley Powell, *The Exploration of the Colorado River and Its Canyons* (Penguin Classics, 2003), 123.

PAGE 58: *that of my own sensory elations* "sensory elations" taken from C. K. Williams, "Manure," in *All at Once* (Farrar, Straus and Giroux, 2014), 21.

PAGE 60: *a process known as stream piracy* See Wayne Rainey, *Carving Grand Canyon* (Grand Canyon Association, 2005), 127.

PAGE 62: Gregory Crampton, *Land of Living Rock* (Knopf, 1972), 7, 10.

PAGES 62–64: Buffalo Bill Cody story, the evolution of "heroic nomenclature," and the evolution of the name of Deer Creek came from Nancy Brian, *River to Rim: A Guide to Place Names along the Colorado River in Grand Canyon from Lake Powell to Lake Mead* (Earthquest Press, 1992).

PAGE 64: *spoken in English by a Japanese tourist*   This tidbit about adopting the word "butte" was ripped from George R. Stewart, *Names on the Land: A Historical Account of Place-Naming in the United States* (Lexicos, 1983).

PAGE 65: *initial baptism*   Saul Kripke, *Naming and Necessity* (Harvard University Press, 1982).

PAGE 68: Much of the information on the Supai layer, and indeed, much of the geological information in this book, came from Lon Abbott and Terri Cook, *Hiking the Grand Canyon's Geology* (Mountaineers Books, 2004).

PAGE 72: *most awful bellow of a thunderous roar*   Zane Grey, *Tales of Lonely Trails* (Harper & Brothers, 1922), 78.

PAGE 72: *final grand leap into the inner gorge*   Edward Abbey, *Desert Solitaire: A Season in the Wilderness* (Simon & Schuster, 1968), 196.

PAGE 77: *violent distaste for discipline of any kind*   Wallace Stegner, *Beyond the Hundredth Meridian: John Wesley Powell and the Second Opening of the West* (Houghton Mifflin, 1954), 44.

PAGE 79: *and other mundane activities*   See Ellen Dissanyake, *Homo Aestheticus* (University of Washington Press, 1995), 195.

PAGE 82: *In this manner the days passed*   Respectfully adopted from James Hamilton Peterson, *Playing with Water: Passion and Solitude on a Philippine Island* (New Amsterdam Books, 1998), 50.

PAGE 82: See Munro Leaf, *The Story of Ferdinand*; W. Somerset Maugham, *The Razor's Edge*; Jack London, *Martin Eden*; and Hunter S. Thompson, *The Proud Highway: Saga of a Desperate Southern Gentleman, 1955–1967*.

PAGE 84: Wallace Stegner, "A Sense of Place," in *Where the Bluebird Sings to the Lemonade Springs: Living and Writing in the West* (Modern Library, 2002).

PAGE 84: *conserving nature as we conserve ourselves*   John Daniel, *The Far Corner* (Counterpoint, 2009), 28.

PAGE 84: *take responsibility from there*   Gary Snyder, *Turtle Island* (New Directions, 1974), 84.

PAGE 85: *what was going on in the world*   Gary Snyder, *A Place in Space* (Counterpoint, 2008), 9.

PAGE 85: *we are space-needing...devastated, simplified ecosystems* Paul Shepard, *The Others: How Animals Made Us Human* (Island Press, 1997), 317.

PAGES 86–87: *Belonging is the pivot...in a terrain of unique geology* Erik Erikson, as quoted in Paul Shepard, *Traces of an Omnivore* (Island Press, 1996), 105.

PAGES 87–88: The John Haines and Paul Bowles "rooted" anecdotes are taken from Lawrence Buell's "The Place of Place," in *Writing for an Endangered World* (Harvard University Press, 2009), 74.

PAGE 90: Stephen Hirst, *I Am the Grand Canyon: The Story of the Havasupai People* (Grand Canyon Association, 2006).

PAGE 91: All information on Waluthma, and much of this essay's information about the Havasupai, is garnered from Stephen Hirst, *I Am the Grand Canyon: The Story of the Havasupai People* (Grand Canyon Association, 2006), 92.

PAGE 92: Mike Anderson, *Living at the Edge: Explorers, Exploiters, and Settlers of the Grand Canyon Region* (Grand Canyon Association, 1998), 72. For general history of National Park Service consolidation, see Philip Burnham, *Indian Country, God's Country: Native Americans and the National Parks* (Island Press, 2000).

PAGE 93: *undergoing conquest and never fully escaping its consequences* Patricia Limerick, *Legacy of Conquest: The Unbroken Past of the American West* (W. W. Norton, 1987), 190.

PAGE 94: *There is not a trail...their knowledge is unerring*   John Wesley Powell, *Exploration of the Colorado River*, 164.

PAGE 94: Polynesian sailor information gleaned from Dennis Kawaharda, *Voyaging Chiefs of Hawai'i*, 1994, www2.hawaii.edu/~dennisk/voyaging_chiefs/voyagingintro.html.

PAGE 95: *talking about the kind of knowing...your all-but-unknown ancestors have put into it*   Wallace Stegner, "A Sense of Place," in *Where the Bluebird Sings to the Lemonade Springs: Living and Writing in the West* (Modern Library, 2002).

PAGE 96: *we seem unlikely to make much progress* William Cronon, "The Trouble with Wilderness; or Getting Back to the Wrong Nature," in *Uncommon Ground: Rethinking the Human Place in Nature* (W. W. Norton, 1995), 69–90.

PAGE 97: *the relationship Grand Canyon has with the Havasupai and Hualapai…relationships with our tribal neighbors* Janet R. Balsom, "Inclusion in NPS Management at Grand Canyon: Tribal Involvement and Integration," in *Crossing Boundaries in Park Management: Proceedings of the 11th Conference on Research and Resource Management in Parks and on Public Lands*, ed. David Harmon (Hancock, MI: George Wright Society, 2001).

PAGE 103: *In the canyon…in the present* Eliot Porter, *The Place No One Knew: Glen Canyon on the Colorado* (Gibbs Smith, 2000), 8.

PAGE 104: *the deep, simple necessities in which life renews itself* Rainer Maria Rilke, *Letters to a Young Poet*, rev. ed. (W. W. Norton, 1993), 14.

PAGES 105–107: Abbey information comes from *Confessions of a Barbarian: Selections from the Journals of Edward Abbey* (Little, Brown, 1994) and *Adventures with Ed: A Portrait of Abbey* (University of New Mexico Press, 2003), by Jack Loeffler, and *Edward Abbey: A Life* (University of Arizona Press, 2003), by James M. Cahalan, his most reliable biographer.

PAGE 105: *My wives got sick and tired of the constant moving around and the poverty level income* See Cahalan, *Edward Abbey*, 93.

PAGE 106: *I don't believe in doing work I don't want to do in order to live the way I don't want to live* See Edward Abbey, *The Fool's Progress* (Henry Holt and Co, 1998), 17.

PAGE 106: *a blinding and terrible beauty which obliterated everything but the image of itself* See Edward Abbey, *Black Sun* (HarperPerennial Modern Classics, 2014), 174.

PAGE 107: *seasons come and go in a small rectangle of walled-in space we called our yard* From "Manhattan Twilight, Hoboken Night," in *The Serpents of Paradise: An Ed Abbey Reader* (Macmillan, 1996), 86.

PAGE 119: *because it's there* George Mallory quoted in "Climbing Mount Everest Is Work for Supermen," *New York Times*, March 18, 1923.

PAGE 119: *because we are insane*   Warren Harding quoted in *CBS Evening News* broadcast, November 19, 1970.

PAGE 119: *At best...very hard to climb*   David Roberts, *The Mountain of My Fear* (Vanguard Press, 1968), 32.

PAGE 120: *A species of hope...illuminates the rest of life*   William Debuys, *The Walk* (Trinity University Press, 2009), 1.

PAGE 126: *my hands grew to the sledge*   Respectfully adopted from Hayden Carruth, "Song: So often, so long I have thought," in *Collected Shorter Poems* (Copper Canyon Press, 1992), 219.

PAGE 127: *everything not a necessity an encumbrance*   Wilfred Thesiger, *Arabian Sands* (Penguin Classics, 2008), 37.

PAGE 129: *spectacle too strange to be real...an unbelievable fact* Joseph Wood Krutch, *The Grand Canyon: Today and All Its Yesterdays* (Sloane, 1958), 4.

PAGE 129: *wilderness of rocks*   Actually about the Canyonlands region, but whatever. John Wesley Powell, *Exploration of the Colorado River*, 58.

PAGE 129: *sublimest thing on earth*   Clarence E. Dutton, *Tertiary History of the Grand Cañon District* (University of Arizona Press, 2001), 143.

PAGE 129: *seemingly irrational geography of space and rock*   Ellen Meloy, in Barry Lopez and Debra Gwartney, eds., *Home Ground: A Guide to the American Landscape* (Trinity University Press, 2006), 78.

PAGE 137: *fore-defeated challengers of oblivion*   Robinson Jeffers, "To the Stone-Cutters," in *The Selected Poetry of Robinson Jeffers* (Stanford University Press, 2002).

PAGE 139: *paraphrasing of the Mahabharata*   David James Duncan, *River Teeth: Stories and Writings* (Bantam, 1996), 157.

PAGE 139: *spinning a sledge in circles*   is indebted to Carl Sandburg's poem "Haze."

PAGE 141: *grip on earth of outspread feet*   Robert Frost, "Two Tramps in Mudtime."

PAGE 142: *I declined it...the beginnings of evil*   Henry David Thoreau, *Walden*, 67.

PAGE 145: *The only people…spiders across the stars* Jack Kerouac, *On the Road* (Penguin Books, 1999), 5.

PAGE 149: *the Book of Revelation's "sea of glass mingled with fire"* Rev. 15:2–3, New King James Version.

PAGE 155: *the Southwest monsoons should be called chubascos* See Craig Childs, *The Secret Knowledge of Water* (Backbay Books, 2000), 200.

PAGE 158: *cowered like dogs…woman in childbirth* *The Epic of Gilgamesh*, ed. and trans. Maureen Gallery Kovacs (Stanford University Press, 1989), tablet XI, lines 1–203.

PAGE 160: *In human time…the veil of our illusion* Keith Heyer Meldahl, *Rough-Hewn Land: A Geologic Journey from California to the Rocky Mountains* (University of California Press, 2011), 4.

PAGE 162: *a stream moving two miles an hour…will carry particles a million times as great* Wallace Stegner, *Beyond the Hundredth Meridian: John Wesley Powell and the Second Opening of the West* (Houghton Mifflin, 1954), 96.

PAGES 163–64: *108,000 square miles of…land* Kevin Fedarko, *The Emerald Mile: The Epic Story of the Fastest Ride in History through the Heart of the Grand Canyon* (Scribner, 2014), 11.

PAGE 164: *Estimates on the exact annual size of this load range from 45 million tons to nearly 200 million tons* The Glen Canyon Institute claims that, on average, 100 million tons of sediment are deposited into Lake Powell annually. Gwendolyn L. Waring (*A Natural History of the Intermountain West: Its Ecological and Evolutionary Story* ([University of Utah Press, 2011]) cites 91 million tons. Helen C. Fairley (*Changing River: Time, Culture, and the Transformation of Landscape in the Grand Canyon*, USGS report [2004]) says that, pre-dam, "on average, roughly 76 million tons of sediment were transported past the gauge at Lees Ferry every year."

PAGE 165: *the cyclic melting of the Quaternary Ice Ages produced flood after flood* See Wayne Ranney, *Carving Grand Canyon* (Grand Canyon Association, 2005), and Julia Rosen, "Colorado River Researchers Find Signs of Ancient, Devastating Floods," *Los Angeles*

Times, June 19, 2014, latimes.com/science/sciencenow/la-sci-sn-colorado-floods-20140618-story.html.

PAGE 165: *more than a hundred dams*   See Julia Rosen, "Colorado River Researchers Find Signs of Ancient, Devastating Floods," *Los Angeles Times*, June 19, 2014, www.latimes.com/science/sciencenow/la-sci-sn-colorado-floods-20140618-story.html.

PAGE 165: *little more than a giant plumbing system*   Kevin Fedarko, *The Emerald Mile: The Epic Story of the Fastest Ride in History through the Heart of the Grand Canyon* (Scribner, 2014), 14.

PAGE 166: *a lothesome little stream…slime and salt*   Jack Sumner quote. See Edward Dolnick, *Down the Great Unknown: John Wesley Powell's 1869 Journey of Discovery and Tragedy through the Grand Canyon* (HarperCollins, 2002), 234.

PAGE 166: *carried greater…sediment per quart*   Gwendolyn L. Waring, *A Natural History of the Intermountain West*, 20.

PAGES 167–68: *However, according to a 2011 USGS report*   See T. S. Melis, ed., "Effects of Three High-Flow Experiments on the Colorado River Ecosystem Downstream from Glen Canyon Dam," *US Geological Survey Circular 1366* (2011): 147.

PAGE 168: *The Colorado's modern notoriety…most litigated river in the entire world*   Marc Reisner, *Cadillac Desert* (Penguin Books, 1993), 120.

PAGE 170: *the thousand cubic miles of rock that the river has excavated*   As estimated in Michael P. Ghiglieri and Thomas M. Myers, *Over the Edge: Death in Grand Canyon* (Puma Press, 2001), 274.

PAGE 170: *Fifty thousand cubic miles of sediment may lie buried under the Gulf of California*   See James Lawrence Powell, *Grand Canyon: Solving Earth's Grandest Puzzle* (Pi Press, 2005), 214.

PAGE 171: *heart-breaking beauty…break for it*   Robinson Jeffers, *The Collected Poetry of Robinson Jeffers, 1920–1928* (Stanford University Press, 1988), 239.

PAGE 184: *five earthquakes of magnitude 5.0 or bigger since 1900*   From the David S. Brumbaugh, "Earthquakes and Seismicity of the Grand Canyon Region," in *Grand Canyon Geology*, ed. Stanley S. Beus and Michael Morales (Oxford University Press, 2002), 346.

PAGE 184: *bulge four to forty inches toward it*   Gary Lockhart, *The Weather Companion: An Album of Meteorological History, Science, and Folklore* (Wiley Science Editions, 1998), 66.

PAGE 184: *mysteries that fit into no pattern*   J. B. Jackson, "A Pair of Ideal Landscapes" in *The People, Place, and Space Reader* (Routledge, 2014), 259.

PAGE 185: *possess their own existence*   Richard Evans Schultes, *Plants of the Gods*, 2nd ed. (Healing Arts Press, 2001), 71.

PAGE 187: *The plants sing to us*   Wade Davis, *One River* (Simon & Schuster, 1997), 197.

PAGE 187: Walt Whitman, "When I Heard the Learn'd Astronomer."

PAGE 187: *one impulse from a vernal wood*   William Wordsworth, "The Tables Turned."

PAGE 188: *on the summit…do not understand*   John Wesley Powell, *Exploration of the Colorado River*, 7–9.

PAGE 188: *perennial, never consummated project of interpretation* Susan Sontag, "Against Interpretation," in *Against Interpretation and Other Essays* (Picador, 2001).

PAGE 189: *The fact that…the small and the familiar*   Joseph Wood Krutch, *The Desert Year* (Penguin Books, 1960), 119.

PAGE 190: *80 percent of the earth's history is lost in the Canyon's unconformities*   Keith Heyer Meldahl, *Rough-Hewn Land* (University of California Press, 2011), 221.

PAGE 192: *We don't see things as they are, we see them as we are*   Well, sort of Anaïs Nin. In *Seduction of the Minotaur*, Nin wrote: "Lillian was reminded of the Talmudic words: 'We do not see things as they are, we see them as we are.'" As to the real origin, see http://quoteinvestigator. com/2014/03/09/as-we-are.

PAGE 214: *so admirably designed…delight from the most apathetic beholder*   Clarence E. Dutton, *Tertiary History of the Grand Cañon District* (University of Arizona Press, 2001), 177.

PAGE 215: *There is only one question: / how to love this world*   Mary

Oliver, "Spring," in *New and Selected Poems*, vol. 1 (Beacon Press, 2004), 68.

PAGE 216: *when you surrender you stretch out like the world* Pablo Neruda, "Body of a woman, white hills, white thighs," from *Neruda and Vallejo: Selected Poems*, edited by Robert Bly (Beacon Press, 1993), 18.

PAGE 218: *mono-no-ware, the beautiful sadness of temporality* See Sam Hammill, introduction to Hayden Carruth, *Toward the Distant Islands* (Copper Canyon Press, 2006), x.

PAGE 219: *in time already gone* *Confessions of Saint Augustine.*

PAGE 221: *the end of all our exploring…for the first time* T. S. Eliot, *Four Quartets* (Mariner Books, 1968), 59.

PAGE 224: *powerful, directionless, hungry…energies of transformation* Robert Hass, introduction to *The Ecopoetry Anthology*, ed. Ann Fisher-Wirth and Laura-Gray Street (Trinity University Press, 2013), 13.

PAGE 224: *Remove the sandals…holy ground* Exodus 3:5, New American Bible

PAGE 227: *Nature preservation…advanced in a reluctant, vacillating way* Richard West Sellars, *Preserving Nature in the National Parks* (Yale University Press, 1999), xiii.

PAGE 228: *The region…shall be forever unvisited and undisturbed* Joseph Ives, "Report upon the Colorado River of West" (Government Printing Office, 1861).

PAGE 229: *industrial tourism* Edward Abbey, *Desert Solitaire*, 47.

PAGE 230: *annual appropriations from Congress, which make up nearly 88 percent of the National Park Service budget, declined 8 percent* After adjusting for inflation, according to December 2015 report from the GAO. See Phil Taylor, "The Park Service's Befuddled Funding," *High Country News*, August 22, 2016.

PAGE 240: *those US senators blocking more-stringent overflight regulations* Harry Reid and John McCain, for the record.

PAGE 241: *Walker Percy called the "symbolic complex"* See Walker Percy, "The Loss of the Creature," in *The Message in the Bottle: How Queer Man Is, How Queer Language Is, and What One Has to Do with the Other* (New York: Picador, 1975), 46.

PAGE 246: *If there were water...there is no water*   T. S. Eliot, "The Waste Land."

PAGE 248: *For all the toil...communion of the stars*   Mary Austin, *The Land of Little Rain* (Modern Library, 2003), 10.

PAGE 250: *the USGS conducted a study of springs*   See Stephen A. Monroe et al., "Chemical Characteristics of Ground-Water Discharge along the South Rim of Grand Canyon in Grand Canyon National Park, Arizona, 2000–2001," USGS Scientific Investigations Report 2004–5146.

PAGE 251: *looked just ghastly...water is the better for it*   George Steck quoted at http://photographic-exploration.com/steck/gs05.htm.

PAGE 251: *tributary streams occupy only 0.003 percent of the area of Grand Canyon*   See "Assessment of Spring Chemistry along the South Rim of Grand Canyon in Grand Canyon National Park, Arizona," USGS Factsheet 096-02.

PAGE 253: *beautiful, but apparently incongruous idea...everlasting duration*   Thomas Cole, "Essay on American Scenery," *American Monthly* 1 (January 1836): 1–12.

PAGE 259: *At the same time... We can never have enough of nature*   Henry David Thoreau, *Walden: or, Life in the Woods* (Penguin Classics, 1983), 366.

PAGE 259: *It is too big for us...aspired to but never attained*   John C. Van Dyke, *The Grand Canyon of the Colorado* (Kessinger, 2010), 218.

PAGES 260–61: *Statistical projections estimate...in the park altogether*   Susan Lamb, *Grand Canyon: Vault of Heaven* (Grand Canyon Association, 1995), 38.

PAGE 262: *Wilderness offers a taste...of hunting, gathering, wandering*   Edward Abbey, "Thus I Reply to Rene Dubos," in *Down the River* (Plume, 1991), 92.

PAGE 262: *People don't get it...you gotta leave the map behind*   John Krakauer, from the Sundance Channel series *Iconoclasts*, episode 13, aired October 25, 2007.

PAGE 262: *To be lost is...a matter of getting lost*   Rebecca Solnit, *A Field Guide to Getting Lost* (Viking, 2005), 6.

PAGE 264: *likely the most astounding hiking feat in southwest canyoneering history*   Tom Myers, "Down the Gorge with Uncle George," in *A Rendezvous of Grand Canyon Historians* (Grand Canyon Historical Society, 2012), 112.

PAGE 264: *the Canyon becomes...this fanatic possessiveness*   Bill Beer, *We Swam Grand Canyon: The True Story of a Cheap Vacation That Got a Little Out of Hand* (15 Minute Press, 2008), 78.

PAGE 266: *what Harvey Butchart described as "perfect and total wilderness"*   Harvey Butchart, *Grand Canyon Treks* (Spotted Dog Press, 1996), 181.

PAGE 268: *A descent into the Canyon...upward to the narrowed sky*   From *John L. Stoddard's Lectures*, vol. 10 (Geo. L. Shuman and Co., 1910).

PAGE 277: Edward Abbey, "The Crooked Wood," in *The Journey Home* (Plume, 1991), 206–8.

PAGE 277: *In rain country...more geologic than biologic*   Scott Thybony, *Burntwater* (University of Arizona Press, 2015), 63.

PAGE 278: *far out on the very...depths of another*   Abbey, *The Journey Home* (Plume, 1991), xiv.

PAGE 278: *ideal for reading and writing...every 15 minutes or so*   Edward Abbey, "Fire Lookout," in *Abbey's Road* (Plume, 1991), 176.

PAGE 278: *A man or woman...the National Park Service*   Edward Abbey, *Cactus Country* (Little, Brown, 1973), 62.

PAGE 279: *If we go far...replace yourself again*   Keith Basso, *Wisdom Sits in Places: Landscape and Language among the Western Apache* (University of New Mexico Press, 1996), 59.

PAGE 280: *how to live a full, meaningful, joyous life*   From *Confessions of a Barbarian: Selections from the Journals of Edward Abbey* (Johnson Books, 2003), 113.

PAGE 280: *I made no bones about it*   See Louise Teal, *Breaking Into the Current: Boatwomen of the Grand Canyon* (University of Arizona Press, 1996), xi.

PAGE 280: *I've not been a very good family man or father*   See James M. Cahalan, *Edward Abbey: A Life* (University of Arizona Press, 2003), 273.

ACKNOWLEDGMENTS

Wendell Berry wrote, "No product can be the equal of its source. The source is infinite, the product finite." The Canyon has far exceeded my task of writing about it, so too is my portrayal of Trails flawed. The biggest fault is that due to the constraints of narrative and word count, all too many of the crew either don't appear or appear as peripheral players, though many of them worked longer and harder on Trails than I. For that I apologize, and offer much love and thanks to all my Traildog companions: Bill, Richie, Chris, Jake, Damon, Dyer, T. Mill, Dowell, Shayne, Gibson, Shannon, Roark, Cullen, Doc, Marmac, Francis (RIP), LTB, Luke, Chad, Dabney, EG, Stan, Evonne, Miguel, JP, Tim W., Kenton.

Much love to all the Ranchers, river runners, trail runners, desert rats, dirtbags, and other Canyon folk whose knowledge and passion have helped me love and know the Canyon.

Special thanks and acknowledgments to the editors of *Creative Nonfiction*, *High Desert Journal*, *Hawk and Handsaw*, *High Country News*, *Flyaway*, and *Terrain.org* for publishing some of the work that appears in this book.

The utmost thanks to Alison Hawthorne Deming for her

guidance, wisdom, and friendship; my UAMFA community for their support and camaraderie; John Daniel, Bradley and Frank Boyden, and the Margery Boyden Wilderness Writing Residency for the invaluable gift of time in a wild place in which to write; Jenny Marder Fadoul for her editorial insights; my aunt Betty, who gifted me the laptop on which 95 percent of this was written; and The Spring Creek gang for giving me shelter and succor.

Thanks to Tom Payton, Marguerite Avery, Sarah Nawrocki, and all those at Trinity University Press. Thanks to Char Miller. Thanks to Colleen Hyde at the Grand Canyon National Park Museum Collection.

To Jedediah, Olga, Joaquin, Niko; Patty and Robin; Emory; and so many others who have encouraged and lifted me in these long years.

To Mom and Dad, for a lifetime of support and encouragement and so much more. I love you.

To Fiona Wren, for reminding me of what matters, and how to live right.

And, finally, to Kelly E. Gleason: there was never a doubt.

NATHANIEL BRODIE is the coeditor, with Charles Goodrich and Frederick J. Swanson, of *Forest Under Story: Creative Inquiry in an Old-Growth Forest*. He lives with his wife and daughter in Portland, Oregon.